The
Philosopher's
TOOLKIT

For Rick O'Neil, colleague and friend, in memoriam

The Philosopher's TOOLKIT

A Compendium of Philosophical Concepts and Methods

Julian Baggini
and
Peter S. Fosl

BLACKWELL PUBLISHING
350 Main Street, Malden, MA 02148-5020, USA
9600 Garsington Road, Oxford OX4 2DQ, UK
550 Swanston Street, Carlton, Victoria 3053, Australia

First published 2003 by Blackwell Publishing Ltd

11   2007

Library of Congress Cataloging-in-Publication Data

Baggini, Julian.
    The philosopher's toolkit : a compendium of philosophical concepts
and methods / Julian Baggini and Peter S. Fosl
        p. cm.
    Includes bibliographical references and index.
    ISBN 0-631-22873-X (alk. paper) — ISBN 0-631-22874-8 (pbk. : alk. paper)
    1. Reasoning. 2. Methodology. I. Fosl, Peter S. II. Title.

    BC177 .B19 2003
    101—dc21

                                    2002001568

ISBN-13: 978-0-631-22873-8 (alk. paper) — ISBN-13: 978-0-631-22874-5 (pbk. :
alk. paper)

A catalogue record for this title is available from the British Library.

Set in 10 on 12.5 pt Plantin
by Ace Filmsetting Ltd, Frome, Somerset
Printed and bound in India
by Replika Press Pvt. Ltd

The publisher's policy is to use permanent paper from mills that operate a sustainable
forestry policy, and which has been manufactured from pulp processed using
acid-free and elementary chlorine-free practices. Furthermore, the publisher ensures
that the text paper and cover board used have met acceptable environmental
accreditation standards.

For further information on Blackwell Publishing, visit our website:
www.blackwellpublishing.com

Contents

Preface

Philosophy can be an extremely technical and complex affair, one whose terminology and procedures are often intimidating to the beginner and demanding even for the professional. Like that of surgery, the art of philosophy requires mastering a body of knowledge, but it also requires acquiring precision and skill with a set of instruments or tools. *The Philosopher's Toolkit* may be thought of as a collection of just such tools. Unlike those of a surgeon or a master woodworker, however, the instruments presented by this text are conceptual, tools that can be used to analyse, manipulate, and evaluate philosophical concepts, arguments and theories.

The *Toolkit* can be used in a variety of ways. It can be read cover to cover by those looking for instruction on the essentials of philosophical reflection. It can be used as a course book on basic philosophical method or critical thinking. It can also be used as a reference book to which general readers and more advanced philosophers can turn in order to find quick and clear accounts of the key concepts and methods of philosophy. The aim of the book, in other words, is to act as a conceptual toolbox from which all those from neophytes to master artisans can draw instruments that would otherwise be distributed over a diverse set of texts and require long periods of study to acquire.

The book is divided into seven sections, which include an Internet resources section (see Contents). These sections progress from the basic tools of argumentation to sophisticated philosophical concepts and principles. The text passes through instruments for assessing arguments to essential laws, principles and conceptual distinctions. It concludes with a discussion of the limits of philosophical thinking.

Each of the first six sections contains a number of compact entries comprising an explanation of the tool it addresses, examples of the tool in use and guidance about the tool's scope and limits. Each entry is cross-referenced to other related entries. Suggestions for further reading are included, and those particularly suitable for novices are marked with an asterisk.

Becoming a master sculptor requires more than the ability to pick up and use the tools of the trade: it requires flair, talent, imagination and practice. In the same way, learning how to use these philosophical tools will not turn you into a master of the art of philosophy overnight. What it will do is equip you with many skills and techniques that will help you philosophize better.

Acknowledgements

We are indebted to Nicholas Fearn, who helped to conceive and plan this book, and whose fingerprints can still be found here and there. Thanks to Jack Furlong and Tom Flynn for their help with the entries on radical critique and to the anonymous reviewers for their thorough scrutiny of the text. Thanks to Jeff Dean at Blackwell for nurturing the book from a good idea in theory to, we hope, a good book in practice. We would also like to thank the on-screen editor, Eldo Barkhuizen, for his remarkably thorough work. Thanks also to Peter's wife and children – Catherine Fosl, Isaac Fosl-Van Wyke and Elijah Fosl – for their patient support.

chapter 1

Basic Tools for Argument

1.1 Arguments, premises and conclusions

Philosophy is for nit-pickers. That's not to say it is a trivial pursuit. Far from it. Philosophy addresses some of the most important questions human beings ask themselves. The reason philosophers are nit-pickers is that they are concerned with the way in which beliefs we have about the world either are or are not supported by rational argument. Because their concern is serious, it is important for philosophers to demand attention to detail. People reason in a variety of ways using a number of techniques, some legitimate and some not. Often one can discern the difference between good and bad arguments only if one scrutinizes their content and structure with supreme diligence.

Argument.

What, then, is an argument? For many people, an argument is a contest or conflict between two or more people who disagree about something. An argument in this sense might involve shouting, name-calling, and even a bit of shoving. It might – but need not – include reasoning.

Philosophers, by contrast, use the term 'argument' in a very precise and narrow sense. For them, an argument is the most basic complete unit of reasoning, an atom of reason. An 'argument' is an inference from one or more starting points (truth claims called a 'premise' or 'premises') to an end point (a truth claim called a 'conclusion').

Argument vs. explanation.

'Arguments' are to be distinguished from 'explanations'. A general rule to keep in mind is that arguments attempt to demonstrate *that* something is true; explanations attempt to show *how* something is true. For example, consider encountering an apparently dead woman. An explanation of the woman's death would undertake to show *how* it happened. ('The existence of water in her lungs explains the death of this woman.') An argument would undertake to demonstrate *that* the person is in fact dead ('Since her heart has stopped beating and there are no other vital signs, we can conclude that she is in fact dead.') or that one explanation is better than another ('The absence of bleeding from the laceration to her head combined with water in the lungs indicates that this woman died from drowning and not from bleeding.')

The place of reason in philosophy.

It is not universally realized that reasoning comprises a great deal of what philosophy is about. Many people have the idea that philosophy is essentially about ideas or theories about the nature of the world and our place in it. Philosophers do indeed advance such ideas and theories, but in most cases their power and scope stems from their having been derived through rational argument from acceptable premises. Of course, many other regions of human life also commonly involve reasoning, and it may sometimes be impossible to draw clean lines distinguishing philosophy from them. (In fact, whether or not it is possible to do so is itself a matter of heated philosophical debate!)

The natural and social sciences are, for example, fields of rational inquiry that often bump up against the borders of philosophy (especially in consciousness studies, theoretical physics, and anthropology). But theories composing these sciences are generally determined through certain formal procedures of experimentation and reflection with which philosophy has little truck. Religious thinking sometimes also enlists rationality and shares an often-disputed border with philosophy. But while religious thought is intrinsically related to the divine, sacred or transcendent – perhaps through some kind of revelation, article of faith, or religious practice – philosophy, by contrast, in general is not.

Of course, the work of certain prominent figures in the Western philosophical tradition presents decidedly non-rational and even anti-rational dimensions (for example, that of Heraclitus, Kierkegaard, Nietzsche,

Heidegger and Derrida). Furthermore, many wish to include the work of Asian (Confucian, Taoist, Shinto), African, Aboriginal and Native American thinkers under the rubric of philosophy, even though they seem to make little use of argument.

But, perhaps despite the intentions of its authors, even the work of non-standard thinkers involves rationally justified claims and subtle forms of argumentation. And in many cases, reasoning remains on the scene at least as a force to be reckoned with.

Philosophy, then, is not the only field of thought for which rationality is important. And not all that goes by the name of philosophy may be argumentative. But it is certainly safe to say that one cannot even begin to master the expanse of philosophical thought without learning how to use the tools of reason. There is, therefore, no better place to begin stocking our philosophical toolkit than with rationality's most basic components, the subatomic particles of reasoning – 'premises' and 'conclusions'.

Premises and conclusions.

For most of us, the idea of a 'conclusion' is as straightforward as a philosophical concept gets. A conclusion is, literally, that with which an argument concludes, the product and result of a chain of inference, that which the reasoning justifies and supports.

What about 'premises'? In the first place, in order for a sentence to serve as a premise, it must exhibit this essential property: it must make a claim that is either true or false. Sentences do many things in our languages, and not all of them have that property. Sentences that issue commands, for example, ('Forward march, soldier!'), or ask questions ('Is this the road to Edinburgh?'), or register exclamations ('Holy cow!'), are neither true nor false. Hence it is not possible for them to serve as premises.

This much is pretty easy. But things can get sticky in a number of ways.

One of the most vexing issues concerning premises is the problem of implicit claims. That is, in many arguments key premises remain unstated, implied or masked inside other sentences. Take, for example, the following argument: 'Socrates is a man, so Socrates is mortal.' What's left implicit is the claim that 'all men are mortal'.

In working out precisely what the premises are in a given argument, ask yourself first what the claim is that the argument is trying to demonstrate. Then ask yourself what other claims the argument relies upon (implicitly or explicitly) in order to advance that demonstration.

Indicators.

Sometimes certain words and phrases will indicate premises and conclusions. Phrases like 'in conclusion', 'it follows that', 'we must conclude that' and 'from this we can see that' often indicate conclusions. ('The DNA, the fingerprints and the eyewitness accounts all point to Smithers. It follows that she must be the killer.') Words like 'because' and 'since', and phrases like 'for this reason' and 'on the basis of this', often indicate premises. (For example, 'Since the DNA, the fingerprints and the eyewitness accounts all implicate Smithers, she must be the killer.')

Premises, then, compose the set of claims from which the conclusion is drawn. In other sections, the question of how we can justify the move from premises to conclusion will be addressed (see 1.4 and 4.7). But before we get that far, we must first ask, 'What justifies a reasoner in entering a premise in the first place?'

Grounds for premises?

There are two basic reasons why a premise might be acceptable. One is that the premise is itself the conclusion of a different, solid argument. As such, the truth of the premise has been demonstrated elsewhere. But it is clear that if this were the only kind of justification for the inclusion of a premise, we would face an infinite regress. That is to say, each premise would have to be justified by a different argument, the premises of which would have to be justified by yet another argument, the premises of which . . . *ad infinitum.* (In fact, sceptics – Eastern and Western, modern and ancient – have pointed to just this problem with reasoning.)

So unless one wishes to live with the problem of the infinite regress, there must be another way of finding sentences acceptable to serve as premises. There must be, in short, premises that stand in need of no further justification through other arguments. Such premises may be true by definition. (An example of such a premise is 'all bachelors are unmarried'.) But the kind of premises we're looking for might also include premises that, though conceivably false, must be taken to be true for there to be any rational dialogue at all. Let's call them 'basic premises'.

Which sentences are to count as basic premises depends on the context in which one is reasoning. One example of a basic premise might be, 'I exist'. In most contexts, this premise does not stand in need of justification. But if, of course, the argument is trying to demonstrate that I exist, my existence cannot be used as a premise. One cannot assume what one is trying to argue for.

Philosophers have held that certain sentences are more or less basic for various reasons: because they are based upon self-evident or 'cataleptic' perceptions (Stoics), because they are directly rooted in sense data (positivists), because they are grasped by a power called intuition or insight (Platonists), because they are revealed to us by God (Jewish, Christian and Islamic philosophers), or because we grasp them using cognitive faculties certified by God (Descartes, Reid, Plantinga). In our view, a host of reasons, best described as 'context' will determine them.

Formally, then, the distinction between premises and conclusions is clear. But it is not enough to grasp this difference. In order to use these philosophical tools, one has to be able to spot the explicit premises and make explicit the unstated ones. And aside from the question of whether or not the conclusion follows from the premises, one must come to terms with the thornier question of what justifies the use of premises in the first place. Premises are the starting points of philosophical argument. As in any edifice, intellectual or otherwise, the construction will only stand if the foundations are secure.

See also

1.2 Deduction
1.3 Induction
1.9 Axioms
1.10 Definitions
3.6 Circularity
6.1 Basic beliefs
6.6 Self-evident truths

Reading

*Nigel Warburton, *Thinking From A to Z*, 2nd edn (2000)
*Patrick J. Hurley, *A Concise Introduction to Logic*, 7th edn (2000)

1.2 Deduction

The murder was clearly premeditated. The only person who knew where Dr Fishcake would be that night was his colleague, Dr Salmon. Therefore, the killer must be . . .

Deduction is the form of reasoning that is often emulated in the formulaic drawing-room denouements of classic detective fiction. It is the most rigorous form of argumentation there is, since in deduction, the move from premises to conclusions is such that if the premises are true, then the conclusion *must* also be true. For example, take the following argument:

1. Elvis Presley lives in a secret location in Idaho.
2. All people who live in secret locations in Idaho are miserable.
3. Therefore Elvis Presley is miserable.

[handwritten margin notes: (E → I), (I & M), (E & M)]

If we look at our definition of a deduction, we can see how this argument fits the bill. If the two premises are true, then the conclusion must also be true. How could it not be true that Elvis is miserable, if it is indeed true that all people who live in secret locations in Idaho are miserable, and Elvis is one of these people?

You might well be thinking there is something fishy about this, since you may believe that Elvis is not miserable for the simple reason that he no longer exists. So all this talk of the conclusion having to be true might strike you as odd. If this is so, you haven't taken on board the key word at the start of this sentence, which does such vital work in the definition of deduction. The conclusion must be true *if* the premises are true. This is a big 'if'. In our example, the conclusion is, I believe, not true, because one or both (in this case both) premises are not true. But that doesn't alter the fact that this is a deductive argument, since if it turned out that Elvis does live in a secret location in Idaho and that all people who lived in secret locations in Idaho are miserable, it would necessarily follow that Elvis is miserable.

The question of what makes a good deductive argument is addressed in more detail in the section on validity and soundness (1.4). But in a sense, everything that you need to know about a deductive argument is contained within the definition given: a (successful) deductive argument is one where, if the premises are true, then the conclusion must also be true.

But before we leave this topic, we should return to the investigations of our detective. Reading his deliberations, one could easily insert the vital, missing word. The killer must surely be Dr Salmon. But is this the conclusion of a successful deductive argument? The fact is that we can't answer this question unless we know a little more about the exact meaning of the premises.

First, what does it mean to say the murder was 'premeditated'? It could mean lots of things. It could mean that it was planned right down to the last detail, or it could mean simply that the murderer had worked out what she would do in advance. If it is the latter, then it is possible that the murderer did not know where Dr Fishcake would be that night, but, coming across him by chance, put into action her premeditated plan to kill him. So it could be the case that both premises are true (the murder was premeditated, and

Dr Salmon was the only person who knew where Dr Fishcake would be that night) but that the conclusion is false (Dr Salmon is, in fact, not the murderer). Therefore the detective has not formed a successful deductive argument.

What this example shows is that, although the definition of a deductive argument is simple enough, spotting and constructing successful ones is much trickier. To judge whether the conclusion really *must* follow from the premises, we have to be sensitive to ambiguity in the premises as well as to the danger of accepting too easily a conclusion that seems to be supported by the premises, but does not in fact follow from them. Deduction is not about jumping to conclusions, but crawling (though not slouching) slowly towards them.

See also

1.1 Arguments, premises and conclusions
1.3 Induction
1.4 Validity and soundness

Reading

*John Shand, *Arguing Well* (2000)
Fred R. Berger, *Studying Deductive Logic* (1977)

1.3 Induction

I (Julian Baggini) have a confession to make. Once, while on holiday in Rome, I visited the famous street market, Porta Portese. I came across a man who was taking bets on which of the three cups he had shuffled around was covering a die. I will spare you the details and any attempts to justify my actions on the grounds of mitigating circumstances. Suffice it to say, I took a bet and lost. Having been budgeted so carefully, the cash for that night's pizza went up in smoke.

My foolishness in this instance is all too evident. But is it right to say my decision to gamble was 'illogical'? Answering this question requires wrangling with a dimension of logic philosophers call 'induction'. Unlike deductive inferences, induction involves an inference where the conclusion follows from the premises not with necessity but only with probability (though even this formulation is problematic, as we will see).

Defining induction.

Often, induction involves reasoning from a limited number of observations to wider, probable generalizations. Reasoning this way is commonly called 'inductive generalization'. It is a kind of inference that usually involves reasoning from past regularities to future regularities. One classic example is the sunrise. The sun has risen regularly so far as human experience can recall, so people reason that it will probably rise tomorrow. (The work of the Scottish philosopher David Hume [1711–76] has been influential on this score.) This sort of inference is often taken to typify induction. In the case of my Roman holiday, I might have reasoned that the past experiences of people with average cognitive abilities like mine show that the probabilities of winning against the man with the cups is rather small.

But beware: induction is not essentially defined as reasoning from the specific to the general.

An inductive inference need not be past–future directed. And it can involve reasoning from the general to the specific, the specific to the specific or the general to the general.

I could, for example, reason from the *more general*, past-oriented claim that no trained athlete on record has been able to run 100 m in under 9 seconds, to the *more specific* past-oriented conclusion that my friend had probably not achieved this feat when he was at university, as he claims.

Reasoning through *analogies* (see 2.4) as well as *typical examples* and *rules of thumb* are also species of induction, even though none of them involves moving from the specific to the general.

The problem of induction.

Inductive generalizations are, however, often where the action is. Reasoning in experimental science, for example, depends on them in so far as scientists formulate and confirm universal natural laws (e.g. Boyle's ideal gas law) on the basis of a relatively small number of observations. The tricky thing to keep in mind about inductive generalizations, however, is that they involve reasoning from a 'some' in a way that only works with *necessity* for an 'all'. This type of inference makes inductive generalization fundamentally different from deductive argument (for which such a move would be illegitimate). It also opens up a rather enormous can of conceptual worms. Philosophers know this conundrum as the 'problem of induction'. Here's what we mean.

Take the following example (Example A):

1. *Some* elephants like chocolate.
2. This is an elephant.
3. Therefore, this elephant likes chocolate.

This is *not* a well-formed deductive argument, since the premises could be true and the conclusion still be false. Properly understood, however, it may be a strong inductive argument – for example, if by 'some' elephants one means 'all but one' and if the conclusion is interpreted to mean 'it is *probably* the case that this elephant likes chocolate'.

On the other hand, consider this rather similar argument (Example B):

1. *All* elephants like chocolate.
2. This is an elephant.
3. Therefore, this elephant likes chocolate.

Though similar in certain ways, this one is, in fact, a well-formed deductive argument, not an inductive argument at all. The problem of induction is the problem of how an argument can be good reasoning as induction but be poor reasoning as a deduction. Before addressing this problem directly, we must take care not to be misled by the similarities between the two forms.

A misleading similarity.

Because of the kind of general similarity one sees between these two arguments, inductive arguments can sometimes be confused with deductive arguments. That is, although they may actually look like deductive arguments, some arguments are actually inductive. For example, an argument that the sun will rise tomorrow might be presented in a way that might easily be taken for a deductive argument:

1. The sun rises every day.
2. Tomorrow is a day.
3. Therefore the sun will rise tomorrow.

Because of its similarity with deductive forms, one may be tempted to read the first premise as an 'all' sentence:

The sun rises on *all* days (every 24-hour period) that there ever have been and ever will be.

The limitations of human experience, however (the fact that we can't experience every single day), justify us in forming only the less strong 'some' sentence:

> The sun has risen on every day (every 24-hour period) that humans have recorded their experience of such things.

This weaker formulation, of course, enters only the limited claim that the sun has risen on a small portion of the total number of days that have ever been and ever will be; it makes no claim at all about the rest.

But here's the catch. From this weaker 'some' sentence one cannot construct a well-formed deductive argument of the kind that allows the conclusion to follow with the kind of certainty characteristic of deduction. In reasoning about matters of fact, one would like to reach conclusions with the certainty of deduction. Unfortunately, induction will not allow it.

The uniformity of nature?

Put at its simplest, the problem of induction can be boiled down to the problem of justifying our belief in the uniformity of nature. If nature is uniform and regular in its behaviour, then events in the *observed* past and present are a sure guide to unobserved events in the *unobserved* past, present and future. But the only grounds for believing that nature is uniform are the *observed* events in the past and present. We can't seem to go beyond the events we observe without assuming the very thing we need to prove – that is, that unobserved parts of the world operate in the same way as the parts we've observed. (This is just the problem to which Hume points.) Believing, therefore, that the sun may *possibly not* rise tomorrow is, strictly speaking, *not* illogical, since the conclusion that it must rise tomorrow does *not* inexorably follow from past observations.

A deeper complexity.

Acknowledging the relative weakness of inductive inferences (compared to those of deduction), good reasoners qualify the conclusions reached through it by maintaining that they follow not with necessity but *with probability*. But does this fully resolve the problem? Can even this weaker, more qualified formulation be justified? Can we, for example, really justify the claim that, on the basis of uniform and extensive past observation, it is *more probable* that the sun will rise tomorrow than it won't?

The problem is that there is no deductive argument to ground even this qualified claim. To deduce this conclusion successfully we would need the premise 'what has happened up until now *is more likely* to happen tomorrow'. But this premise is subject to just the same problem as the stronger claim that 'what has happened up until now *is certain* to happen tomorrow'. Like its stronger counterpart, the weaker premise bases its claim about the future only on what has happened up until now, and such a basis can be justified only if we accept the uniformity (or at least general continuity) of nature. But the uniformity (or continuity) of nature is just what's in question!

A groundless ground?

Despite these problems, it seems that we can't do without inductive generalizations. They are (or at least have been so far!) simply too useful to refuse. They compose the basis of much of our scientific rationality, and they allow us to think about matters concerning which deduction must remain silent. We simply can't afford to reject the premise that 'what we have so far observed is our best guide to what is true of what we haven't observed', even though this premise cannot itself be justified without presuming itself.

There is, however, a price to pay. We must accept that engaging in inductive generalization requires that we hold an indispensable belief which itself, however, must remain in an important way ungrounded.

See also

1.1 Arguments, premises and conclusions
1.2 Deduction
1.7 Fallacies
2.4 Analogies
3.14 Hume's Fork

Reading

*David Hume, *A Treatise of Human Nature* (1739–40), bk 1

1.4 Validity and soundness

In his book *The Unnatural Nature of Science* the eminent British biologist Lewis Wolpert argued that the one thing that unites almost all of the sciences is that they often fly in the face of common sense. Philosophy, however, may exceed even the sciences on this point. Its theories, conclusions and terms can at times be extraordinarily counter-intuitive and contrary to ordinary ways of thinking, doing and speaking.

Take, for example, the word 'valid'. In everyday speech, people talk about someone 'making a valid point' or 'having a valid opinion'. In philosophical speech, however, the word 'valid' is reserved exclusively for arguments. More surprisingly, a valid argument can look like this.

1. All blocks of cheese are more intelligent than any philosophy student.
2. Meg the cat is a block of cheese.
3. Therefore Meg the cat is more intelligent than any philosophy student.

All utter nonsense, you may think, but from a strictly logical point of view it is a perfect example of a valid argument. What's going on?

Defining validity.

Validity is a property of well-formed deductive arguments, which, to recap, are defined as arguments where the conclusion is in some sense (actually, hypothetically, etc.) presented as following from the premises *necessarily* (see 1.2). A valid deductive argument is one for which the conclusion follows from the premises in that way.

The tricky thing, however, is that an argument may possess the property of validity even if its premises or its conclusion are not in fact *true*. Validity, as it turns out, is essentially a property of an argument's *structure*. And so, with regard to validity, the *content* or truth of the statements composing the argument is irrelevant. Let's unpack this.

Consider structure first. The argument featuring cats and cheese given above is an instance of a more general argumentative structure, of the form

1. All Xs are Ys.
2. Z is an X.
3. Therefore Z is a Y.

In our example, 'block of cheese' is substituted for X, 'things that are more intelligent than all philosophy students' for Y, and 'Meg' for Z. That makes our example just one particular instance of the more general argumentative form expressed with the variables X, Y and Z.

What you should notice is that one doesn't need to attach any meaning to the variables to see that this particular structure is a valid one. No matter what we replace the variables with, it will always be the case that *if* the premises are true (although in fact they might not be), the conclusion *must* also be true. If there's any conceivable way possible for the premises of an argument to be true but its conclusion simultaneously be false, then it is an invalid argument.

What this boils down to is that the notion of validity is content-blind (or 'topic-neutral'). It really doesn't matter what the content of the propositions in the argument is – validity is determined by the argument having a solid, deductive structure. Our example is then a valid argument because *if* its ridiculous premises were true, the ridiculous conclusion would also have to be true. The fact that the premises are ridiculous is neither here nor there when it comes to assessing the argument's validity.

The truth machine.

From another point of view we might consider that deductive arguments work a bit like sausage machines. You put ingredients (premises) in, and then you get something (conclusions) out. Deductive arguments are the best kind of sausage machine because they *guarantee* that when you put good ingredients (all true premises) in, you get a quality product (true conclusions) out.

A good machine with good ingredients is called a sound argument. Of course if you don't start with good ingredients, deductive arguments don't guarantee a good end product. Invalid arguments are not desirable machines to employ. They provide no guarantee whatsoever for the quality of the end product. You might put in good ingredients (true premises) and sometimes get a high-quality result (a true conclusion). Other times good ingredients might lead to a poor result (a false conclusion).

Stranger still (and very different from sausage machines), with invalid deductive arguments, you might sometimes put in poor ingredients (one or more false premises) but actually end up with a good result (a true conclusion). Of course, in other cases with invalid machines you put in poor ingredients and end up with rubbish. The thing about invalid machines is that you don't know what you'll get out. With valid machines, when you put in good ingredients (though *only* when you put in good ingredients), you have a guarantee. In sum:

INVALID ARGUMENT
Put in false premise(s) → get out either true or false conclusion
Put in true premise(s) → get out either true or false conclusion

VALID ARGUMENT
Put in false premise(s) → get out either true or false conclusion
Put in true premise(s) → get out only true conclusion

Soundness.

To say an argument is valid, then, is not to say that its conclusion must be accepted as true. The conclusion must be accepted *only if* (1) the argument is valid *and* (2) the premises are true. This combination of valid argument plus true premises (and therefore true conclusion) is called a 'sound' argument. Calling it sound is the highest endorsement one can place on an argument. If you accept an argument as sound you are really saying that you must accept its conclusion. This can be shown by the use of another valid, deductive argument. If you say that an argument is sound you are saying two things that may be understood as premises:

1. If the premises of the argument are true, then the conclusion must also be true. (That is to say, you're maintaining that the argument is valid.)
2. The premises of the argument are (in fact) true.

If you regard these two as premises, you can produce a deductive argument that concludes with certainty:

3. Therefore, the conclusion of the argument is true.

For a deductive argument to pass muster, it must be valid. But being valid is not sufficient to make it a sound argument. A sound argument must not only be valid; it must have true premises as well. It is, strictly speaking, only sound arguments whose conclusions we *must* accept.

Importance of validity.

This may lead you to wonder why, then, the concept of validity has any importance. After all, valid arguments can be absurd in their content and false in the conclusions – as in our cheese and cats example. Surely it is soundness that matters.

Keep in mind, however, that validity is a required component of soundness, so there can be no sound arguments without valid ones. Working out whether or not the claims you make in your premises are true, while important, is simply not enough to ensure that you draw true conclusions. People make this mistake all the time. They forget that one can begin with a set of entirely true beliefs but reason so poorly as to end up with entirely false conclusions. They satisfy themselves with starting with truth. The problem is that starting with truth doesn't guarantee that one ends with it.

Furthermore in launching criticism, it is important to grasp that understanding validity gives you an additional tool for evaluating another's position. In criticizing another's reasoning you can either

1. *attack the truth of the premises from which he or she reasons,*
2. *or show that his or her argument is invalid, regardless of whether or not the premises deployed are true.*

Validity is, simply put, a crucial ingredient in arguing, criticizing and thinking well. It is an indispensable philosophical tool. Master it.

See also

1.1 Arguments, premises and conclusions
1.2 Deduction
1.5 Invalidity

Reading

Aristotle (384–322 BCE), *Prior Analytics*
*Patrick J. Hurley, *A Concise Introduction to Logic*, 7th edn (2000)
Fred R. Berger, *Studying Deductive Logic* (1977)

1.5 Invalidity

Given the definition of a valid argument, it may seem obvious what an invalid one looks like. Certainly, it is simple enough to define an invalid argument: it is one where the truth of the premises does not guarantee the truth of the conclusion. To put it another way, if the premises of an invalid argument are true, the conclusion may still be false.

To be armed with an accurate definition, however, may not be enough to enable you to make use of this tool. The man who went looking for a horse equipped only with the definition 'solid-hoofed, herbivorous, domesticated mammal used for draught work and riding' (*Collins English Dictionary*) discovered as much to his cost. One needs to understand the definition's full import.

Consider this argument:

1.   Vegetarians do not eat pork sausages.
2.   Ghandi did not eat pork sausages.
3.   Therefore Ghandi was a vegetarian.

If you're thinking carefully, you'll probably have noticed that this is an invalid argument. But it wouldn't be surprising if you and a fair number of readers required a double take to see that it is in fact invalid. And if one can easily miss a clear case of invalidity in the midst of an article devoted to a careful explanation of the concept, imagine how easy it is not to spot invalid arguments more generally.

One reason why some fail to notice that this argument is invalid is because all three propositions are true. If nothing false is asserted in the premises of an argument and the conclusion is true, it is easy to think that the argument is therefore valid (and sound). But remember that an argument is valid *only if* the truth of the premises *guarantees* the truth of the conclusion. In this example, this isn't so. After all, a person may not eat pork sausages yet not be a vegetarian. He or she may, for example, be a Muslim or Jew. He or she simply may not like pork sausages but frequently enjoy turkey or beef.

So the fact that Ghandi did not eat pork sausages does *not*, in conjunction with the first premise, guarantee that he was a vegetarian. It just so happens that he was. But, of course, since an argument can only be sound if it is valid, the fact that all three of the propositions it asserts are true does *not* make it a sound argument.

Remember that validity is a property of an argument's structure. In this case, the structure is

1.   All Xs are Ys
2.   Z is a Y
3.   Therefore Z is an X

where X is substituted for 'vegetarian', Y for 'person who does not eat pork sausages' and Z for 'Ghandi'. We can see why this structure is invalid by replacing these variables with other terms that produce true premises, but a clearly false conclusion. (Replacing terms creates what philosophers call a new 'substitution instance' of the argument form.) If we substitute X for 'Cat', Y for 'meat eater' and Z for 'the president of the US', we get:

1. All cats are meat eaters.
2. The president of the US is a meat eater.
3. Therefore the president of the US is a cat.

The premises are true but the conclusion clearly false. Therefore this cannot be a valid argument structure. (You can do this with various invalid argument forms. Showing that an argument form is invalid by substituting sentences into the form that give true premises but a false conclusion is what philosophers call showing invalidity by 'counterexample'. See 3.8)

It should be clear therefore that, as with validity, invalidity is not determined by the truth or falsehood of the premises but by the logical relations among them. This reflects a wider, important feature of philosophy. Philosophy is not just about saying things that are true; it is about making true claims that are grounded in good arguments. You may have a particular viewpoint on a philosophical issue, and it may just turn out that you are right. But, in many cases, unless you can show you are right by the use of good arguments, your viewpoint is not going to carry any weight in philosophy. Philosophers are not just concerned with the truth, but with what makes it the truth and how we can show that it is the truth.

See also

1.2 Deduction
1.4 Validity and soundness
1.7 Fallacies

Reading

*Patrick J. Hurley, *A Concise Introduction to Logic*, 7th edn (2000)
*Irving M. Copi, *Introduction to Logic*, 10th edn (1998)

1.6 Consistency

Of all the philosophical crimes there are, the one you really don't want to get charged with is inconsistency. Consistency is the cornerstone of rationality. What then, exactly, does consistency mean?

Consistency is a property characterizing two or more statements. If one holds two inconsistent beliefs, then, at root, this means one is asserting both that X is true *and* X is in the same sense and at the same time not true. More broadly, one holds inconsistent beliefs if one belief contradicts another or the beliefs in question together imply contradiction or contrariety.

In short, two or more statements are *consistent* when it is possible for them all to be true at the same time. Two or more statements are *inconsistent* when it is not possible for them all to be true at the same time.

A single sentence, however, can be self-contradictory when it makes an assertion that is necessarily false – often by conjoining two inconsistent sentences.

Apparent and real inconsistency: the abortion example.

At its most flagrant, inconsistency is obvious. If I say, 'All murder is wrong' and 'That particular murder was right', I am clearly being inconsistent, because the second assertion clearly contradicts the first. I am, in effect, saying both that 'all murder is wrong' and 'not all murder is wrong' – a clear inconsistency.

But sometimes inconsistency is difficult to determine. Apparent inconsistency may actually mask a deeper consistency – and vice versa.

Many people, for example, agree that it is wrong to kill innocent human beings (persons). And many of those same people also agree that abortion is morally acceptable. One argument against abortion is based on the claim that these two beliefs are inconsistent. That is, critics claim that it is inconsistent to hold both that 'It is wrong to kill innocent human beings' and that 'It is permissible to destroy living human embryos and foetuses.'

Defenders of the permissibility of abortion, on the other hand, may retort that properly understood the two claims are not inconsistent. One could, for example, claim that embryos are not human beings in the sense normally understood in the prohibition (e.g. conscious or independently living or already-born human beings). Or a defender of abortion might change the prohibition itself to make the point more clearly (e.g. by claiming that it's wrong only to kill innocent human beings that have reached a certain level of development, consciousness or feeling).

Exceptions to the rule?

But is inconsistency always undesirable? Some people are tempted to say it is not. To support their case, they present examples of beliefs that intuitively seem perfectly acceptable yet seem to match the definition of inconsistency given. Two examples might be:

It is raining, and it is not raining.
My home is not my home.

In the first case, the inconsistency may be only apparent. What one may really be saying is not that it is raining and not raining, but rather that it is neither properly raining nor not raining, since there is a third possibility – perhaps that it is drizzling, or intermittently raining – and that this other possibility most accurately describes the current situation.

What makes the inconsistency only apparent in this example is that the speaker is shifting the sense of the terms being employed. Another way of saying the first sentence, then, is that 'In one sense it is raining, but in another sense of the word it is not.' For the inconsistency to be real, the relevant terms being used must retain the same meaning throughout.

This equivocation in the meanings of the words show that we must be careful not to confuse the logical form of an inconsistency – asserting both X and not X – with ordinary language forms that appear to match it but really don't. Many ordinary language assertions that both X and not X are true turn out, when analysed carefully, not to be inconsistencies at all. So be careful before accusing someone of inconsistency.

But, when you do unearth a genuine logical inconsistency, you've accomplished a lot, for it is impossible to defend the inconsistency without rejecting rationality outright! Perhaps there are poetic, religious and philosophical contexts in which this is precisely what people find it proper to do.

Poetic, religious or philosophical inconsistency?

What about the second example we present above – 'My home is not my home.' Suppose that the context in which the sentence is asserted is in the diary of someone living under a horribly violent and dictatorial regime – perhaps by George Orwell's character Winston Smith in *1984* as he writes in his diary. Literally, the sentence is self-contradictory, internally inconsistent. It seems to assert both that 'This is my home' and that 'This is not my home.' But the sentence also seems to carry a certain poetic sense, to convey how absurd the world seems to the speaker, how alienated he or she feels from the world in which he or she exists.

The Danish existentialist philosopher philosopher Søren Kierkegaard (1813–55) maintained that the Christian notion of the incarnation ('Jesus is God, and Jesus was a man') is a paradox, a contradiction, an affront to reason, but nevertheless true. Existentialist philosopher Albert Camus (1913–60) maintained that there is something fundamentally 'absurd' (perhaps inconsistent?) about human existence.

Perhaps, then, there are contexts in which inconsistency and absurdity paradoxically make sense.

Consistency ≠ truth.

Be this as it may, inconsistency in philosophy is generally a serious vice. Does it follow from this that consistency is philosophy's highest virtue? Not quite. Consistency is only a minimal condition of acceptability for a philosophical position. Since it is often the case that one can hold a consistent theory that is inconsistent with another, equally consistent theory, the consistency of any particular theory is no guarantee of its truth. Indeed, as French philosopher-physicist Pierre Maurice Marie Duhem (1861–1916) and the American philosopher Willard Van Orman Quine (1908–2000) have maintained, it may be possible to develop two or more theories that are (1) internally consistent, (2) yet inconsistent with each other, and also (3) perfectly consistent with all the data we can possibly muster to determine the truth or falsehood of the theories.

Take as an example the so-called problem of evil. How do we solve the puzzle that God is supposed to be good but there is awful suffering in the world? A number of theories can be advanced that may solve the puzzle but are inconsistent with one another. One can hold that God does not exist. Or one can hold that God allows suffering for a greater good. Although each solution may be perfectly consistent with itself, they can't both be right, as they are inconsistent with each other. One asserts God's existence, and the other denies it. Establishing the consistency of a position, therefore, may advance and clarify philosophical thought, but it probably won't settle the issue at hand. We need to appeal to more than consistency if we are to decide between the competing positions. How we do this is a complex and controversial subject of its own.

See also

1.12 Tautologies, self-contradictions and the law of non-contradiction
3.28 Sufficient reason

Reading

José L. Zalabardo, *Introduction to the Theory of Logic* (2000)
Fred R. Berger, *Studying Deductive Logic* (1977)
Pierre M. M. Duhem, *La théorie physique, son object et sa structure* (1906)

1.7 Fallacies

The notion of 'fallacy' will be an important instrument to draw from your toolkit, for philosophy often depends upon identifying poor reasoning, and a fallacy is nothing other than an instance of poor reasoning – a faulty inference. Since every invalid argument presents a faulty inference, a great deal of what one needs to know about fallacies has already been covered in the entry on invalidity (1.5). But while all invalid arguments are fallacious, not all fallacies involve invalid arguments. Invalid arguments are faulty because of flaws in their form or structure. Sometimes, however, reasoning goes awry for reasons not of form but of content.

All fallacies are instances of faulty reasoning. When the fault lies in the form or structure of the argument, the fallacious inference is called a 'formal' fallacy. When it lies in the content of the argument, it is called an 'informal' fallacy. In the course of philosophical history philosophers have been able to identify and name common types or species of fallacy. Oftentimes, therefore, the charge of fallacy calls upon one of these types.

Formal fallacies.

One of the most common types of inferential error attributable to the form of argument has come to be known as 'affirming the consequent'. It is an extremely easy error to make and can often be difficult to detect. Consider the following example:

1. If Fiona won the lottery last night, she'll be driving a red Ferrari today.
2. Fiona is driving a red Ferrari today.
3. Therefore Fiona won the lottery last night.

Why is this invalid? It is simply this: as with any invalid argument, the truth of the premises does not guarantee the truth of the conclusion. Drawing this conclusion from these premises leaves room for the *possibility* that the conclusion is false, and if any such possibility exists, the conclusion is not guaranteed.

One can see that such a possibility exists in this case by considering that it is *possible* that Fiona is driving a Ferrari today for reasons *other* than her winning the lottery. Fiona may, for example, have just inherited a lot of money. Or she may be borrowing the car, or perhaps she stole it. (Her driving the Ferrari for other reasons does not of course render the first premise false. Even if she's driving it because she in fact inherited a lot of money, it still might be true that *if* she had instead won the lottery she *would have* gone out and bought a Ferrari just the same. Hence the premises and conclusion might all be true but the conclusion will not *follow with necessity* from the premises.

The source of this fallacy's persuasive power lies in an ambiguity in ordinary language concerning the use of 'if'. The word 'if' is sometimes used to imply 'if and only if' but sometimes means simply 'if'. Despite their similarity, these two phrases have very different meanings.

As it turns out, the argument would be valid if the first premise were stated in a slightly different way. Strange as it may seem, while the argument about Fiona above is deductively invalid, substituting either of the following statements for the first premise in that argument will yield a perfectly valid argument.

If Fiona's driving a red Ferrari today, she won the lottery last night.
Only if Fiona won the lottery last night will she be driving a red Ferrari today.

Because 'if' and 'only if' are ordinarily used in rather vague ways (that don't distinguish the usages above), philosophers redefine them in a very precise sense. Mastering philosophical tools will require that you master this precise usage as well (see 4.5).

In addition, because fallacies can be persuasive and are so prevalent, it will be very useful for you to acquaint yourself with the most common fallacies. (The masked man [3.17] and genetic [3.12] fallacies have their own entries in this book. Others are delineated in the texts listed below.) Doing so can inoculate you against being taken in by bad reasoning. It can also save you some money.

Informal fallacies.

The 'gambler's fallacy' is both a dangerously persuasive and a hopelessly flawed species of inference. The fallacy occurs when someone is, for example, taking a bet on the tossing of a fair coin. The coin has landed heads up four times in a row. The gambler therefore concludes that the next time it is tossed, it is more likely to come up tails than heads (or the reverse). But what the gambler fails to realize is that each toss of the coin is unaffected by the tosses that have come before it. No matter what has been tossed beforehand, the odds remain 50-50 for every single new toss. The odds of tossing eight heads in a row are rather low. But if seven heads in a row have already been tossed, the chances of the sequence of eight in a row being completed (or broken) on the next toss is still 50-50.

What makes this an informal rather than a formal fallacy is that we can actually present the reasoning here using a valid form of argument.

1. If I've already tossed seven heads in a row, the probability that the eighth toss will yield a head is less than 50-50 — that is, I'm due for a tails.
2. I've already tossed seven heads in a row.
3. Therefore the probability that the next toss will yield a head is less than 50-50.

The flaw here is not with the *form* of the argument. The form is valid; logicians call it *modus ponens*, the way of affirmation. It is the same form we used in the valid Fiona argument above. Formally, it looks like this:

If P, then Q.
P
Therefore, Q.

The flaw rendering the gambler's argument fallacious instead lies in the content of the first premise – the first premise is simply false. The probability of the next individual toss (like that of all individual tosses) is and remains 50-50 no matter what toss or tosses preceded it. But people mistakenly believe that past flips of coins somehow affect future flips. There's no formal problem with the argument, but because this factual error remains so common and so easy to commit, it has been classified as a fallacy and given a name. It is a fallacy, but only informally speaking.

Sometimes ordinary speech deviates from these usages. Sometimes any widely held, though false, belief is described as a fallacy. Don't worry. As the philosopher Ludwig Wittgenstein said, language is like a large city with lots of different avenues and neighbourhoods. It is all right to adopt different usages when one inhabits different parts of the city. Just keep in mind where you are.

See also

1.5 Invalidity
3.12 Genetic fallacy
3.17 Masked man fallacy
4.5 Conditional/Biconditional

Reading

*S. Morris Engel, *With Good Reason: An Introduction to Informal Fallacies*, 5th edn (1974)
*Irving M. Copi, *Informal Fallacies* (1986)
*Patrick J. Hurley, *A Concise Introduction to Logic*, 7th edn (2000)

1.8 Refutation

Samuel Johnson was not impressed by Bishop Berkeley's argument that matter did not exist. In his *Life of Johnson* (1791) James Boswell reported that, when discussing Berkeley's theory with him, Johnson once kicked a stone with some force and said, 'I refute it thus.'

Any great person is allowed one moment of idiocy to go public. Johnson's refutation wildly missed Berkeley's point, since the bishop would never have denied that one could kick a stone. But not only did Johnson's refutation formally fail; it also contained none of the hallmarks of a true refutation.

To refute an argument is to show that is wrong. If one merely disagrees with an argument or denies its soundness, one is not refuting it, although in everyday speech people often talk about refuting a claim in just this way. So how can one really refute an argument?

Refutation tools.

There are two basic ways of doing this, both of which are covered in more detail elsewhere in this book. One can show that the argument is invalid: the conclusion does not follow from the premises as claimed (see 1.5). One can show that one or more of the premises are false (see 1.4).

A third way is to show that the conclusion must be false and that therefore, even if one can't identify what is wrong with the argument, something must be wrong with it (see 3.23). This last method, however, isn't strictly speaking a refutation, as one has failed to show *what* is wrong with the argument, only *that* it must be wrong.

Inadequate justification.

Refutations are powerful tools, but it would be rash to conclude that in order to reject an argument *only* a refutation will do. We may be justified in rejecting an argument even if we have not strictly speaking refuted it. We may not be able to show that a key premise is false, for example, but we may believe that it is inadequately justified. An argument based on the premise that 'there is intelligent life elsewhere in our universe' would fit this model. We can't show that the premise is actually false, but we can argue that we have no good reasons for believing it to be true and good grounds for supposing it to be false. Therefore we can regard any argument that depends on this premise as dubious and rightly ignore it.

Conceptual problems.

More contentiously, we might also reject an argument by arguing that it utilises a concept inappropriately. This sort of problem is particularly clear in cases where a vague concept is used as if it were precise. For instance, one might argue that the government is only obliged to provide assistance to those who do not have enough to live on. But given that there can be no precise formulation of what 'enough to live on' is, any argument must be inadequate that concludes by making a sharp distinction between those who have enough and those who don't. The logic of the argument may be impeccable and the premises may appear to be true. But if we use vague concepts in precise arguments we inevitably end up with distortions.

Using the tool.

There are many more ways of legitimately objecting to an argument without actually refuting it. The important thing is to know the clear difference between refutation and other forms of objection and to be clear what form of objection one is offering.

See also

1.4 Validity and soundness
1.5 Invalidity
3.3 Bivalence and the excluded middle

Reading

*Theodore Schick, Jr, and Lewis Vaughn, *How to Think about Weird Things: Critical Thinking for a New Age*, 3rd edn (2002)

1.9 Axioms

Obtaining a guaranteed true conclusion in a deductive argument requires both (1) that the argument be valid, and (2) that the premises be true. Unfortunately, the procedure for determining whether or not a premise is true is much less determinate than the procedure for assessing an argument's validity.

Defining axioms.

Because of this indeterminacy, the concept of an 'axiom' becomes a useful philosophical tool. An axiom is a proposition that acts as a special kind of premise in a certain kind of rational system. Axiomatic systems were first formalized by the geometer Euclid (*fl.* 300 BCE) in his famous work the *Elements*. Axioms in such systems are initial claims that stand in need of no justification – at least from within the system. They are simply the bedrock of the theoretical system, the basis from which, through various steps of deductive reasoning, the rest of the system is derived. In ideal circumstances, an axiom should be such that no rational agent could possibly object to its use.

Axiomatic vs. natural systems of deduction.

It is important to understand, however, that not all conceptual systems are axiomatic – not even all rational systems. For example, some deductive systems try simply to replicate the procedures of reasoning that seem to have unreflectively or naturally developed among humans. This type of system is called a 'natural system of deduction'; it does not posit any axioms but looks instead for its formulae to the practices of ordinary rationality.

First type of axiom.

As we have defined them, axioms would seem to be pretty powerful premises. Once, however, you consider the types of axiom that there are, their power seems to be somewhat diminished. One type of axiom comprises premises that are true by definition. Perhaps because so few great philosophers have been married, the example of 'all bachelors are unmarried men' is usually offered as the paradigmatic example of this. The problem is that no argument is going to be able to run very far with such an axiom. The axiom is purely tautological, that is to say, 'unmarried men' merely repeats in different words the meaning that is already contained in 'bachelor'. (This sort of proposition is sometimes called – following Immanuel Kant – an 'analytic' proposition. See 4.3.) It is thus a spectacularly uninformative sentence (except to someone who doesn't know what 'bachelor' means') and is therefore unlikely to help yield informative conclusions in an argument.

Second type of axiom.

Another type of axiom is also true by definition, but in a slightly more interesting way. Many parts of mathematics and geometry rest on their axioms, and it is only by accepting their basic axioms that more complex proofs can be constructed. For example, it is an axiom of Euclidean geometry that the shortest distance between any two points is a straight line. But while these axioms are vital in geometry and mathematics, they merely define what is true within the particular system of geometry or mathematics to which they belong. Their truth is guaranteed, but only in the context within which they are defined. Used in this way, their acceptability rises or falls with the acceptability of the theoretical system as a whole. (One might call these propositions, 'primitive' sentences within the system.)

Axioms for all?

Some may find the contextual rendering of axiom we've given rather unsatisfactory. Are there not any 'universal axioms' that are both secure and informative in all contexts, for all thinkers, no matter what? Some philosophers have thought so. The Dutch philosopher Baruch (also known as Benedictus) Spinoza (1632–77) in his *Ethics* (1677) attempted to construct an entire metaphysical system from just a few axioms, axioms that he believed were virtually identical with God's thoughts. The problem is that most would agree that at least some of his axioms seem to be empty, unjustifiable and parochial assumptions.

For example, one axiom states that 'if there be no determinate cause it is impossible that an effect should follow' (*Ethics*, bk 1, pt 1, axiom 3). But as John Locke (1632–1704) pointed out, this claim is, taken literally, pretty uninformative since it is true by definition that all effects have causes. What the axiom seems to imply, however, is a more metaphysical claim – that all events in the world are effects that necessarily follow from their causes.

Hume, however, points out that we have no reason to accept this claim about the world. That is to say, we have no reason to believe that events can't occur without causes (*Treatise*, bk 1, pt 3, §14). Certainly, by definition, an effect must have a cause. But for any particular *event*, we have no reason to believe it has followed necessarily from some cause. Medieval Islamic philosopher al-Ghazali (1058–1111) advanced a similar line (*The Incoherence of the Philosophers*, 'On Natural Science', Question One ff.)

Of course, Spinoza seems to claim that he has grasped the truth of his axioms through a special form of intuition (*scientia intuitiva*), and many philosophers have held that there are basic, self-evident truths that may serve as axioms in our reasoning. But why should we believe them?

In many contexts of rationality, therefore, axioms seem to be a useful device, and axiomatic systems of rationality often serve us well. But the notion that those axioms can be so secure that no rational person could in any context deny them seems to be rather dubious.

See also

1.1 Arguments, premises and conclusions
1.10 Definitions
1.12 Tautologies, self-contradictions and the law of non-contradiction
6.6 Self-evident truths

Reading

Euclid, *Elements*
Al-Ghazali, *The Incoherence of the Philosophers*
*Benedictus Spinoza, *Ethics* (1677)

1.10 Definitions

If, somewhere, there lies written on tablets of stone the ten philosophical commandments, you can be sure that numbered among them is the injunction to 'define your terms'. In fact, definitions are so important in philosophy that some have maintained that definitions are ultimately all there is to the subject.

Definitions are important because without them, it is very easy to argue at cross-purposes or to commit fallacies involving equivocation. As the exploits of a recent US president show, if you are, for example, to debate the ethics of extramarital sex, you need to define what precisely you mean by 'sex'. Otherwise, much argument down the line, you can bet someone will turn around and say, 'Oh, well, I wasn't counting *that* as sex.' Much of our language is ambiguous, but if we are to discuss matters in as precise a way as possible, as philosophy aims to do, we should remove as much ambiguity as possible, and adequate definitions are the perfect tool for helping us do that.

Free trade example.

For example, I may be discussing the justice of 'free trade'. In doing so I may define free trade as 'trade that is not hindered by national or international law'. By doing so I have fixed the definition of free trade for the purposes of my discussion. Others may argue that they have a better, or alternative, definition of free trade. This may lead them to reach different conclusions about its justice. Setting out definitions for difficult concepts and reflecting on their implications comprises a great deal of philosophical work.

The reason why it is important to lay out clear definitions for difficult or contentious concepts is that any conclusions you reach properly apply only to those concepts (e.g. 'free trade') *as defined*. My clear definition of how I will use the term thereby both helps and constrains my discussion. It helps it because it gives a determinate and non-ambiguous meaning to the term. It limits it because it means that what I conclude does not necessarily apply to other uses of the term. As it turns out, much disagreement in life results from the disagreeing parties, without their realizing it, meaning different things by their terms.

Too narrow or too broad?

This is why it is important to find a definition that does the right kind of work. If one's definition is *too narrow* or idiosyncratic, it may be that one's findings cannot be applied as broadly as could be hoped. For example, if one defines 'man' to mean bearded, human, male adult, one may reach some rather absurd conclusions – for example, that Native American males are not men. A tool for criticism results from understanding this problem. In order to show that a philosophical position's use of terms is inadequate, point to a case that ought to be covered by the definitions it uses but clearly isn't.

If, on the other hand, a definition is *too broad*, it may lead to equally erroneous or misleading conclusions. For example, if you define wrongdoing as 'inflicting suffering or pain upon another person' you would have to count the administering of shots by physicians, the punishment of children and criminals, and the coaching of athletes as instances of wrongdoing. Another way, then, of criticizing someone's position on some philosophical topic is to indicate a case that fits the definition he or she is using but which they would clearly not wish to include under it.

A definition is like a property line; it establishes the limits marking those instances to which it is proper to apply a term and those instances to which it is not. The ideal definition permits application of the term to just those cases to which it should apply – and to no others.

A rule of thumb.

It is generally better if your definition corresponds as closely as possible to the way in which the term is ordinarily used in the kinds of debates to which your claims are pertinent. There will be, however, occasions where it is appropriate, even necessary, to coin special uses. This would be the case where the current lexicon is not able to make distinctions that you think are philosophically important. For example, we do not have a term in ordinary language that describes a memory that is not necessarily a memory of something the person having it has experienced. Such a thing would occur, for example, if I could somehow share your memories: I would have a memory-type experience, but this would not be of something that I had actually experienced. To call this a memory would be misleading. For this reason, philosophers have coined the special term 'quasi-memory' (or q-memory) to refer to these hypothetical memory-like experiences.

A long tradition.

Historically many philosophical questions are, in effect, quests for adequate definitions. What is knowledge? What is beauty? What is the good? Here, it is not enough just to say, 'By knowledge I mean . . .' Rather, the search is for a definition that best articulates the concept in question. Much of the philosophical work along these lines has involved conceptual analysis or the attempt to unpack and clarify the meanings of important concepts. What is to count as the best articulation, however, requires a great deal of debate. Indeed, it is a viable philosophical question as to whether such concepts actually can be defined. For many ancient and medieval thinkers (like Plato and Aquinas), formulating adequate definitions meant giving verbal expression to the very 'essences' of things – essences that exist independently of us.

Many more recent thinkers (like some pragmatists and post-structuralists) have held that definitions are nothing more than conceptual instruments that organize our interactions with each other and the world, but in no way reflect the nature of an independent reality.

Some thinkers have gone so far as to argue that all philosophical puzzles are essentially rooted in a failure to understand how ordinary language functions. While, to be accurate, this involves attending to more than just definitions, it does show just how deep the philosophical preoccupation with getting the language right runs.

See also

1.9 Axioms
3.4 Category mistakes
3.9 Criteria

Reading

*Plato (c.428–347 BCE), *Meno, Euthyphro, Theatetus, Symposium*
J. L. Austin, *Sense and Sensibilia* (1962)
Michel Foucault, *The Order of Things* (1966)

1.11 Certainty and probability

Seventeenth-century French philosopher René Descartes (1596–1650) is famous for claiming he had discovered the bedrock upon which to build a new science that could determine truths with absolute certainty. The bedrock was an idea that could not be doubted, the *cogito* ('I think') – *je pense donc je suis* ('I think therefore I am', popularly rendered *cogito ergo sum*). Descartes reasoned that it is impossible to doubt that you are thinking, for even if you're in error or being deceived or doubting, you are nevertheless thinking, and if you are thinking, you exist.

Ancient Stoics like Cleanthes (*ob.* 232 BCE) and Chrysippus (280–207 BCE) maintained that we experience certain impressions of the world and morality that we simply cannot doubt – experiences they called 'cataleptic impressions'. Later philosophers like the eighteenth century's Thomas Reid (1710–96) believed that God guarantees the veracity of our cognitive faculties. His contemporary Giambattista Vico (1688–1744) reasoned that we can be certain about things human but not about the non-human world. More recently the Austrian philosopher Ludwig Wittgenstein (1889–1951) tried to show how it simply makes no sense to say that one doubts certain things.

Others have come to suspect that there may be little or nothing we can know with certainty and yet concede that we can still figure things out with some degree of probability. Before, however, you go about claiming to have certainly or probably discovered philosophical truth, it will be a good idea to give some thought to what each concept means.

Types of certainty.

'Certainty' is often described as a kind of feeling or mental state (perhaps as a state in which the mind believes some X without any doubt at all), but doing so simply renders a psychological account of the concept. It fails to define when we are *warranted* in feeling this way. A more philosophical account of certainty would add the claim that a proposition is certainly true when it is impossible for it to be false – and certainly false when it is impossible for it to be true. Sometimes propositions that are certain in this way are called 'necessarily true' and 'necessarily false'.

The sceptical problem.

The main problem, philosophically speaking, thinkers face is in establishing that it is in fact impossible for any candidate for certainty to have a different truth value. Sceptical thinkers have been extremely skilful in showing how virtually any claim might possibly be false even though it appears to be true (or possibly true though it appears to be false). In the wake of sceptical scrutiny, most would agree that absolute certainty in advancing truth claims remains unattainable. Moreover, even if achieving this sort of certainty were possible, while it may be that all that's philosophically certain is true, clearly not all that's true is certain.

But if you can't have demonstrable certainty, what is the next best thing? To give a proper answer to this question would require a much larger study of the theory of knowledge. But it is worth saying a little about the answer that most commonly springs to mind: probability.

Probability is the natural place to retreat to if certainty is not attainable. As a refuge, however, it is rather like the house of sticks the pig flees to from his house of straw. The problem is that probability is a precise notion that cannot be assumed to be the next best thing to certainty.

Objective and subjective probability.

We can distinguish between objective and subjective probability. Objective probability is where what will happen is genuinely indeterminate. Radioactive decay could be one example. For any given radioactive atom, the probability of it having decayed over the period of its half-life is 50-50. This means that, if you were to take ten such atoms, it is likely that five will have decayed over the period of the element's half-life and five will not have decayed. On at least some interpretations, it is genuinely indeterminate which atoms will fall into which category.

Subjective probability refers to cases where there may be no actual indeterminacy, but some particular mind or set of minds makes a probability judgement about the likelihood of some event. These subjects do so because they lack complete information about the causes that will determine the event. Their ignorance requires them to make a probabilistic assessment, usually by assigning a probability based on the number of occurrences of each outcome over a long sequence in the past.

So, for example, if I toss a coin, cover it and ask you to bet on heads or tails, the outcome has already been determined. Since you don't know what it is, you have to use your knowledge that heads and tails over the long run fall 50-50 to assign a 50 per cent probability that it is a head and a 50 per cent probability that it is a tail. If you could see the coin, you would know that, in fact, it was 100 per cent certain that it was whichever side was facing up.

The odds set by gamblers and handicappers at horse races are also species of subjective probability. The posted odds record simply what the many people betting on the race subjectively believe about the outcome.

Certainty and validity.

If you have a sound deductive argument, then its conclusion follows from the premises with certainty. Many inquirers, however, demand not only that conclusions *follow* with certainty but that the conclusions themselves be true. Consider the difference between the following arguments:

1. If it rained last night, England will probably win the match.
2. It rained last night.
3. Therefore, England will probably win the match.

1. All humans are mortal.
2. Socrates was a human.
3. Therefore, Socrates was mortal.

The conclusion of the first argument clearly enters only a probable claim. The conclusion of the second argument in contrast to the first, enters a much more definite claim. But here's the rub: both examples present valid deductive arguments. Both arguments possess valid forms. Therefore in both arguments the conclusion *follows* with certainty – i.e. the truth of the premises *guarantees* the truth of the conclusion – even though the *content* of one conclusion is merely probable while the other is not.

You must therefore distinguish between (1) whether or not the conclusion of an argument *follows* from the premises with certainty, and (2) whether or not the conclusion of an argument advances a *statement* whose truth is itself certain.

Philosophical theories.

But what about philosophical theories? It would seem that if certainty in philosophical theories were attainable, there would be little or no dispute among competent philosophers about which are true and which false – but, in fact, there seems to be a lot of dispute. Does this mean that the truth of philosophical theories is essentially indeterminate?

Some philosophers would say no. For example, they would say that although there remains a great deal of dispute, there is near unanimous agreement among philosophers on many things – for example, that Plato's theory of forms is false and that mind–body dualism is untenable.

Others of a more sceptical bent are, if you'll pardon the pun, not so certain about the extent to which anything has been proven, at least with certainty, in philosophy. Accepting a lack of certainty can be seen as a matter of philosophical maturity.

See also

1.1 Arguments, premises and conclusions
1.2 Deduction
1.4 Validity and soundness
1.5 Invalidity
1.9 Axioms

Reading

*Brad Inwood and Lloyd P. Gerson, *Hellenistic Philosophy: Introductory Readings*, 2nd edn (1988)
Giambattista Vico, *Scienza nuova* (1725)
Ludwig Wittgenstein, *On Certainty* (1969)

1.12 Tautologies, self-contradictions and the law of non-contradiction

Tautologies and self-contradictions fall at opposite ends of a spectrum: the former is a sentence that's necessarily true and the latter a sentence that's necessarily false. Despite being in this sense poles apart, they are actually intimately related.

In common parlance, 'tautology' is a pejorative term used to deride a claim because it purports to be informative but in fact simply repeats the meaning of something already understood. For example, consider: 'A criminal has broken the law.' This statement might be mocked as a tautology since it tells us nothing about the criminal to say he has broken the law. To be a lawbreaker is precisely what it means to be a criminal.

In logic, however, 'tautology' has a more precisely defined meaning. A tautology is a statement in logic such that it will turn out to be true in every circumstance – or, as some say, in every possible world. Tautologies are 'necessary' truths.

Take, for example:

P or not-P

If P is true the statement turns out to be true. But if P is false, the statement still turns out to be true. This is the case for *whatever* one substitutes for P: 'today is Monday', 'atoms are invisible' or 'monkeys make great lasagna'. One can see why tautologies are so poorly regarded. A statement that is true regardless of the truth or falsehood of its components can be considered to be empty, since its content does no work.

This is not to say that tautologies are without philosophical value. Understanding tautologies helps one to understand the nature and function of reason and language.

Valid arguments as tautologies.

As it turns out, all valid arguments can be restated as tautologies – that is, hypothetical statements in which the antecedent is the conjunction of the premises and the consequent the conclusion. That is to say, every valid argument may be articulated as a statement of this form: 'If W, X, Y are true, then C is true', where W, X and Y are the argument's premises and C is the conclusion. When any valid argument is substituted into this form, a tautology results.

Law of non-contradiction.

In addition, the law of non-contradiction — a cornerstone of philosophical logic – is also a tautology. The law may be formulated this way.

   Not (P and not-P)

The law is a tautology since, whether P is true or false, the complete statement will turn out to be true.

   The law of non-contradiction can hardly be said to be uninformative, since it is the foundation upon which all logic is built. But, in fact, it is not the law itself that's informative so much as any attempt to break it.

   Attempts to break the law of non-contradiction are themselves contradictions, and they are obviously and in all circumstances wrong. A contradiction flouts the law of non-contradiction, since to be caught in a contradiction is to be caught asserting both that something is true and something is false at the same time – asserting both P and not-P. Given that the law of non-contradiction is a tautology, and thus in all circumstances true, there can be nothing more clearly false than something that attempts to break it.

   The principle of non-contradiction has also been historically important in philosophy. The principle underwrote ancient analyses of change and plurality and is crucial to Parmenides of Elea's sixth century BCE proclamation that 'what is is and cannot not be'. It also seems central to considerations of identity – for example in Leibniz's claim that objects that are identical must have all the same properties.

Self-refuting criticism.

One curious and useful feature of the law of non-contradiction is that any attempt to refute it presupposes it. To argue that the law of non-contradiction is false is to imply that it is not also true. In other words, the critic *presupposes* that what he or she is criticizing can be either true or false *but not both true and false*. But this presupposition is just the law of non-contradiction itself – the same law the critic aims to refute. In other words, anyone who denies the principle of non-contradiction simultaneously affirms it. It is a principle that cannot be rationally criticized, because it is presupposed by all rationality.

To understand why a *tautology* is necessarily, and in a sense at least, uninformatively true and why a *self-contradiction* is necessarily false is to understand the most basic principle of logic. The *law of non-contradiction* is where those two concepts meet and so is perhaps best described as the keystone, rather than cornerstone, of philosophical logic.

See also

1.4 Validity and soundness
1.6 Consistency
3.19 Paradoxes
3.16 Leibniz's law of identity
3.27 Self-defeating arguments

Reading

*Patrick J. Hurley, *A Concise Introduction to Logic*, 7th edn (2000)
Aristotle, *Posterior Analytics*, bk 1, ch. 11:10
Aristotle, *Interpretation*, esp. chs 6–9

chapter 2
Further Tools for Argument

2.1 Abduction

No, we're not talking about kidnapping but, rather, an important dimension of scientific and ordinary as well as philosophical rationality. Consider the following example.

A man is found in a cabin in a remote forest, with all the doors and windows securely locked from the inside, hanging dead from a noose. A suicide note lies on the table nearby. What would best explain this set of facts? Abduction, a term coined by the American pragmatist philosopher Charles Sanders Peirce (1839–1914), is a tool to do just that.

Abduction is a process of reasoning used to decide which explanation of given phenomena we should select, and so, naturally, it is also called 'argument to the best explanation'. Often we are presented with certain experiences and are called upon to offer some sort of explanation for them. But the problem we frequently face is that a body of data does not determine or force us to accept only one explanation. Unsettling as it seems, some philosophers have even argued that for *every possible* body of evidence there will *always* be a variety of explanations consistent with it. This is just the claim that Duhem and Quine have advanced. Whether or not their claim is true, however, in cases where we do face a set of alternative explanations, our task as good reasoners must be to decide which one of those explanations *best* fits the evidence. That's where abduction comes in. To understand how it works, let's return to our example.

If you think about it, although the man's death seems on the face of it to be an open and shut case of suicide, there are other possible explanations for it, some more fanciful than others. Perhaps the man was rehearsing a drama about suicide, had locked the doors for privacy and things had gone terribly wrong. Or perhaps the CIA has developed teletransporters, had killed the man, set things up to look like a suicide and left without using the doors. Perhaps a demonic spirit lived in the woods nearby, magically entered the room, killed him, and then vanished. These alternative explanations may seem ludicrous, but all are consistent with the evidence. Therefore it cannot be the case that the evidence leaves suicide as the *only possible* explanation.

So, which explanation should we choose? Philosophers thinking about abduction have developed a number of key principles of selection – though note that a good deal of interesting controversy surrounds them. Think of the following list as a set of tools you can use to select among competing theories.

Simplicity: when possible, go with the least complicated explanation, the one that requires the fewest and most direct causal sequences, the fewest claims about what exists, and that speculates about things beyond the evidence as little as possible. (Medieval philosopher William of Ockham is famous for developing this idea. See 3.18.)

Coherence: when possible, go with the explanation that's consistent with what we already believe to be true.

Testability or predictive power: when possible, go with the theory that allows you to make predictions that can be confirmed or disconfirmed (see 3.29).

Comprehensiveness in scope: when possible, go with the explanation that leaves the fewest loose ends, that explains the most and leaves the least unexplained.

Another way of saying all this is simply to say, 'Choose the explanation characterized by features closest to those of an open and shut case.'

Consider the possibility that the victim of our hanging was an actor who died an accidental death. That claim would predict that he should own a script, perhaps have been a member of a theatre troupe, or told his friends that he was involved in a play. But in examining the room and his home, interviewing his friends, checking local theatre groups, we find no such evidence. That is to say, investigation fails to confirm the prediction and finds an improbable absence of evidence.

Investigating the teletransportation explanation similarly fails to produce confirming evidence, the facts of government security render it exceedingly difficult to test, and it contradicts our background knowledge about the technological abilities of the US government.

The demonic spirit explanation requires us to believe in a kind of supernatural being for which we have no evidence.

Suicide as an explanation, on the other hand, is simple. It requires us to posit the existence of neither supernatural spirits nor secret, illegal government conspiracies involving unknown but incredibly advanced technologies. It allows us to make predictions that can be tested. (For example, that the man had been depressed and under stress. Let's say investigation shows him to have recently been fired, bankrupt and divorced.) Unlike the actor theory it doesn't predict the existence of things (like scripts) that we can't find. It is consistent with our background knowledge of common human behaviour. And it explains all the facts before us.

The problem of enumerative induction.

But here's the problem that continues to gnaw at philosophers: it is still *possible* that the other explanations are true. Therefore, it is *possible* not only that these principles of abduction *fail to guarantee* that our selection of explanations will be the truth. It is also possible that these principles will at least sometimes serve as an *obstacle* to our acquiring true beliefs. Sceptics love to point this out.

For example, if we encounter a series of numbers 1, 2, 3, 4, 5, 6 our principles of abduction would lead us to conclude that the next will be 7. That is, our background experience and our past testing has led us to explain satisfactorily the advance of the sequence as a process of simply adding one to the last number to produce the next. But it is possible that the next number in the series is actually any number. The process might be following a rule of add one five times, then add ten. In that case the next number will be 16. In short, our selection of 7 would have been the best we could do using the principles of abduction and the evidence available to us, but it would nevertheless have been wrong. And for *any* sequence of numbers, the next may *always* reveal that our preceding conclusions about the rules governing the sequence have been wrong.

It is easy to see, then, why Peirce's method of abduction is appealing to pragmatists but troubling to realists, who maintain that science discloses the single nature of independent reality. From a pragmatic point of view, the methods of abduction are not based on the supposition that truth about an independent reality can be irrefutably established, but on the idea that we have to make the best of truth that we can, given the limits of evidence and the demands of life. Peirce himself held that the evident convergence of scientific theories as well as their usefulness suggests that abduction ultimately leads explanations to converge upon a single truth. Many, however, remain unconvinced.

See also

1.6 Consistency
3.1 Alternative explanations
3.18 Ockham's Razor
3.28 Sufficient reason
3.29 Testability

Reading

Charles Sanders Peirce, 'Pragmatism and Pragmaticism', in *Collected Works of Charles Sanders Peirce* (1960), vol. 5
Peter Lipton, *The Inference to the Best Explanation* (1991)
Pierre M. M. Duhem, *La théorie physique, son object et sa structure* (1906)

2.2 Hypothetico-deductive method

In an episode of the hilarious British chat-show parody, *Knowing Me, Knowing You*, the host, Alan Partridge, is arguing with a major novelist about the existence of Sherlock Holmes. Partridge is under the illusion that Sherlock Holmes was a real person who not only solved crimes, but wrote about them as well. Eventually, the exasperated author asks Partridge, 'If Sherlock Holmes was a real person, how could he describe, in intimate details, the circumstances of his own death?' There is a pregnant pause. 'The Nobel prize for literature,' replies Partridge. 'You've never won it, have you?'

Grandiose though it may seem, the author was, in essence, making use of the 'hypothetico-deductive', 'covering law', or 'deductive-nomological' method. This is a procedure that many philosophers of science – most notably Karl Popper (1902–94) and Carl Gustav Hempel (1905–97) – have argued lies at the heart of scientific enquiry. It works by starting with a hypothesis, say, that lead is heavier than water. If this is true then it is possible to deduce certain other true claims that follow from it. The most obvious is that lead sinks in water. By then seeing if, in fact, lead does sink in water, one tests the original hypothesis. The results of the experiment may, in the strongest case, prove or disprove the hypothesis; in weaker cases, the result provides evidence for or against it.

The procedure is very widely applicable, as can be seen in the case of hapless Alan Partridge. In this instance, from the hypothesis that the Sherlock Holmes detective novels were autobiographical, certain other facts follow.

One is that it would not be possible for the books to describe the circumstances of the death of their author. The fact that they do therefore proves
that the hypothesis is false.

The basic principle of the hypothetico-deductive method is therefore 'Start
with a hypothesis and a set of given conditions, deduce what facts follow
from them, and then conduct experiments to see if these facts hold and hence
whether the hypothesis is true or false.'

That something like the hypothetico-deductive method is a useful tool in
enquiry generally and science in particular is not in doubt. But its limitations have become much more apparent over the last century and a certain
amount of caution needs to be exercised in using it.

The problem of assumptions.

One reason for this is that the apparently straightforward relationship between the hypothesis and what follows from it is often not very straightforward at all. Even in Partridge's case, had Holmes really existed and planned
his own murder, for example, and the plan been successfully executed, he
could have described the circumstances of his own death. He would also
have been able to describe his own death if he had been clairvoyant. What
this shows is that what we take to follow from the hypothesis depends upon
a wide range of *assumptions* about what else is normal or true. This is a
problem in the philosophical use of the method, because successful philosophical arguments have to make minimal assumptions about what else is
true. In the philosophy of science, it is a problem because one can often only
assume what is needed to make the method work if one has already accepted
the broad theoretical framework within which the hypothesis is being tested.

Testability problems.

A second set of problems stems from the method not easily generating tests
that are able to settle the question of the hypothesis's truth. Typically this is
true of *universal claims*, such as 'no human is immortal'. No matter how
many humans you slay to see if this hypothesis is true, it always remains
logically possible that one of the surviving humans is immortal, or that the
experimenter herself is the immortal one. For this reason, Popper thought
one can falsify but not fully verify many important universal claims. Hence the
universal claim that all swans are white can be falsified by pointing out a black
swan, but no matter how many white swans one finds it always remains possible
that the next swan encountered will not be white.

Problems also arise because of *technical limitations on testability*. I may, for example, be able to deduce from a set of hypotheses what would happen to the orbits of the other planets if Jupiter were suddenly to double in mass, but I am technically unable to construct a procedure to test that claim.

The hypothetico-deductive method is a useful tool, therefore, but it doesn't have quite the depth and power it may at first appear to possess.

See also

1.2 Deduction
3.1 Alternative explanations

Reading

Carl Gustav Hempel, 'Deductive-Nomological vs. Statistical Explanation', in *Minnesota Studies in the Philosophy of Science* 3 (1962)
Carl Gustav Hempel and Paul Oppenheim, 'Studies in the Logic of Explanation', in *Philosophy of Science* 15 (1948)
Karl Popper, *The Logic of Scientific Discovery* (1934, 1959)

2.3 Dialectic

According to Plato's Socrates (*Apology* 38a), the life of philosophical examination is the best life, and, moreover, the unexamined life is not worth living. A great deal of philosophical examination has taken the form of 'dialectic' (*dialektikē*). It is a kind of thinking that pops up again and again in the history of philosophy. But what exactly is dialectic and how does one take part in it?

In a nutshell, dialectical thinking is a sort of philosophical dialogue – a back and forth process between two or more points of view. There are various ways one might formulate this process. One way would be like this:

1. One party advances a claim.
2. Some other party advances a contrary claim, or the other launches into a critical analysis of the claim, looking for incoherencies or logical inconsistencies or absurd implications in the claim.
3. The first party attempts to defend, to refine or to modify the original claim in the light of the challenge brought by the other.

4.   The other responds to the first party's defence, refinement or modification.
5.   Ultimately, a more sophisticated and/or accurate understanding of the issue at hand emerges.

You can see, then, that dialectical thinking involves some 'other' and some sort of opposition or contrariety between the various thinkers engaged in the process. This sort of opposition is often thought of as the 'negative moment' of the first claim.

Otherness and oneness.

The dialectical process is also often thought of as acting as a sort of engine for philosophical progress – perhaps as the most powerful sort. By struggling through a series of negative moments and resolutions to them, dialecticians believe that understanding of the truth emerges. Typically, dialecticians hold that thinking begins in a murky, incoherent morass of many, different, *other* opinions – some having a glimmer or partial grasp on the truth. Through confrontations with these *others* and their negativity, a more complete and comprehensive grasp of the *one* or *oneness* that is truth emerges. Hence, for Plato, upon the wings of dialectic we can transcend the *many* images of the truth to grasp of the *one* 'form' of which those images are copies, as for instance in his famous image of the 'Divided Line' (*Republic* 532d). Georg Wilhelm Friedrich Hegel (1770–1831) maintains that while some of us individuals caught up in history may gain a partial understanding of the things, 'the true is the whole' (*das wahr ist das ganzen*). Hence dialectic can be said to aim at wholeness or unity, while 'analytic' thinking divides that with which it deals into parts. The great German philosopher Immanuel Kant (1724–1804), however, famously argued in the section of his *Critique of Pure Reason* (1781) entitled 'Transcendental Dialectic' that when it comes to metaphysics, thinking fails to achieve wholeness, completion and truth, but yields instead only endless, irresolvable conflict and illusion.

Hegel.

Hegel has, in fact, become misleadingly associated with perhaps the most well-known model of dialectic. According to this model, one begins with a 'thesis' against which is opposed an 'antithesis'. The result of their confrontation is a 'synthesis' which subsumes and resolves the apparent conflict between the thesis and the antithesis in an upward, transcending motion called 'sublation' (*Aufhebung*), resulting in a condition that is *aufgehoben* or literally 'thrown upwards'.

SYNTHESIS

↑

(sublation)

↑

THESIS ↔ ANTITHESIS

The trouble is, Hegel didn't really use this model. He did regard history as a dialectical process characterized by the opposition of negative moments as well as *aufgehoben* moments of progress, but he did not formalize the process in terms of theses and antitheses. It was instead the poet Johann Christoph Friedrich von Schiller (1759–1805) who developed that model and an influential fellow philosopher, Jacob Gottlieb Fichte (1762–1814), who deployed it with vigour.

Dialectical materialism.

Karl Marx (1818–83) and Friedrich Engels (1820–95) have also been associated with a way of understanding the world called 'dialectical materialism'. The term is not their own but originated with Russian Marxist Georgii Plekhanov in 1891. Engels did, however, characterize his own and Marx's thought as 'materialist dialectics' and contrasted it against the Hegelians' 'idealist dialectics'. As with the Hegelians, Marx and Engels regarded history as a progressive, dialectical process driven by the clash of oppositions. But for Marx and Engels the process entails not the clash of theories and ideas but instead the struggle of economic classes. While, then, for Hegel the result of the dialectical process is 'absolute knowledge' (*das absolute Wissen*) of the comprehensive whole of truth, for Marx and Engels the result of the material dialectic is the perfect, classless society they describe as 'communism'. Soviet theorists advanced this idea.

See also

5.1 Class critique

Reading

*Plato, *Republic*
Jacob Gottlieb Fichte, *The Science of Knowledge* (1794–5)
Gustav A. Wetter, *Dialectical Materialism: A Historical and Systematic Survey of Philosophy in the Soviet Union* (1958, 1973)

2.4 Analogies

Indisputably, one of the most famous texts in the history of Western philosophy is Plato's *Republic*. While this text is well known for the vision it presents of an ideal political order, careful readers will know that Plato's character Socrates articulates his theory of the just *polis* as an analogy for the justice of the human soul or mind (*Republic* 368b–369b). The text is, in fact, full of analogies. Socrates describes a cave where humans are kept literally in the dark about reality. He describes a ship of fools, piloted not by someone with nautical understanding but by those clever enough to gain power. Perhaps because he can't seem to formulate his grasp of it in any other way, he tries to convey the nature of transcendent reality by comparing it to the sun. Similarly, medieval philosopher Thomas Aquinas (1224–74) held that while we remain unable to formulate God's nature *literally* in language, it is nevertheless possible to attribute properties like 'good' and 'one' to God through a process called *analogical* predication.

It is hard to get a grip on abstract ideas such as truth or reality, but people can easily relate to cities, ships, celestial objects and cave dwellers. Analogies make it possible for us to engage our imaginations in philosophical thought. This is one reason why analogies are such useful philosophical tools.

Analogies in reasoning.

Analogies, of course, have many uses in our lives. They advance ideas in poetry, fiction, film, morals, religion, government and sport. One of their most important uses may be found in the law. When lawyers cite precedents in making their cases, they are appealing to arguments from analogy. In short they are saying, 'The present case is analogous to this past case, so the court should rule now in the same way it did then.' Legal opponents will, of course, try to show that the present case is not analogous to that previous case and that therefore the ruling ought to be otherwise.

Reasoning in empirical science may also be thought of as relying upon analogies. Whenever we encounter a new phenomenon and explain it by appeal to a general law based upon past experience, we rely on the claim that the new phenomenon is analogous to those of the past. Indeed, the eighteenth-century philosopher David Hume writes, 'All our reasonings concerning matters of fact are founded on a species of Analogy' (*Enquiry concerning Human Understanding*, 82). Kant goes so far as to claim that analogy makes possible the representation of necessary connections among perceptions in ordinary experience.

Argument and illustration.

Analogies can serve two different functions in philosophy. Sometimes, as is often the case in Plato, for example, they serve simply to illustrate. When Socrates compares the Good with the sun, he is simply using the image of the sun to help bring to life his arguments about the Good. On other occasions, however, the analogy can be an integral part of an argument. Consider one of the most popular arguments for the existence of God, the 'argument from design', which has been advanced by many thinkers, from the ancient Stoics to British theologian William Paley (1743–1805). The argument holds that just as an artefact such as a watch implies the existence of an artisan, so the universe implies the existence of a divine creator. Here the analogy with the watch is not meant simply to illustrate a point. Rather, the analogy is supposed to show why we should conclude that the universe has a creator.

Strong and weak.

Analogical reasoning, then, is both powerful and important. There are, however, dangers. Analogies can mislead as well as illuminate. Analogies can be weak as well as strong. But how can we tell the difference? Consider the following tools for discriminating strong from weak analogies:

Strong Analogy: an analogy is strong when the things compared (1) share a large or decisive number of relevant similarities and (2) do *not* exhibit a large or decisive number of relevant differences.

Weak Analogy: an analogy is weak when the things compared (1) do *not* share a share a large or decisive number of relevant similarities or (2) do exhibit a large or decisive number of relevant differences.

Consider the argument from design. Is the analogy at the heart of the argument a strong or a weak one? As Cicero (106–43 BCE) and Hume point out, there are a number of crucial dissimilarities between an artefact and the universe. For example, we *experience* the making of artefacts by artisans, but none of us has ever witnessed the creation of a universe, and it doesn't seem that any of us ever will. Therefore, while certain similarities do exist between artefacts and the universe, their argumentative force is countered by relevant dissimilarities.

A good analogy should compare things exhibiting similarities whose number and relevance exceeds that of any dissimilarities between them. Beautiful and wise-sounding phrases such as 'The flower that refuses to turn to the sun will never open' are simply not enough.

See also

2.6 Intuition Pumps
2.9 Thought experiments
2.11 Useful fictions

Reading

*Plato, *Republic*
*David Hume, *Enquiry concerning Human Understanding* (1748); *Dialogue concerning Natural Religion* (1779)
Ralph McInerny, *The Logic of Analogy* (1961)
Emmanuel Kant, *Critique of Judgment* (1790)

2.5 Anomalies and exceptions that prove the rule

One of the more baffling sayings in the English-speaking world is that 'the exception proves the rule'. At first sight, this looks plain nonsense: if the rule states that 'all swans are white' and I find a black swan, that doesn't prove the rule, it disproves it.

Whenever something enduring appears to be so patently false, one should invoke the principle of charity (see 3.21) and ask whether it really means what it appears to. In this case, the apparent absurdity is a consequence of a change of linguistic usage. In its old-fashioned sense 'prove' means to test, not to confirm. Once this etymological fact is acknowledged, our tired old saying becomes much more interesting.

In what sense can exceptions be used to 'prove' or 'test' a rule, rather than just show it to be false? Some possible answers to this question can be seen in how one could respond to exceptions to rules proposed by Hume.

In Hume's empirical philosophy, he proposed a general rule that all our 'ideas' (by which he roughly meant thoughts and other mental representations) are derived from 'impressions' (by which he roughly meant sense and feeling). Further, he claimed that 'the most lively thought is still inferior [i.e. less vivid] to the dullest perception' (*Enquiry concerning Human Understanding*, 2).

There appear to be exceptions to both of these rules. One Hume himself discussed. He asks us to imagine a person who has never seen a particular shade of blue. What if we were to place before this person a series of shades of blue, each one next to its most similar shade, so that we have a range of subtle gradations. If we were to remove the shade that the person had never seen, would they be able to imagine this missing shade, which they had never actually seen? Hume admits they could, which means that in a least one case, a person can have an idea without ever having the corresponding impression.

Weakening the rule.

How did Hume respond to this exception to his rule? Far from seeing it as disproving his theory, he writes, '[this] instance is so singular, that it is scarcely worth our observing'. A charitable rendering of this remark might hold that the exception reveals something about the nature of the rule. That is to say, Hume never put forward the rule as an absolute, exceptionless description of all of nature. Rather, it is a rule that describes a general pattern in the overwhelming majority of cases – but not in all of them. Rules need not be absolute – they may sometimes admit exceptions.

Amending and defending a rule.

Phenomena that don't fit the pattern described by a rule are often called 'anomalies' – literally non-lawful things. Weakening the rule to make room is one way to deal with them. Another way of coping with anomalies is to show how, properly understood, they really don't break the rule in question. Consider the following example.

Sometimes a survivor of trauma reports being unaware of the traumatic events at the time they occurred, only to suffer extremely vivid flashbacks later. In this case, the later idea (the recollection) appears to be more vivid than the original impression (the actual traumatic experience).

This phenomenon seems to violate Hume's rule. But perhaps Hume can save his rule by showing that there is something extraordinary or 'exceptional' about this case. For example, he might reformulate his rule such that it holds true *except* in cases where the resulting idea is modified by some additional, supervening mechanism (such as a post-traumatic reaction). Similarly, Isaac Newton's (1642–1727) law of motion claims that a body in motion will remain in motion – *except* in cases where the body in question is acted upon by an external force.

In short, the very fact that we can show that something which appears to falsify the rule is in some important way different from cases where the rule normally applies shows that the rule is sound. Because we've found that the case of post-traumatic flashbacks is *exceptional* it doesn't falsify the general rule. By definition an 'exception' is something to which the rule does not apply; and moreover, something can only be an 'exception' if the rule has already been established!

Fallacy of accident.

There's even a special fallacy associated with applying a general rule inappropriately to a particular case. It is called 'accident'. The fallacy of accident is applying a general rule inappropriately to a particular case.

For example, if someone claimed that the right of free speech gives citizens the right to threaten each other's lives, you could accuse her of this fallacy. Since the rule that the government may not interfere with free speech applies only to speech with political value, it does not protect threats, or harassment, slander or abuse. Similarly, Newton's law that bodies in motion remain in motion does not apply to moving bodies acted upon by external forces.

The proving of rules by exceptions, therefore, can be understood, not as a piece of nonsense, but as a sound procedure in rational enquiry. Whenever a rule appears to admit of an exception, there is a need to revisit the rule, to decide if the status of the rule needs reconsidering; if the substance of the rule needs amending or reinterpretation; or whether it just needs to be abandoned. Anomalies can often be dismissed as mere exceptions or as phenomena that only appear to violate the rule. But just how many anomalies can we tolerate before we ought to abandon a rule entirely? Answering this question is no simple matter.

See also

3.8 Counterexamples
3.21 Principle of charity

Reading

*David Hume, *An Enquiry concerning Human Understanding* (1748)
*Thomas Kuhn, *The Structure of Scientific Revolutions* (1962)
G. P. Baker and P. M. S. Hacker, *Scepticism, Rules and Language* (1984)

2.6 Intuition pumps

Many ideas in science and philosophy are difficult to grasp. To help us on our way, both scientists and philosophers have made use of metaphor and imagery.

Plato's conception of 'the Good' in the *Republic*, for example, is extremely abstract and obscure, but by encouraging us to think of the Good as like the sun in Book 7, we are enabled to get some kind of grip on the idea. Just as the sun is that which makes physical objects visible, we are told, so the Good is that which makes the world intelligible.

More recently, the concept of 'person-stages' has been introduced to the philosophy of personal identity. This is again an odd idea, but to help us understand it, we are often given a simpler analogue. Think of a carrot, for example, which is a single object one can take a slice out of at any stage, thus seeing what that carrot is at a particular point in space. Imagine a person's whole life in a similar way, as a single object extended in time *and* space, and at any one point in time, we are able to see what that person is at that particular point in time by examining that 'time-slice' or 'person-stage'.

Both the carrot and the sun are examples of intuition pumps. They are not philosophical arguments, but rather images, stories or analogies that give us something vivid and concrete to help us understand what would otherwise be obscure and abstract.

Use of the tool.

But why call them 'intuition pumps' rather than just metaphors or analogies? The reason can be seen in the phrase's origins. Like 'Quakers' and 'Methodists', the perfectly dignified name of intuition pump owes its existence to a piece of derogatory coinage. Daniel C. Dennett (1942–) introduced the term in a criticism of John R. Searle's (1932–) famous 'Chinese room' argument. Dennett's claim was that, despite its name, this wasn't an argument at all, it was a mere 'intuition pump'. The point of the term is to make clear the distinction between arguments that might make use of analogies and analogies that aren't in fact part of an argument at all but simply devices that assist our comprehension.

It is extremely useful to be able to recognize and use intuition pumps. When used well, they can be a powerful tool in aiding the understanding. The theory of functionalism, for example, can be very hard to fathom when one hears it explained in terms of inputs and outputs. But if we start thinking about the brain as like a piece of computer hardware and the mind like the program that is running in it, it is much easier to begin to see what the theory is getting at.

Problems.

However, intuition pumps can lead us astray. Sometimes what is in fact no more than an intuition pump may appear to us as an argument. This is arguably the case with a famous passage in John Locke's work. Locke asks whether, if we had the souls of ancient Greeks, but knew nothing of their lives, we would consider ourselves to be the same persons they were. On the basis of their intuitions most answer this question in the negative, but notice that *no argument has been put forward* that we are not, in fact, the same persons as those ancient Greeks. All Locke has done is taken a question where people's intuitions are not clear ('Is memory necessary for personal identity?') and answered it with a hypothetical situation where their intuitions are stronger. This makes the question under consideration much more vivid, but it is not to be confused with offering an argument. Both readers and writers can equally fall into this confusion.

Being able, then, clearly to distinguish intuition pumps from arguments is a useful tool. Equally useful is recognizing that intuition pumps are no more than aids to comprehension. They don't always function as strict analogies. So you have to be careful how you draw the parallel from the intuition pump to what is being explained.

Perhaps the most notorious example of failing to do this is Richard Dawkins's use of the term the 'selfish gene'. In calling the gene selfish, Dawkins is merely trying to help us understand that the gene does not do what is best for the organism as a whole – it merely duplicates itself. But in taking the term too literally, people have misunderstood both Dawkins and the consequences of accepting a gene-centred understanding of evolution. Perhaps this shows that the intuition pump he chose was not a good one. At the very least, it shows the danger of employing this particular expository tool.

See also

2.4 Analogies
2.9 Thought experiments

Reading

*Richard Dawkins, *The Selfish Gene* (1990)
Daniel C. Dennett, 'The Milk of Human Intentionality', *Behavioural and Brain Sciences* 3 (1980)
*John Searle, *Minds, Brains, and Science* (1984)

2.7 Logical constructions

> The average Briton spends one hour a day surfing the Internet.

What is philosophically interesting about this sentence is that it expresses something that clearly has a truth value (it is either true or false), but the two things it refers to – the Internet and the average Briton – do not exist in a straightforward way. You can't have a chat with the average Briton and you can't catch any fish with the Internet. So in what sense does either exist?

Both the average Briton and the Internet are logical constructions. That is to say, although there is no single thing that exists in either case, the existence of both can be described in terms of a variety of other things, the existence of which is unproblematic.

Type 1: the Internet.

Take the Internet first. There seems something odd about thinking of the Internet as a single thing, since one is unable to say about the Internet what one would normally be expected to say about a normal object. One cannot say how big it is, how much it weighs, where its boundaries are, and so on. The Internet certainly exists in some sense – I use it virtually everyday. The mystery is dissolved once we describe the Internet in terms of the many other things and their activities that it *comprises*. The Internet springs into existence when computers, servers, telephone lines and satellites work together in a certain way. None of these objects is at all mysterious, and they exist in the standard, straightforward way. So we can see the Internet as a logical construction – something that is really no more than many other things working together in a certain way, but which for convenience we can refer to as a single entity. In the same way we might talk about the Renaissance, the Catholic Church or the US, all of which are logical constructions that *comprise* various unproblematic material things and events.

Type 2: the average Briton.

The average Briton is a logical construction in a different way. This fictional person is an *abstraction*, constructed from taking all the statistics about all Britons and finding their *mean average*. Unlike the Internet, the average Briton cannot be used or engaged as one does the Internet or the Catholic Church. Nevertheless, it is still a logical construction, since facts about the average Briton can be described in terms of facts about a large number of real people, whose existence is unproblematic. Again, for convenience's sake we can refer to this abstraction as a single entity, although it is more accurate not to think of it as a single thing, but as a logical construction built up from many other things.

A complication.

Although the idea of a logical construction may appear to be quite straightforward, a little reflection shows that its introduction opens up a particularly wriggly can of worms. The problem is with logical constructions of the first sort – constructions rather than abstractions. The worry is that all sorts of things we don't take to be logical constructions could, on some understandings, turn out to be just that. Take a simple object like a table. Doesn't science tell us that there really doesn't exist a single, simple entity such as a table? Rather, what fundamentally exists are mere atoms (which in turn are mere collections of subatomic particles). If science is right, then isn't a table a logical construction? While it may be convenient to talk about the table as if it were a single object, perhaps it is just a collection of many smaller objects. Or perhaps theories about atoms and quarks are logical constructions we invent to explain something more fundamental: namely, the things that compose our ordinary, common life-world. The distinction between theory and the prior things that theory is about becomes difficult to maintain – perhaps for good reason.

See also

2.8 Reduction
2.11 Useful fictions

Reading

*Bertrand Russell, *The Problems of Philosophy* (1912)
Bertrand Russell, 'Logical Atomism', in *The Philosophy of Logical Atomism*,
  ed. D. F. Pears (1985)

2.8 Reduction

It is not clear when 'reductionist' became a term of abuse, but, in general discourse, at least, that seems to be where it has ended up. A reductionist is seen as someone who takes what is complex, nuanced and sophisticated and breaks it down into something simplistic, sterile and empty. So, for example, a reductionist takes the complex web of human motivation and reduces it to a Darwinian survival instinct or a Freudian expression of repressed desires. On this view, the reductionist is the crude simplifier.

It would be wildly unfair, however, to dismiss reductionism on the basis of these caricatures. Reductionism is a much more respectable process than many of its critics maintain. Reductionism is simply the process of explaining one kind of phenomenon in terms of the simpler, more fundamental phenomena that underlie both it and other phenomena.

Simplified water.

Reductionism is an indispensable tool in science. As everyone learned at school, in order to understand why water bubbles and evaporates at 100°C, you need to understand what is going on at the molecular level – the increase in the Brownian motion of the H_2O. This is a paradigmatic example of reductionism at work. The phenomenon of boiling water is explained in terms of the simpler, more fundamental phenomena of Brownian motion. It is simpler, not in the sense that it is easier to understand, but because it describes what happens to the many parts that make up the more complex whole. Moreover, Brownian motion explains not only boiling water but the behaviour of many other phenomena related to solids, gases and liquids – for example the pressure changes in chlorine gas as it is heated and the expansion of concrete bridges. The appeal to Brownian motion is more fundamental because the Brownian motion explains why the water bubbles and evaporates, not the other way around.

Application in philosophy.

Reductionism has been extremely successful in science. But what is its role in philosophy? There are several major philosophical questions for which reductionist solutions have been offered. One example is the question of what knowledge is. Knowledge seems to be different from mere belief, but the concept of knowledge itself does not seem precise enough to indicate what this difference is. One reductionist account of knowledge is that it is justified true belief. Here, the single, amorphous concept of knowledge is explained in terms of three, simpler constitutive features: knowledge comprises a *belief* that is both *justified* and *true*. The reductionist can take these further by giving reductive accounts of what justification, belief and truth each in turn comprise. Moreover, where we began with two distinct types of thought (knowing and believing), reductionism shows how we may be dealing with various types of belief only.

The many and the one.

Indeed, philosophy and science are often said to have begun in a reductionist moment – Thales of Miletus's (*c.* 620–*c.* 555 BCE) famous assertion that 'all is water'. The genius of Thales's claim is that it reduces the vast multiplicity of natural phenomena (leaves, animals, rocks, clouds, shells, fire, hair, etc.) to a single principle – what the ancient Greeks called an *archē*. Whether it appears in Thales's original philosophical gesture, in Newton's explaining the multifarious kinds of motion in the universe with a mere three laws, or Einstein's all-embracing $E = mc^2$, this reductionist gesture is basic to philosophy and science.

Ethics.

Reductionist accounts can also be found in ethics. 'Good', like 'knowledge', is a concept that many do not think is self-explanatory. We have some idea of what goodness is, but there seems to be scope for disagreement among competent users of the word as to what it actually means. A reductive account of goodness may explain it in terms of its simpler, more fundamental features. So, for example, a utilitarian account is essentially reductive because it explains goodness in terms of what increases happiness and decreases suffering and pain. These features are all simpler than goodness, since there is greater clarity about their meaning: 'increasing happiness' has a precision of meaning that 'being good' does not. It also provides an explanation for why good things are good, in that we can all see why happiness is a good thing and pain bad.

Ordinary language opposition.

Reductionism certainly has a good pedigree in philosophy, but it is also not difficult to see why some oppose it. It is not at all obvious why all questions in philosophy should best be answered reductively. Maybe you just can't specify what it means to know something by breaking the concept down into its simpler, constitutive parts. Wittgenstein and the ordinary-language philosophers such as Oxford professor J. L. Austin (1911–60) argued that words like 'knowledge' are to be understood in terms of the way in which they function in communities of competent language users. One cannot describe this in reductive terms. One can identify certain recurrent features of the use of the word, some of which may even be essential. But one cannot expect to be able to boil down the list of rules for the correct application of a word to a finite list of specific conditions. If one did this, something of the meaning of knowledge would be lost – one would have failed to 'save the phenomena'.

A heuristic device.

One needn't always choose between reductive and non-reductive approaches. One could use reductionism as a *heuristic device*. Here, one would attempt the reduction, not because one believes that the phenomenon being explained can be fully understood in terms of something simpler but because the process of reductive explanation reveals interesting things from which one can learn. So, for example, returning to knowledge as justified true belief, one could reject the view that a full account of what knowledge is can be given by no more than this reductive analysis. But one could accept that the attempt to make the reduction reveals the importance of the ideas of justification and truth for the concept of knowledge. This is reductionism as a tool in the full sense of the word – it is something to be used for what it can reveal, not something that is itself a recipe for truth-finding.

See also

Reading

Patricia S. Churchland, *Neurophilosophy: Towards a Unified Science of Mind–Brain* (1986)
C. A. Hooker, 'Toward a General Theory of Reduction', *Dialogue* 20 (1981)
Ernest Nagel, *The Structure of Science* (1961)

2.9 Thought experiments

There is a long-running fight going on in philosophy between those who think there is an important continuity between philosophy and the sciences and those who think philosophy is a very different form of enquiry. When the division is put in these terms, it is easy to imagine that, on the one side, you have the hard-nosed, dry-brained, scientistic philosophers and, on the other, the artistic, creative poet-philosophers. But in fact, on both sides a great deal of use has been made of a curious literary-scientific hybrid – fictional thought experiments.

Philosophers use fictions in analogies (2.4) and intuition pumps (2.6), but perhaps their most striking usage is to be found in thought experiments (aka *Gedanken* experiments). Thought experiments are aptly named since their aim is to mimic the method of scientific experiments but in thought alone.

Experimental method.

It is helpful to begin by thinking about what happens in a standard scientific experiment. Imagine an experiment to find out how a soap powder bleaches. In normal use, there are several factors that may cause the soap powder to act in a certain way. These will include its active ingredients, the type and temperature of the water in which the ingredients are dissolved, the materials being cleaned, and the machinery – if any – used to do the cleaning. Any experiment that could hope to discover what *caused* bleaching would have to be devised in such a way as to ensure that the crucial factors were properly isolated from the other variables. So if, for example, the hypothesis is that it is the chlorine that does the bleaching, the experiment needs to show that *if all the other factors remain the same* the presence or absence of the chlorine will determine whether the soap powder bleaches.

Put more simply, the aim of a scientific experiment is to *isolate the crucial variables* – the factors which, if present, cause a certain effect that would not occur in their absence and does occur in their presence.

Thought experiments are based on the same principle. The difference is that the variables being tested in a thought experiment need not or cannot, for whatever reason, actually be isolated. Rather, the variables are altered merely in imagination.

Possible worlds and Twin Earth.

Some of the most outlandish-sounding examples of thought experiments involve possible worlds. Perhaps the best-known argument that invokes a possible world is Hilary Putnam's (1926–) argument about meaning and reference. Putnam asks us to imagine a possible world that he calls 'Twin Earth'. On Twin Earth, everything is just like it is on Earth. There are human beings, they eat, drink, listen to Britney Spears and occasionally kill each other (not that those last two facts are in any way connected). But there is one difference: what Twin Earthers call 'water' is not H_2O, but another complex chemical compound, which we can call XYZ.

Some say that if it looks like a duck, walks like a duck and quacks like a duck, then it is a duck. But Putnam argues that, from our perspective, whatever XYZ is, it just isn't water. What we call water is H_2O, and XYZ isn't H_2O. Therefore, though we may both have clear, refreshing liquids, which we both call water and that both function like water, Twin Earth water just isn't Earth water. Just because it has the same name it doesn't mean it is the same stuff.

Mapping the conceptual universe.

Putnam's argument is intriguing and could be discussed at much greater length. But our interest here is simply with how the idea of a possible world is used in the argument. The thought experiment alters one variable in the real world – changing it so that the chemical compound for what functions as water isn't H_2O – and seeing what the consequences of that are for the meaning of the word 'water'. Scientists, too, have used thought experiments. Einstein used them thinking out his theories of relativity. The difference between the thought experiments in science and philosophy, however, is that those in science often lead to physical experimentation. For philosophers, however, in most cases physical experimentation is unnecessary because what one is exploring is not the terrain of the physical but the conceptual universe. Reasoning out the leads of our imagination is often sufficient for concepts.

Some have argued that thought experiments do little more than test out our intuitions and that this is an unreliable method of doing philosophy. But despite these doubts about the reliability of thought experiments as an argumentative tool, they continue to fascinate and engage as few other forms of philosophical argumentation can.

See also

2.6 Intuition pumps
2.11 Useful fictions

Reading

Hilary Putnam, 'Meaning and Reference', *Journal of Philosophy* 70, 19 (1973)
Yu Shi, 'Early Gedanken Experiments Revisited', *Annalen der Physik* 9, 8 (2000)
A. I. Miller, 'Einstein's First Steps Toward General Relativity: Gedanken Experiments and Axiomatics', *Physics in Perspective* 1, 1 (1999)

2.10 Transcendental arguments

There is one figure who keeps popping up throughout the history of philosophy like a bad penny. No matter what you do, you just don't seem to be able to keep him away. The name of this Banquo at the philosophical banquet is the sceptic.

The sceptic is like the truculent child who just keeps asking, 'But how do you know?' or (more precociously) 'How can you be sure?' You think that other people have thoughts, but how can you be sure they're not just robots behaving as though they had thoughts? You think that an apple exists independently of people who perceive it, but how can you be sure that there is nothing to an apple other than what we perceive of it – its distinctive tastes, smells, feels, colours and sounds? You think there is a single truth to the matter, but how can you be sure there aren't just a variety of 'truths'?

All this relentless scepticism can be very wearing and very hard, if not impossible, to refute comprehensively. One strategy to employ against the sceptic is *transcendental argument*. Despite its name, this sort of argument has nothing to do with Eastern religion or meditation. It is, rather, a cool, calm analytic procedure most notably used by Emmanuel Kant (1724–1804).

Defining it.

Kant was deeply troubled by scepticism, and the threat he saw from it in the writings of Hume awoke him from his 'dogmatic slumbers'. To answer the sceptic, he reasoned using this procedure.

1. Whatever the sceptic says, it is given that we have certain experiences.
2. Given we have these experiences, we must then ask *what must be the case in order for these experiences to be possible.*

This is the simple essence of any transcendental argument: it starts with what is given in experience and then reasons from this to what must be true *in order to make experience possible.* Transcendental argument, then, tries to circumvent scepticism by making its starting assumptions nothing more than the facts of experience – it makes no assumptions about the nature of these experiences, whether they are caused by an independent reality or so on. If successful, the sceptic's 'How can you be sure?' challenges seem thereby to be sidestepped or found to be pointless.

Despite its strength, there remain at least two significant limitations to this strategy.

The status of experience.

The first is that the sceptic can still ask, 'How can you be sure you have these experiences?' One might construe this challenge as empty. After all, even if Descartes was wrong to conclude that he existed from the fact that he was thinking, he might have better observed, along the lines Franz Brentano (1838–1917) later would, that there is thinking or consciousness. As long as a transcendental argument genuinely starts from what is given in experience and doesn't smuggle in other assumptions, it is surely starting from incontrovertible premises. The problem, here, however, is that it's not clear that there is any pure 'given' in experience. That is, all experience seems to be interpreted experience, bound up with various assumptions about what's going on. (Consider how many assumptions and interpretations are at work in calling an experience a 'thought' – or even calling it 'experience'.)

The quality of transcendental reasoning.

Secondly, the sceptic can ask, 'How can you be sure your reasoning from the facts of experience is sound?' Such scepticism about the very possibility of good reasoning is as fundamental a challenge to philosophy as one can get, and raises issues about the limits of argumentation. Kant himself emphasized that his reasoning is not to be taken as a demonstration or deductive proof of the truth of the transcendental claims he makes. Rather, he says that his 'transcendental deduction' ought to be regarded more along the lines of something that might persuade a law court. And even more weakly, he argues that even though we can't be sure that he's right we ought to think about the world, ourselves, and the divine 'as if' (*als ob*) his claims are true. At best, therefore, transcendental argument provides a limited victory over the sceptic.

Copernican revolution.

In Kant's case, employing the method of transcendental deduction resulted in a major shift – a 'Copernican revolution' in metaphysics – in the way in which he saw the relationship between knowledge and the world. By starting with our experience, he shifted the direction of fit: whereas previously it was assumed that our understanding had to fit the way the world was, Kant argued it was the world that had to conform to the nature of our understanding.

Some have seen this shift as having exacted a tremendous cost. The transcendental method provided a response to the sceptic; it also resulted in a revision of our understanding of philosophy that some find just as threatening. Since Kant, many philosophers have been engrossed not in determining the nature of the world and ourselves as they are *in themselves* but, rather, *how our experience of them is conditioned* by our cognitive faculties, our languages, our histories, and our practices.

Transcendental arguments continue to be employed by philosophers, Kantian and otherwise. For example, John Searle has offered what he views as a transcendental argument for external realism – the view that there is a real world that exists independently of our experiences. His argument works by taking as its given the fact that ordinary discourse is meaningful. If, for example, we agree to meet at a certain place and time, that is meaningful. Searle's argument is that, since this is meaningful, and it is only meaningful if external realism is true, external realism is therefore true. Searle's argument derives from Wittgenstein's famous private language argument, which holds that language can only be meaningful if we live in a shared, public world – since language is meaningful, we do live in such a world. Transcendental arguments, then, are very much alive and well and still a useful part of the repertoire of argumentative techniques.

See also

1.2 Deduction
6.7 Scepticism

Reading

Immanuel Kant, *Critique of Pure Reason* (1781), A84, B116 ff.
*Ludwig Wittgenstein, *Philosophical Investigations* (1953)

2.11 Useful fictions

Trail through the history of philosophy and you'll find some interesting persons and artefacts. Jean-Jacques Rousseau (1712–78) talked about the 'social contract', an agreement by which we all manage to live together. John Rawls (1921–) talked about the 'ideal observer', the person who designed the political arrangements of the world from behind a 'veil of ignorance', not knowing what position in that society the observer would occupy. And Friedrich Wilhelm Nietzsche (1844–1900) talked about the *Übermensch* (overhuman), who would be able to overcome the nihilistic culture we endure and embrace the eternal recurrence, living this life again and again for eternity.

There is no museum where the social contract or the veil of ignorance are on display, nor a gallery where faithful likenesses of the overman and the ideal observer hang. These are all fictions – ideas that do not attempt to describe anything real in the world, nor even prescriptions for things we ought to bring into the world. So what place do these have in a discipline supposed to be all about truth?

Different from most thought experiments.

Useful fictions can be viewed as a subspecies of thought experiment (2.9), but they have enough distinctive features to merit recognition in their own right. Thought experiments are generally a means to an end, in the sense that they are invoked as part of an argument, and, once the argument has reached its conclusion, one moves on. Many useful fictions, on the other hand, serve a purpose beyond this.

Take Rawls's ideal observer – a device in part derived from Adam Smith's

(1723–90) fiction the 'impartial spectator'. The point of this fictional person is that, in order to design a just society, one must adopt the viewpoint of an ideal observer. Rawls advances arguments for why this is so. If one accepts these arguments, one is left with the ideal observer as a figure to which one must constantly return when deciding substantive matters of what is just. So, for example, if one takes a Rawlsian line and wants to know whether the US should increase spending on Social Security, one needs to ask, 'What would the ideal observer say?' The useful fiction must be maintained in order for it to do its work.

Similar things could be said about the social contract. If one accepts that there is an implicit social contract and that there is a need for it, in deciding whether the state is justified in acting in a certain way towards its citizens, one must consider whether such action is sanctioned by the contract. Like a lawyer, one needs to consult the clauses in the fictitious contract to see if it has been breached.

Use in explanation.

Some useful fictions are maintained merely as explanatory tools. In evolutionary theory, for example, it can be useful to run with the fictions *that genes act selfishly*, or that features of an organism should be understood by reference to their *purpose*. Both of these are in a sense fictions, because genes can't really be selfish, since they are not motivated by any interests at all, and what drives evolution is not a goal or purpose but random mutations and how these make the organism more or less fit to reproduce. For explanatory purposes, however, it can be useful to adopt the fictions of selfishness and purpose.

Caution!

Keep in mind that this kind of useful fiction is perilous. Whereas there is no danger of any but the most foolish believing that the social contract or the ideal observer really exist, too much talk of selfish genes or purpose in evolution can lead people to mistake these fictions for facts. Useful fictions are most useful when they are most clearly fictions.

See also

2.9 Thought experiments
2.7 Logical constructions

Reading

*Adam Smith, *The Theory of Moral Sentiments* (1759)
*Jean-Jacques Rousseau, *The Social Contract* (1762)
*John Rawls, *A Theory of Justice* (1971)

chapter 3
Tools for Assessment

3.1 Alternative explanations

There are quite a lot of people who have dedicated much of their time to the private study of philosophy outside academia. The result for some of them is a new theory, sometimes of considerable range and scope. For example, some believe to have discovered the ultimate nature of reality, or morality or both. But when they come to try to get their work read, they often find no one is willing to publish them. What could explain this? It could be that their ideas are ahead of their time, or too complex for publishers to understand. Maybe academic philosophy is too insular and refuses to listen to outside voices. Perhaps the theory is too threatening.

It is difficult to decide in any particular case what the true explanation is. But one is very unlikely to have hit upon the right answer if one has failed to countenance credible alternative explanations. The writer who concludes that the establishment must have vested interests, but who hasn't considered that his work may not be very good or original has clearly been premature in reaching a conclusion. Lack of quality is clearly one possible reason for a publisher turning down a manuscript. So unless this explanation is properly considered, any other conclusion will have been reached too hastily.

Looking for alternative explanations is something we often do when we find the only explanations we do have are outlandish or lack credibility. But it is worth seeking out alternative explanations even when we seem to have a perfectly good one. Generally what we should want is the best explanation. The only way to be sure we have the best, however, is to investigate the alternatives and see if any are better.

Free-will example.

Many debates in philosophy can be seen as ongoing quests to find better explanations. Take the issue of free will. At its crudest level, the question is, 'Do we have the freedom to choose what we want to do, or are all our choices determined by prior events?' For example, when I choose a cup of tea over a cup of coffee, could I really have chosen the coffee, or was it somehow inevitable, given all that has happened in the past, that I would choose the tea?

Framed in this way, it seems we are being offered two explanations of our behaviour: that it is freely determined by our own choices, or fully determined by past events with no room for our personal choice. Much of the progress that has been made in this debate has not simply been about deciding which of these explanations is right, but about finding alternative explanations that offer a richer account of what decisions entail. One trend has been called 'compatiblism', the view that it is possible to see human actions as being essentially free and at the same time the inevitable consequence of past actions. This works by understanding free will as the ability to act free from *external* coercion, rather than past causes *per se*. So we act freely if our acts are voluntary – in accord with our natures and desires – even if those acts causally originated in past events.

This is a fruitful way to conduct the debate, and it has led to a proliferation of alternative explanations. For example, Daniel Dennett, in his *Elbow Room* (1984), distinguishes between several concepts of free will, all of which provide alternative explanations for how human freedom does or does not have a credible place in our understanding of how the world works.

As this example shows, among the benefits of looking for alternative explanations is that the account one gives can often, as a result, be a richer one. On first glance, the explanations available may provide a clear choice. But on reflection this apparent clarity may be no more than a simplistic distortion.

Good advice for prosecutors.

Making a point of considering alternative explanations can also prevent us from jumping to conclusions to which we are led by our prejudices, ambitions or self-interest. A prosecutor may find it desirable and in her self-interest to pursue charges against a vulnerable suspect, but carefully considering alternative explanations of the evidence at hand may lead her to take the time to explore other possibilities and discover that the suspect is actually innocent.

In summary, looking for alternative explanations rather than settling for one that looks ok as it is makes it more likely that we have got the best explanation and often leads to a richer, more complete account of what it is we are trying to explain.

See also

3.8 Counterexamples
3.28 Sufficient reason

Reading

Theodore Schick, Jr, and Lewis Vaughn, *How to Think about Weird Things: Critical Thinking for a New Age*, 3rd edn (2002)

3.2 Ambiguity

Many people are nervous about trading over the Internet. How can you tell whether the site to which you are submitting your credit card information is bona fide or bogus? A woman bothered by this question was pleased to see advertised a bogus e-traders guide and sent off for it straight away. However, when she got it, she found that all that the book contained was a few drawings. When she rang the publishers to complain, they replied, 'But madam, we did tell you very clearly that our guide was bogus.' Unfortunately, the woman had fallen prey to a faulty inference produced through an ambiguity in the grammar of the product's name. Such an error is called an 'amphiboly'.

In this case, the problem lies with the phrase 'bogus e-traders guide'. In this instance, the ambiguity is in the scope of the adjective 'bogus'. It could apply simply to 'e-traders', in which case the book would be a guide to bogus e-traders, or it could apply to the noun phrase 'e-traders guide', in which case it is the guide, rather than the e-traders it describes, that is bogus.

'A' cause for 'everything'.

Such ambiguities can be philosophically significant. In a famous debate, British philosopher Bertrand Russell (1872–1970), for example, accused the Jesuit philosopher Frederick Charles Copleston (1907–94) of making a logical error when he argued that God must be the cause of everything that exists. 'Every man who exists has a mother,' said Russell, 'and it seems to me your argument is that therefore the human race must have a mother.' This is simply an analogy. What Russell was really accusing Copleston of doing was arguing from the fact that each individual thing ('everything') has a cause (a unique individual, different cause) to the conclusion the whole of all things ('everything' in a different sense) has a cause (a single, same cause). The ambiguity in 'everything has a cause' may be rooted in the various possible meanings of either 'everything' or 'a cause'. Consider again this sentence:

1.   Everything has a cause.

This sentence could mean any one of the following three statements:

a.   Each individual thing has a different, individual cause unique to it.
b.   Each individual thing has the same single cause.
c.   The totality of things has a single cause.

Russell's argument is that this ambiguity had been missed and that Copleston's reasoning works only if you take sentence 1 to mean either 'b' or 'c'. But these two are the least plausible readings of the ambiguity, according to Russell.

Ambiguity ≠ vagueness.

Be clear that ambiguity is not the same as vagueness. When something is vague it is out of focus. It is unclear in the sense that one can't be sure what it is at all, even what the alternatives are. When the meaning of something is ambiguous, the alternatives can be made very clear, though it may remain difficult to decide which to select. Consider the following ambiguous statement:

2.   I like Brown.

Here, since the capital tells us that 'Brown' is a proper name, we face these distinct possibilities:

a.   I like a person whose surname is 'Brown'.
b.   I like Brown, the university in Rhode Island.
c.   I like some other thing whose name is Brown.

Now, for contrast, consider this rather vague statement:

3.   What this society needs is to be better.

Here it seems indeterminate as to precisely what this means at all, even what
the relevant alternatives are.

Clarity and rationality.

Removing ambiguity is important for two reasons. First, where there is ambiguity there is a danger of being misunderstood. If one wants to express an
argument clearly, one therefore needs to make it as difficult to misunderstand
as possible, and that requires removing ambiguity. Second, ambiguities may
lead to errors in reasoning, since an argument may work if the ambiguity is
resolved in one direction, but not if it is resolved in another. But if the argument only works if the resolution requires interpreting the ambiguity wrongly,
the argument just doesn't do the work it is supposed to do. Copleston's argument works on one reading of the ambiguous claim that everything has a
cause, but this is not the reading to which Copleston would want to commit
himself.

See also

3.21 Principle of charity
4.4 Categorical/Modal

Reading

*Bertrand Russell, *Why I Am Not a Christian* (1957)
*René Descartes, *Principles of Philosophy* (1644), pt 1, Principle 45

3.3 Bivalence and the excluded middle

One of the joys and frustrations of philosophy is that, no matter how long
you do it, you can't avoid coming back to fundamentals. This is particularly
striking in logic, where the most basic propositions form the foundations of
all the more complex advances, and so must be checked to see if they're still

up for the job on a regular basis.

The principle of the excluded middle provides a clear example of this. The principle may be formulated this way:

For any statement P, P or not-P must be true.

So, to give a mundane example, if we say 'Fred is dead', then either 'Fred is dead' or 'Fred is not dead' must be true.

This principle is itself entailed by an even more fundamental one, that of *bivalence*, which states that:

Every statement is true or false, *and* there is no other alternative.

With our example, it means the statement 'Fred is dead' is either true or false – there's no middle ground. The principles of bivalence and the excluded middle are not equivalent, since the latter involves the concept of negation ('not'), whereas the former does not. But the principle of the excluded middle is entailed by the principle of bivalence, and there is a close relationship between the two.

Too simple?

The principle of bivalence plays a foundational role in logic. It has, however, come under sustained attack by critics who argue that it is just too simplistic to say everything must be true or false. Surely some things are partly true and partly false. Forcing everything into the straightjacket of bivalence seriously distorts the world.

The problem is most acute in the case of *vague* concepts. Take for example, the idea of thinness. For many people, it seems to be neither straightforwardly true nor false that people are thin or not thin. We prefer to say people are quite thin, or a bit on the thin side. What we don't think is that there are three categories of people, thin, fat and average, and that everyone definitely falls into one category. Rather, thinness and fatness set two ends of a spectrum, with many shades of grey in between.

The plausibility of this view is shown in the Sorites paradox. Adapted to our example, the paradox is generated by considering a fat person. We can ask the question of this person, if he lost 1 g of weight, would he still be fat? The answer is surely yes – someone does not go from being fat to not fat by dint of losing 1 g. Now we can ask of this person who is 1 g lighter, would losing a further 1 g make him not fat? Again, it seems absurd to say that if there are two people who have only 1 g difference in weight between them one could be fat and one not. But if we continue this line of reasoning, we would eventually end up with someone who weighed, say 40 kg who we would have to say was fat.

It seems that the two ways out of this are to say that there is, in fact, a clear boundary between fat and not fat, as absurd as that may sound. This would enable us to preserve the principle of bivalence. The alternative is to say that fat is a vague concept, and it is often neither straightforwardly true that a person is fat or is not fat. But that defeats the principle of bivalence.

Fuzzy logic.

In recent years, both solutions have had sophisticated champions. A whole discipline of 'fuzzy logic' has developed which attempts to construct a logic that effectively does without the idea of bivalence. At the same time, one of the most lauded books in British philosophy in recent years has been *Vagueness* (1994) by Timothy Williamson, which argues that the principle of bivalence can be preserved, despite its apparently absurd consequences.

While the debate rolls on, one must be sensitive to both sides. In practice, where there is no vagueness in a concept the principle of bivalence is usually accepted by all. But when vague concepts are involved, things are far less clear and a careful path must be trodden.

See also

1.6 Consistency
1.12 Tautologies, self-contradictions and the law of non-contradiction

Reading

Timothy Williamson, *Vagueness* (1994)
*Bart Kosko, *Fuzzy Thinking: The New Science of Fuzzy Logic* (1993)

3.4 Category mistakes

Occasionally, a philosophical tool arrives fully formed, complete with vivid examples and explanations of its use and nature. Such is the case with the category mistake, introduced by Gilbert Ryle (1900–76) in his classic *The Concept of Mind* (1949). Chapter one of that book is the first and often last word about what a category mistake is.

Ryle gives some colourful examples to illustrate the meaning of a category mistake. One is of a foreign tourist who is shown all the colleges, libraries and other buildings of Oxford University but then asks, 'But where is the university?' His mistake was to think that the university was itself a building, like the library and colleges, rather than the institution to which all these buildings belonged.

In another example, he talks about a cricket match, where all the players and their roles are described to another hapless foreigner. 'I do not see whose role it is to exercise *esprit de corps*,' she says. Her mistake is to think that exercising team spirit is exercising a specific function in the game, rather than being a manner in which specific functions are exercised.

In both these examples, the foreigner has made the mistake of thinking of one kind of thing in the wrong terms. The university has been wrongly categorized by the foreigner as a building, whereas it is in fact an institution. Contributing to team spirit has been wrongly categorized as a specific kind of action, rather than a manner of performing a task or series of actions.

Mind and will examples.

Ryle believed that a category mistake lays at the heart of a confusion over the nature of mind. On his view, the mistake made by Descartes, and countless others after him, was to think of mind as if it were a kind of object, rather like a brain, table or flower. Given that this object was clearly not material, in the way that brains, tables or flowers are, it was presumed that it had to be a special kind of object, a ghostly substance of some sort. This, Ryle believed, was a mistake. Mind is not an object at all. Rather, it is a set of capacities and dispositions, all of which can be described without any reference to ghostly substances.

Alleged category mistakes crop up elsewhere in philosophy. Ryle himself also talked about 'the will'. He argued that it was a mistake to think about the will as if it were a distinct part of ourselves, a kind of centre for decision-making where switches are flicked according to whether we choose something or not. The will is not a thing or even a faculty, but shorthand for the manner in which a course of action is undertaken. We act according to or against our will depending on whether we resist or accede to the act, not on whether some part of us comes down one way or another on a decision.

One thing to bear in mind here is that to call something a category mistake is to claim that matter under discussion has been wrongly categorized. Of course, more often than not, it is unclear whether there has been a mistake or not. Then, we have category *disputes*. For example, is goodness something simple and indefinable, or can it be analysed in terms of other properties such as happiness, freedom from pain, and so on? This is a question about whether the good should be categorized as a simple, indefinable property or as a complex, definable one. To say one side in the dispute has made a category mistake is simply to say that you believe they have wrongly categorized something. But to do this one must, of course, show *why* that is the case, otherwise the most you can do is to say you are on one side of a category dispute, not that a genuine category mistake has been made. From the fact that a stranger has mistaken the 'university' for a building it does not follow that mind is a set of dispositions.

See also

3.1 Alternative explanations
3.7 Conceptual incoherence

Reading

*Gilbert Ryle, *The Concept of Mind* (1949)

3.5 *Ceteris paribus*

These two little words can save you a lot of trouble. They will also provide you with a powerful conceptual tool. They mean nothing more technical than 'all other things being equal', but their importance is immense.

Take, for example, a simple thought experiment. Your brain is to be transplanted into another body, taking all your thoughts, memories, personality, and so on. We'll call the resulting person 'Yourbrain'. Meanwhile your body will receive the brain of another, and we'll call that person 'Yourbody'. Before this operation takes place, you are asked to sign over all your bank accounts, property deeds, and so on to Yourbody or Yourbrain. Assuming that you are acting out of self-interest, which person would you choose?

An experienced philosopher would probably assume that this thought experiment contains an implicit *ceteris paribus* clause. That is to say, it is assumed that, apart from the changes that are specifically made by the operation, all other things remain equal. For example, there is no difference between the health or gender of the bodies concerned, one is not uglier than the other, one person is not on the run from the FBI. This *ceteris paribus* clause is important, because the purpose of the thought experiment is to focus the mind on the relative significance of our bodies and our brains for making us the individual people we are. For that reason, these factors need to be isolated from all other variables. Therefore, by declaring *ceteris paribus*, the devisor of the thought experiment can eliminate from consideration any other factor that is not relevant to what he or she is trying to consider.

Limiting the unusual.

When we talk about 'all other things being equal' we often mean no more than 'under normal conditions'. That is to say, we take it that there are no unusual circumstances in the situation we are describing that might affect the reasoning. For example, if we are discussing mass-murder *ceteris paribus*, it is assumed that the murderer was not given an ultimatum stating that if he did not kill 20 people by noon the whole world would be blown up. But the phrase 'under normal conditions' does not capture the full scope of *ceteris paribus*, which, as we have seen, can be invoked in thought experiments where conditions are, by definition, not normal.

In decision procedure.

The *ceteris paribus* principle has a use in assessing the relative merits of two explanations and deciding between them, even where there is no overwhelming evidence for either. For example, are all crop circles formed by aliens or hoaxers? The only sensible way to reach a conclusion is look at the available evidence and ask, *ceteris paribus*, which is the likelier explanation? Of course, in reality, all other things may not be equal – there may, for example, be as yet undiscovered evidence that would prove conclusive. But in the absence of such evidence, we have to focus on what we do know and assume that all other things are equal, until they are shown to be otherwise.

In counter-argument.

Ceteris paribus is also important in moral reasoning where the strength of a counter-argument is being assessed. For example, utilitarians believe that, in any given situation, the morally correct thing to do is that which results in the greatest happiness of the greatest number. A common objection to the theory is to describe a scenario that, although morally repugnant, satisfies the utilitarian criteria of morally correct action. One such case would be that of an innocent person accused of being a serial killer. He has no family or friends, and if he is convicted the angry masses will be appeased. If he is set free, there will be widespread fear and anger, with lynch mobs ready to dispense their own justice. This is all in spite of the fact that the serial killer has stopped killing and psychologists are confident that the killing spree has ended. The utilitarian has to answer the objection that, in such a situation, the best thing to do would be to convict the innocent man, as that results in the greatest overall increase in happiness in the population. But this is clearly unjust.

When faced with this dilemma, there is a great temptation to respond by pointing out some of the other possible negative consequences of convicting the man – such as, that the real serial killer could possibly begin killing again. But the critic can insert a *ceteris paribus* clause, thus ruling that the only considerations should be the ones specified – all other things will remain equal for the purposes of this example. This forces the utilitarian to confront the central dilemma: if increasing happiness means denying justice, should the utilitarian deny justice? The *ceteris paribus* clause thus keeps the focus of the discussion sharply on the relevant features of the argument.

Ceteris paribus clauses are often implicit, but as ever in philosophy, it is a good rule of thumb not to assume that anything will be taken to be the case unless it is clearly stated. So whenever an argument assumes that all other things remain equal, insert a *ceteris paribus* clause and avoid potential confusion.

See also

2.9 Thought experiments
3.18 Ockham's Razor

Reading

John Stuart Mill, *System of Logic: Ratiocinative and Inductive* (1843)

3.6 Circularity

Descartes's *Meditations* occupies a somewhat ambiguous place in academic philosophy. On the one hand, it is generally acknowledged to be a classic. But on the other, it is often presented to first-year students for argumentative target practice. A classic that can be so easily demolished by novices is an odd beast indeed.

The explanation for this is that the easy-to-spot howlers usually turn out, on closer inspection, to touch on fundamental issues in philosophy that need a more thoughtful response than mere dismissal. Bear this in mind when considering the example that follows, and remember that deeper issues lurk behind the apparently obvious mistake.

The Cartesian circle.

Descartes's goal in the *Meditations* is to provide a secure and lasting foundation for knowledge. He believed this foundation could be found in what we 'clearly and distinctly conceive' to be true. Such conceptions are those whose truth is so self-evident and *certain* that no one can seriously doubt them. But just because we're certain about something doesn't mean it is true – does it? How can we be sure that what is certain to our minds is in fact true? The answer is God. If a good God exists, Descartes argues, we can be sure that what we clearly and distinctly conceive to be true actually is true. After all, a good God would not allow us to be systematically deceived about the most basic and self-evident truths. So, in order to justify his claim that what we clearly and distinctly conceive to be true is really true, Descartes undertakes to prove that God exists.

The problem with this is that, in trying to prove that God exists Descartes relies upon those very same clear and distinct ideas. But he cannot know these are reliable until he has proven that God exists. In other words, he assumes in his premises precisely what he wishes to prove in his conclusion – he uses God to justify clear and distinct ideas, and uses clear and distinct ideas to justify belief in God: circular reasoning.

1. Clear and distinct ideas are reliable because God guarantees them.
2. We know God exists because we have a clear and distinct idea that he does.

Definition.

A circular argument, then, may be defined as assuming in the premises just what is to be proved in the conclusion.

Where there are no independent reasons for accepting the significant portions of it, no such argument can be successful. In such cases the circularity is described as being *vicious*.

Non-vicious circularity.

Are all circular arguments vicious? Not necessarily. Consider this example. I am waiting for a bus and a mischievous undergraduate, fresh from her demolition of Descartes, tries to persuade me that I have no good reason to carry on waiting, since my expectation of a bus arriving rests on a circular argument, which runs like this:

1.   How do I know the bus comes at 5pm?
2.   Because the timetable says the bus comes at 5pm.
3.   How do I know the timetable is right?
4.   Because the bus comes at 5pm.
1.   How do I know the bus comes at 5pm?

This line of argument makes it look as though belief in the arrival time of the bus is justified by the timetable but also, circularly, that the reliability of the timetable is justified on the basis of the arrival time of the bus. Hence the argument seems analogous in form to Descartes's.

This is not, however, a viciously circular argument because I have an *independent reason* for accepting both that the timetable is correct and that the bus arrives at 5pm: past experience. Experience has shown that this is a reliable bus company and the timetables posted at bus stops have a record of accuracy. The circle loses its viciousness because in answering either the questions posed by lines 1 and 3 I can appeal to independent evidence. So, for example, the movement from 3 to 4 can bring in a justification that does not rely upon that which we are trying to prove. If line 4 depended *solely* on line 2 (and vice versa), it would be a case of vicious circularity.

The inductive circle?

Philosophers like Hume have wondered whether inductive reasoning rests on a circle. Why should past experience of something's reliability be considered *evidence* for present and future performance? Only if we already accept the principle that past performance gives evidence for performance in the present or future. But why should we accept that principle? Well, because of past experience. But past experience can be considered evidence only if we already accept the principle . . .

Or, as Hume says, 'probability is founded on the presumption of a resemblance betwixt those objects, of which we have had experience, and those, of which we have had none; and therefore 'tis impossible this presumption can arise from probability. The same principle cannot be both the cause and effect of another' (*A Treatise of Human Nature*, bk 1, pt 3, §6).

The point to note here is that in any circular argument the 'a because b' step almost always needs to be unpacked. If this unpacking shows that the justification relies only on things the argument itself is trying to establish, then the circle is vicious; if it does not, the circle is non-vicious.

Whether or not this should accurately be described as breaking the circularity of the argument or simply removing its viciousness is a matter for debate. But at the very least, it shows that some arguments that can be described as circular may not be so useless after all.

See also

1.12 Tautologies, self-contradictions and the law of non-contradiction
3.22 Question-begging
3.25 Regresses

Reading

*René Descartes, *Meditations on First Philosophy* (1641)
*David Hume, *A Treatise of Human Nature* (1739–40)
Alan Gerwitz, 'The Cartesian Circle', *Philosophical Review* 50 (1941)

3.7 Conceptual incoherence

A friend of mine who teaches English as a foreign language once reported a wonderful question a student put to her. He wanted to know which was the correct sentence: 'I will a banana' or 'I would a banana.' Obviously, the answer came as something of a surprise to the student.

Some questions cannot be answered, or puzzles solved, because they just don't make sense. One can only debate, discuss or investigate possibilities that are, in the first place, coherent. That's why a theory of four-sided triangles would not get very far. The concept of 'four-sided triangle' is incoherent, since it contains a self-contradiction. Once we realize this, we can see that many apparently sensible philosophical questions about four-sided triangles are really red herrings. (It doesn't quite mean that all questions are ruled out. For example, one might want to think about the relationship of logically incoherent concepts to other abstractions or impossibilities.)

Woman's true nature example.

Not all instances of logical incoherence are as obvious as four-sided triangles. Janet Radcliffe Richards, in her *The Skeptical Feminist*, presents a fine example of a subtler form of incoherence. Her subject is the nature of women and she considers how the environment in which a woman grows up and lives affects her nature. What is clear is that the environment does have an effect on how women think and behave. But, she argues, it is a mistake to believe that in such circumstances, we see women as they are not, and that if we were to take away these influences, we would find women as they really are. Such a view rests on an assumption that something's true nature is how that thing is in its 'true' environment, or, even worse, in no environment at all.

Both these views suffer from conceptual incoherence. In the second case, it is obvious that all things have to be in some environment or another. Even a vacuum is an environment. So to say that something's true nature is revealed only when it is examined in no environment at all is incoherent, because nothing could ever possibly be in such a situation.

It is also incoherent to think that something's real nature is revealed when it is in its correct environment. First of all, the whole notion of a 'correct environment' is problematic. Isn't the notion of what is correct relative to various concerns? The correct environment for a salmon when cooking one is perhaps a heated oven. The correct environment for its spawning is something else again.

But more importantly, to know something's nature is to know how it is in a *variety* of environments. Iron's nature, for example, is most fully understood if we know how it behaves when it is hot, cold, smashed, left in water, and so on. Knowing how iron behaves when left in conditions optimal to its continued, unchanged existence only gives a partial view of its nature.

Radcliffe Richards's critique shows us that there is something incoherent in the concept of something's true nature being revealed by a lack of, or by a single, optimal environment. It is a concept that, once examined, just doesn't stand up. At first glance, it seems to make sense, but once we look more closely, we can see that it does not.

Incoherence vs. confusion.

There is a question mark over whether instances such as this should be described as literally incoherent or just plain confused. Some might argue that only concepts that contain within them contradictions should be called incoherent. In Radcliffe Richards's example, we might argue that there are no formal contradictions: it is just that on any sensible understanding of what 'true', 'nature' and 'environment' mean, no gloss of 'true nature' in these terms is credible. We might then prefer to talk about 'conceptual confusion' rather than incoherence. Being careful with our words in this way has much to commend it. Nevertheless, in both cases, the force of the critique is very strong. Be the concepts incoherent or confused, they're still not of much use to the careful philosopher. A sewer by any other name smells just as bad.

See also

1.12 Tautologies, self-contradictions and the law of non-contradiction
3.19 Paradoxes

Reading

*Janet Radcliffe Richards, *The Skeptical Feminist* (1980)

3.8 Counterexamples

In everyday life, we often find ourselves asking whether we have done the right thing. Was it right to tell my mother that I never drink, or was it only a white lie? Was it right to have had all those drinks, or did I have such a good time that it does not matter if I woke up the neighbours? When doing philosophy, we are not concerned with only particular cases such as these. Our aim is to discover more general truths, such as whether it can ever be right to tell a lie, or to find what it means for an act to be 'right' or 'wrong' at all.

This generality is what distinguishes philosophical questions from most ordinary questions. The answers philosophers put forward to their questions commonly involve generalizations and universals. They are statements that are supposed to apply to every instance of lying, not just the one in which you lied to your mother about your drinking. But it is because these answers are supposed to have universal application that individual cases become very important again, for an exceedingly powerful tool in philosophical thinking is the skill in deploying particular examples that undermine or at least qualify general claims. From a logical point of view universal claims (e.g. All X are Y) are extremely vulnerable to falsification because it only takes a single contrary instance to falsify them (Here's an X that is not Y). It is just this vulnerability that counterexamples exploit.

Good = pleasant example.

For example, if I were to construct an argument to prove that 'good' acts are those that produce pleasure, I had better be sure that there are no instances in which an act could be deemed good even though it did not produce pleasure. If someone were to take me to task and produce such an instance, they would have cited what is called a 'counterexample'. They might, for instance, suggest that giving money to charity is painful since it leaves me with less money for the finer things in life, yet few would suggest that donating a portion of my salary to the blind would not be a 'good' act. In this case I will either have to renounce my hedonistic theory or else find a way for it to accommodate this counterexample.

I might, however, reply that although I will experience pain as a result of my generosity, those who receive my donation will experience pleasure. I will therein have made an important modification to my initial position (I might alternatively claim that it is a mere clarification): namely, that the pleasurable consequences that make an act 'good' do not necessarily have to be experienced by the act's agent. In this way, counter-examples can perform the role of constructive criticism as well as being used to strike a theory dead. There was, of course, also nothing to stop me from biting the bullet and maintaining that giving money to charity is not a 'good' act at all. This may or may not get me very far. In the face of successive counterexamples and the theorist's responses to them, positions are honed until they are secure or else degraded until they are untenable.

Importance of the strange.

It should be noted that counterexamples can involve some very strange hypothetical scenarios, but although such situations may be unlikely to occur in everyday life, this does not diminish their relevance in a philosophical argument. As a further counterexample to the hedonistic theory of goodness, it might be argued that there are individuals in the world – masochists

– who achieve happiness by inflicting horrendous pain upon themselves. In their case, an act that resulted in their pleasure might not be regarded as good. Such individuals are rare, but if they do indeed achieve happiness through agonizing means, then they present just as pertinent a counterexample as the case of charitable donations. In short, a proposition or theory must be shown to survive even under outlandish conditions if it is to claim universal validity.

Limits of modification.

So far so simple, but thinkers must also take care to preserve the essential nature of a position when subjecting it to trial by counterexample. Whether or not the essential nature of a position has been preserved when presented with a given modification or hypothetical scenario is often controversial. To take a famous example, the status of John Searle's so-called Chinese room has been hotly debated. Supporters of 'strong artificial intelligence' maintain that a computer that passed the Turing Test (where computer responses could not be distinguished from a those of a human, native-language user in a blind test) would not merely be running a simulation of consciousness but would actually count as a full-blown mind possessed of cognitive states and the power of thought.

Against this argument, Searle constructed a counterexample. He imagined a room in which sat a person who understood not a single word of Chinese. Through a letter box the man receives questions written in Chinese characters and responds by looking them up in tables and passing back the symbols indicated by the table to be the appropriate answer. In essence, this is what a computer that apparently 'understood' Chinese would be doing, and, by that rationale, since the man in the room does not understand Chinese, neither would the computer. Both are functioning merely as mindless manipulators of symbols.

The 'systems' reply to the Chinese room charges that Searle's argument changes the nature of the putative possessor of any understanding. The man in the room may not understand Chinese, but the man and the tables within the room taken as a system do. It is the whole room that should be regarded as the language user if there is to be an accurate analogy for a symbol-processing computer. Just as we would not normally locate understanding in a special part of a Chinese speaker's brain, neither should we expect understanding to reside in the computer's CPU, for example. Though the whole, whether person or machine, may understand Chinese, any particular part of it might not. Since the strong artificial intelligence position is not committed to limiting the location of consciousness, it can be argued that Searle's counterexample has altered the essence of the theory it was constructed to test. Defenders of Searle's counterexample must show why this isn't so.

See also

2.4 Analogies
2.9 Thought experiments

Reading

*John R. Searle, *Minds, Brains and Science* (1984)

3.9 Criteria

There's no great philosophical mystery about the meaning of criteria. A standard dictionary definition of a criterion is a 'standard by which something can be judged or decided'.

In this sense of the word, philosophy is full of criteria. Some are expressed in the form 'if and only if' (usually written 'iff'). So if someone argues that a person has knowledge iff what she believes is justified and true, she is offering criteria for knowledge. In other words, something meets the standards of knowledge if it fulfils the conditions of being a justified, true belief.

In other contexts, the language of necessary and sufficient conditions is used. In the above example, if the holding of a belief is justified and true, then all the conditions necessary and sufficient for knowledge are in place.

There is no good reason why, in standard English, either of the above should not be described as setting out the criteria for knowledge. But in philosophy, as in other disciplines, one should become sensitive to facts about usage. There are contexts where philosophers tend to talk about necessary and sufficient conditions rather than criteria and following them in doing this is advisable, just because if everyone is using the same terms, everyone can feel more secure that they are actually talking about the same thing. Philosophers form a community of language users, and this community functions most smoothly if the same words are used in similar contexts.

There are dangers of ignoring this and seeing these conventions as little more than quaint pieces of academic etiquette. What you often find is that a perfectly normal word has become used in one corner of the discipline in a quite specific way. What then happens if you try to use it in another context is that confusion is created – are you using the word in its standard, English sense, or do you have the specialized usage in mind? Such is the case with criteria. This word is now very much associated with the later work of Wittgenstein.

Wittgenstein and criteria.

Wittgenstein's work can be extremely gnomic, and sometimes it seems as though no two people agree on what it actually means. In broad terms, Wittgenstein made use of the idea of criteria for the meaning and use of words. For example, part of the criteria for the correct use of 'pain' is that a person suffering pain behaves in a certain way: by showing distress, for example. The significance of using criteria here is that Wittgenstein is not saying that pain just *is* a certain form of behaviour, nor that such behaviour is a *sign* of pain, which is a private, subjective experience. The idea of criteria implies neither of those things – it merely specifies the standards for correctly using the word 'pain'.

This, Wittgenstein believed, provided a way out of some old philosophical difficulties: How can we know that other people have minds? And how can I avoid solipsism – the idea that only I exist? These problems dissolve because the criteria for the correct use of words like 'pain' and 'minds' are behavioural, but that does not mean that pain and minds *are* only behaviours. Hence the idea of criteria appears to be able to cope with the fact that the inner lives of others are, in a sense, private, but that we have public rules for correctly using language about those lives.

The state of Wittgenstein's scholarship is such that none of the above should be treated as uncontroversial exegesis. Our key point is simply that the notion of criteria has both a special Wittgensteinian sense and an ordinary English sense. In the latter sense, criteria seems to be a word that can be used across a wide range of philosophical discussions. But because of the former, it is wise to ration its usage, employing other words and phrases where they are available, to avoid any confusion between the two. This is an important point, not just about criteria, but about the way in which apparently normal words get associated with particular philosophical positions. One needs to be sensitive to this in order to express one's arguments as clearly and unambiguously as possible.

See also

4.5 Conditional/Biconditional
4.11 Necessary/Sufficient

Reading

John V. Canfield, ed., *The Philosophy of Ludwig Wittgenstein: Criteria* (1986), vol. 7
Stanley Cavell, *The Claim of Reason: Wittgenstein, Skepticism, Morality, and Tragedy* (1979)
Ludwig Wittgenstein, *Last Writings on the Philosophy of Psychology: The Inner and the Outer* (1992)

3.10 Error theory

Human beings are typically loath to abandon long-cherished beliefs in the face of logical argument. Presenting us with the case for an alternative to our views rarely succeeds in convincing us, while attempting to undermine our beliefs in their own terms meets with barely more frequent success. A third approach is sometimes more effective: to show us that, though our position is mistaken, our error was nevertheless an understandable one to have made given the true facts of the matter. In doing this, one would be providing an error theory.

Demanded by revision itself.

An error theory provides a useful accompaniment to a philosophical argument because the burden of proof in any dispute tends to lie with those who would argue against common sense or received or professional opinion. If there is an existing theory, perhaps long held, that seems to explain our experiences adequately, then we are rightly wary of the claims of those who would dislodge it. If we find our beliefs apparently overturned all too quickly and easily, we may actually start to become suspicious of our capacity to form any reliable position. And it is no wonder we'd do so. For while evidence for the new view is being amassed, a wholly different question arises: if the new theory is so succinct, so well-supported and so clearly correct, then how on Earth could we ever have been so dim as to hold our former beliefs in the first place?

One might formulate this demand as a rough principle: the stronger the case for an opposing new theory, the stronger must the explanation be for why one ever held beliefs to the contrary.

Flat Earth example.

While proving the world to be more or less spherical, for instance, we must at the same time produce a convincing explanation of why anyone would ever think it to be flat. If we are to convince our opponents that the world is round, we must begin our case with the plausibility of their assumption. While we present the argument for our own view, we must build a supplementary account that explains how such a fact as the true shape of the Earth could go unnoticed. Astronomers might argue about orbits of the planets and the shadow the Earth casts on the moon, but more simplistic theories tend to base themselves on less sophisticated, supposedly more obvious evidence. The sensation of walking on a flat surface is a very compelling argument for the overall flatness of the Earth, and takes some shifting. In the early days of seafaring, claims that sailors had circumnavigated the globe were sometimes dismissed as hearsay, but one could also have added that, because of the Earth's vast size, its curvature is too gradual to be noticed during a walk in the park. This error theory shows that the view of the Earth as flat was a reasonable one on the strength of the best evidence that was formerly available.

Plausibility not soundness.

The effect is to demonstrate that both accounts, the old and the new, are based on evidence in the same domain. An argument that the Earth is spherical can, of course, be a valid and sound one even if not accompanied by an error theory. What the error theory adds is plausibility. By showing that the new theory takes into account the evidence and concerns of the old, one hopes that the latter's adherents will be persuaded to take a similar view of the new theory.

In this way, adding an error theory provides a powerful instrument to our philosophical toolkit, one that complements the principle of saving the phenomena (see 3.26). Just as our philosophy must preserve the subjective quality of our experience (the phenomena), so must it preserve (to an extent) the logical force of any widely held arguments it overturns. Both practices help philosophers to avoid the charge that their theories simply do not deal with the same material that concerns their opponents.

See also

3.21 Principle of charity
3.26 Saving the phenomena

Reading

*J. L. Mackie, *Ethics: Inventing Right and Wrong* (1977)

3.11 False dichotomy

There is an argument that often crops up in Christian evangelical literature and lectures. Jesus of Nazareth, we are told, claimed to be the Messiah, the Son of God. Either he was telling the truth or he was a liar. There's no evidence that he was a liar, therefore we should accept that he was telling the truth. See you at the prayer meeting.

The argument as it stands does not work because it rests on a false dichotomy. A dichotomy is a distinction between two either/or options. A false dichotomy occurs when we are presented with such a distinction, but the either/or choice does not accurately represent the range of options available.

In this case, there are many more possibilities than (1) Jesus was lying or (2) telling the truth. He could have been (3) mad, and indeed, many versions of this argument present these three choices (a trichotomy?) and reach the same conclusion, since there is no evidence that Jesus was mad.

But there are more possibilities than this: (4) Jesus may have been honestly mistaken, (5) his words may not have been accurately represented in the Gospels, (6) he may have meant in being referred to as the Messiah or the 'Son of man' (Mark 8:29–31) something different from what the argument requires. There are many other possibilities. The argument does not therefore work because it hinges upon us making a choice between a limited range of options when, in reality, there are other reasonable options that have not been considered.

Example: Austin and sensation.

False dichotomies are more often found in everyday arguments than in philosophy. This is because presenting an either/or choice is a typical rhetorical move, employed more often with the aim of persuading people than with actually constructing a good argument. But they do also crop up in philosophy.

One possible example of this comes in arguments concerning perception. It has been observed that when we perceive an object it often appears other than how it actually is. So, for example, a straight stick appears bent in water. Given that the stick is straight, but what is seen is bent, surely in such cases it cannot be the stick itself we are perceiving. From this basic observation, the argument goes on to conclude that what we perceive directly are not objects in the world but internal sense perceptions, or 'sense data'.

The details of the argument are obviously more complicated than this. What we need to focus on is simply a pivotal point in the argument where we are presented with a dichotomy. This dichotomy states (implicitly, if not explicitly) that an object is either perceived as it is, or it is not perceived directly at all. This is the principle that justifies the move from saying that we see a straight stick as bent to the conclusion that in such cases we do not see the stick itself at all.

This is, arguably, a false dichotomy. Why should we accept that the choice is between accepting that an object is perceived as it is or not perceived directly at all? Why is it not possible to perceive an object directly, but incorrectly? What is the sense of 'direct perception' anyway? Is there anything with which this can contrast meaningfully? Questions like these show how the dichotomy the argument depends upon cannot be assumed to be true and on closer examination may fall apart just as easily as the 'Jesus was a liar or a truth teller' dichotomy.

See also

3.3 Bivalence and the excluded middle
3.13 Horned dilemmas

Reading

J. L. Austin, *Sense and Sensibila* (1962)
*Patrick J. Hurley, *A Concise Introduction to Logic*, 7th edn (2000), ch. 3

3.12 Genetic fallacy

As I was walking to catch the train this morning, I caught sight of a headline in a sensationalist tabloid newspaper (let's call it the *Moon*), which claimed, 'Quentin Crisp is Dead'. I believed it to be true and further events have since confirmed that it is indeed true.

When, however, I told my friend about this she asked me how I had found this out. 'I read it in the *Moon*,' I replied. She scoffed and said, 'You can't believe everything you read in there, you know.'

Origin vs. justification.

My friend had thought something like this: (1) The origin of your belief was the *Moon*, (2) the *Moon* is not a reliable source, therefore (3) your belief is not justified. Her reasoning may appear sound, but according to Morris R. Cohen and Ernest Nagel it is an example of the 'genetic fallacy' – confusing the origin of a belief with its justification. For while it may be true that the origin of my belief is an unreliable one, I may still be justified in believing it for other reasons. (If I were, however, to use the fact that the *Moon* reported it as the *justification* of my belief, I may be in trouble.)

In this example, my justifications may include the fact that, though the *Moon* is in general an unreliable source, I have since discovered that other more reliable news services – for example, the BBC – had repeated its claims. It might also be said that, though in general the *Moon* is unreliable, it does not misreport deaths. (In this case, however, it might be said that the source is reliable after all – at least in certain respects.)

The key point is simply that the unreliability of a belief's origin is not itself sufficient to render that belief lacking in justification. Beliefs can be justified in many ways – by our sense experience, by the agreement of authorities, by reasoning from previously accepted premises, and so on. The origin of a belief may have little to do with these justifications. Certainly, the origin of a belief can form part of its justification, as, for example, when the *only* reason I have for believing something is that someone else has told me about it. But there is no necessary link between origin and justification, so nothing can be deduced about the justification of a belief solely from facts about its origin. Sometimes generally incompetent or unreliable sources produce true claims. In more prosaic terms, sometimes even a blind squirrel stumbles across an acorn.

General application.

More generally, the genetic fallacy may be said to occur whenever someone argues directly from facts about origins to facts about something's present nature. So in a broader application of this fallacy, one may consider not only the truth of beliefs but also the properties possessed by things in general. The fact that someone was born to a family of thieves does not prove that he or she is now, decades later, a thief. The fact that one's original political commitments were left wing does not prove that they are so years later.

Example of evolutionary psychology.

This tool is particularly useful when considering the various claims of evolutionary psychology. Evolutionary psychologists claim to be able to explain how it is that human beings developed moral sense. Their argument is essentially that humans who learned how to co-operate and be kind to each other – without being taken advantage of – flourished more than passive 'doves' or aggressive 'hawks'. They also claim that typical differences between the sexes can be explained in evolutionary terms: it increases the survival value of a man's genes if he is promiscuous, risk-taking and high-status-oriented, whereas it increases a woman's genes' survival value if she is faithful, cautious and physically attractive.

Such claims may or may not be true, but too many people have committed a form of the genetic fallacy by taking these accounts of the origins of certain features of human nature and society to be saying things that are straightforwardly true of us now. For example, they argue that, since moral values emerged as effective survival strategies, ethics is about nothing more than survival. But this is only true if one assumes that the nature of ethics as it is now is entirely revealed by an account of its origins. Such an assumption seems false. It confuses the origin of ethics with its justification, and it confuses the origins of moral attributions with their current status.

Similarly, some people believe that the explanation for the different sexual behaviours of men and women somehow *justifies* the sexual double standard where men are forgiven for their philandering while women who behave in the same way are cast as whores. But again, why should it be assumed that explaining the *origin* of a type of behaviour necessarily *justifies* it? The argument is at best incomplete.

Caveat.

Be careful, however, not to conclude that the origins of a thing, claim or belief are always irrelevant to its justification or current character. Sometimes the origins of a thing or belief are telling. What is required, however, in order to sustain the notion that in some specific case origins matter is some solid account of why this is so. Descartes, for instance, argued that because our cognitive capacities originate in God's creation, they are basically reliable; and in advancing this argument he tried to explain why such an appeal to origins is relevant.

Some historical uses.

Despite the potential logical and evidentiary problems of appealing to origins to assess a thing, Nietzsche explicitly embraced a genetic form of criticism against Christian-Platonic morality in his influential 1887 book, *The Genealogy of Morals*. In a modified way he has been followed by French post-structuralist philosopher Michel Foucault (1926–84), who has examined in a critical way the origins and development of ideas of knowledge, punishment, madness and sexuality. Many have held the appeals to origins used by these thinkers to be sound.

The upshot.

The genetic fallacy is, then, in its pure form, about the justification of belief. But, as we have seen, its key insight has a much wider application. Whenever someone confuses the account of something's origin – be it a belief, attitude or behaviour – with its justification, or when someone inappropriately appeals to the origin of a thing to determine the later character or nature of a thing, a form of the genetic fallacy has been committed.

See also

3.15 Is/Ought gap

Reading

Morris R. Cohen and Ernest Nagel, *Logic and Scientific Method* (1934)

3.13 Horned dilemmas

We often hear people arguing that scientific practices, such as genetically modifying organisms, are wrong, because they involve 'tampering with nature'. Not many people can seriously believe this, for the following reasons:

1. If, on the one hand, critics literally mean that *all* tampering with nature is wrong, then they must also be against farming, trying to cure the sick or using wood to build a hut. In this sense, we 'tamper with nature' all the time, and their principle is clearly wrong.
2. If, on the other hand, they think that only *some* specific tampering with nature is wrong, then they do not hold that when science tampers with nature that it is *always* wrong, but that it's wrong when its tampering is of a certain kind. In this case their principle is inconsistent with their criticisms.

3. The principle that they advance, then, is either wrong or inconsistent with their criticisms.

The form this argument makes use of is a very powerful argumentative manoeuvre – a *horned dilemma*.

Definition.

Horned dilemmas attempt to show that the position being criticized could mean one of a number of things, none of which is acceptable. That means the proponent is presented with a 'damned if you do, damned if you don't' choice. In the example above, critics either have to accept that the principle they have advocated has an absurd consequence (that even chopping wood is wrong) or that it doesn't accurately describe the value to which they are appealing. Either way, they have been put on to the back foot.

There are two general forms of this type of dilemma:

Constructive dilemmas
1. (If X, then Y) and (If W, then Z).
2. X or W.
3. Therefore, Y or Z.

Destructive dilemmas
1. (If X, then Y) and (If W, then Z).
2. Not Y or not Z.
3. Therefore, not X or not W.

Horned dilemmas can, however, present more than two choices, the number of which can be used in their alternative name, as a two-pronged or three-pronged (and so on) dilemmas.

Mill example.

There is a nice example of a horned dilemma in the history of philosophy. John Stuart Mill (1806–73) argued in *Utilitarianism* (1863) that the aim of morality was to decrease suffering and increase pleasure. He went on to make a distinction between higher and lower pleasures. Higher pleasures were of the mind, intellect and aesthetic experiences, whereas lower pleasures were those of the body, such as eating and sex. Mill argued that the higher pleasures were superior and that therefore any life that contained some higher pleasures would be better than one containing only lower pleasures, no matter how intense.

The horned dilemma Mill faced was this: Why are higher pleasures superior to lower ones? If it is because they are supposed to be more pleasurable, that seems false, as many people take more pleasure in lower pleasures than higher ones. But if they are superior for some other reason – for example, because they cultivate the self – then Mill is saying that some things, such as self-cultivation, are more important than pleasure, and he has contradicted his own principle that pleasure is the ultimate good.

The choice being presented – between the implausible and that which undermines the position being put forward – is typical of a horned dilemma. In this case, Mill opted for the implausible, arguing that you could show higher pleasures were superior because informed judges – those who had experienced both types of pleasure – would always choose higher over lower pleasures. Whether this is a sufficient response to stop Mill from being impaled on the horn of this particular dilemma is for the reader to decide.

Defensive strategies.

In order to defend your position against a horned dilemma, you may deploy the following strategies:

Grabbing one of the horns. To do this you attack one of the conditionals as false. (Mill did just this by arguing that it is wrong to say that people take more pleasure in lower pleasures.)

Passing through the horns. This strategy aims to show that both alternatives are false. For example, if someone's argument relied upon the claim that we must either go to war or face certain death, one might respond by showing that both alternatives are false. There is another alternative.

Although they appear to be highly negative, horned dilemmas are in fact vital to the process of honing and improving philosophical theories. Used properly, they can reveal the stark choices that have to be made, sometimes about fundamental assumptions. They can be used to force the philosopher to put in the vital details of a too-sketchy thesis or to see that what appeared to be a fruitful line of enquiry has ended in failure. The horned dilemma is a vicious beast but benefits philosophy enormously.

See also

1.6 Consistency
3.23 Reductios

Reading

*John Stuart Mill, *Utilitarianism* (1863)
Patrick J. Hurley, *A Concise Introduction to Logic*, 7th edn (2000), ch. 6

3.14 Hume's Fork

Consider the following two statements:

1.   All criminals have broken the law.
2.   Reggie Kray is a criminal.

You may be equally certain that both statements are true, but, according to Hume, they are true for completely different types of reasons. Understand what that difference is, and you have understood a fundamental distinction between two types of human knowledge.

The first type.

In the first case, the statement 'all criminals have broken the law' is true by definition, since to be a 'criminal' means to be someone who has broken the law. One way of expressing this is to say that the second part of the sentence (the predicate) merely repeats or contains what is already implicit or explicit in the first (the subject). Such statements are known as 'analytical truths', 'necessary truths', or *tautologies*. (Quine, however, has called into question this typology of sentences. See 4.3.)

   One feature of tautologies is that they must be true. To deny their truth is to assert a logical contradiction. The statement 'Not all criminals have broken the law' is self-contradictory and therefore necessarily false, because it asserts that people can be criminals, and thus lawbreakers, without having broken the law. However, this cast-iron seal of truth comes at a cost. The price paid for the certainty of such statements, according to Hume, is that they fail to describe the world. 'All criminals have broken the law', for example, does not describe the world because it does not tell us anything about whether or not criminals exist, which people are criminals, which laws they have broken, and so on. The sentence merely tells us something about what certain words mean. To know that all criminals have broken the law is to know something about the meaning of the words used but nothing about the way the world is.

According to Hume, truths of mathematics and geometry belong in the same category of knowledge as tautologies, a category he called 'the relations of ideas'. 1 + 1 = 2, for example must be true, because, given the meaning of '1', '2', '+' and '=', the statement must be true by definition. 1 + 1 = 2 could only not be true if the numbers and symbols used meant something other than what they actually do, but in that case we'd be dealing with a semantically different statement. The truth of the sum, therefore, flows (whatever that means, as Quine might ask) inexorably from the meanings of the terms found in it.

Such arithmetic statements also share with tautologies the feature that they do not tell us anything about the way the world actually is. They do not, for example, tell you whether or not when you add one drop of water to a second drop of water you get two drops of water, one big drop or something else altogether. Knowledge of such things belongs to Hume's second category, 'matters of fact'.

The second type.

'Reggie Kray is a criminal' belongs in this category, because its truth or falsehood cannot be ascertained simply by attending to the meanings of the words in the sentence. To discover whether this statement is true, we have to look at the world. If it is true that Reggie Kray broke the law, then it is true he is a criminal. It is what goes on in the world that makes such statements true or false, not just what the words mean.

'Matters of fact' are thus informative about the world in a way in which 'relations of ideas' are not. They, however, lack the rock-sure certainty of truths yielded to us by 'relations of ideas'. Whereas 'criminals have broken the law' must be true on pain of contradiction, there is nothing contradictory in saying that 'Reggie Kray is not a criminal'. Unlike relations of ideas, it is *always* logically possible that the opposite of a matter of fact is true. That is why so much ancient mathematics is still fundamentally sound (there was no way it could be wrong) and so much ancient science utterly false (the possibility of error is always inherent in statements that describe the world). That is why judges do not disagree about what a criminal is, but do sometimes execute miscarriages of justice.

Hume's Fork therefore divides human knowledge into two very distinct spheres: (1) the logical certainties of relations of ideas that do not describe the world, and (2) the always provisional matters of fact that do describe the world.

Sceptical import.

If Hume's Fork is accepted, it means that no truths about the real world can ever be demonstrated to be logically necessary. It must always be at least logically possible that the world is other than as it is. This implication is a central feature of Hume's scepticism and one of the principal features of his thought to which German philosopher Immanuel Kant responded in maintaining that some specific fundamental claims in natural science are both necessary and non-analytic – or what he called 'a priori synthetic'.

Nevertheless, the power of Hume's Fork is that from it follows the conclusion that any argument purporting to show that the world *must* be a certain way is sure to be flawed. The history of philosophy is littered with such arguments: arguments that the universe must have a first cause, that time and space must be infinitely divisible, that there must be a god. If Hume is right, all these arguments are unsound. For this reason, Hume's Fork is a very powerful principle and one that, though by no means uncontested, is still considered basically sound by many philosophers today.

See also

1.2 Deduction
1.3 Induction
2.1 Abduction

Reading

*David Hume, *An Enquiry concerning Human Understanding* (1748)
W. V. O. Quine, 'Two Dogmas of Empiricism', in idem, *From a Logical Point of View* (1953)

3.15 Is/Ought gap

Children sometimes decide that stealing toys from their playmates is quicker and easier than saving up their pocket money to buy them. When they are told that they should not do so, their response is sometimes to ask, 'Why not?' 'Because stealing is wrong,' is a perfectly good answer, but it will not always satisfy them. Before resorting to threats of punishment, one might go into further detail: 'It upsets Jimmy when you take his things.' If this might still not satisfy a five-year-old child, it certainly would not satisfy a logician. The assertion 'You should not steal Jimmy's toys' seems to contain something absent from the observation 'Stealing Jimmy's toys upsets him.' The latter is a statement of fact, whereas the former contains a moral prescription.

The logical point.

If you were to construct an argument taking 'Stealing Jimmy's toys upsets him' as your first (and only) premise, it would not be a logically valid argument that concluded, 'Therefore, stealing Jimmy's toys is wrong.' To make the argument valid, you would need to add a second premise: 'Stealing toys is wrong.' You could alternatively add 'Upsetting Jimmy is wrong,' but you would still have added something not present in your first premise – a moral judgement or prescription. The necessity of this second premise is often held to show that one cannot derive an *ought* from an *is*, nor a value from a mere fact.

The meta-ethical point.

The above is true as a matter of pure logical inference. Some philosophers, however, have drawn the more substantive conclusion that ethics is 'autonomous' – that the is/ought gap proves that moral facts are fundamentally different from any other kinds of facts about the world, and so deserve a special treatment of their own. Philosophers who maintain that moral properties like 'good' and 'bad' can be understood without reference to subjective states like beliefs or feelings are called moral realists. The British philosopher George Edward Moore (1873–1958) referred to those who conceive of 'good' as a natural property of things as 'naturalists' and as committing the 'naturalistic fallacy'.

  'Anti-realists', 'moral sceptics' or 'subjectivists', on the other hand, commonly derive their arguments from a section in Hume's *Treatise of Human Nature*, where he notes that moralists 'proceed for some time in the ordinary way of reasoning' with regard to observations concerning human affairs, 'when of a sudden, I am surprised to find that instead of the usual copulations of propositions is and is not, I meet with no proposition that is not connected with an ought, or an ought not'. He continues that 'as this ought or ought not expresses some new relation or affirmation 'tis necessary that it be observed and explained; and at the same time a reason should be given for what seems altogether inconceivable, how this new relation can be a deduction from others which are entirely different from it' (bk 1, pt 1, §1).

This gap between an 'ought' and an 'is' is sometimes held to indicate a fundamental distinction in the world between matters of ethics and any other matters of fact. Some might, for example, use the distinction to refute the claim that 'good' and 'bad' can be reduced to subjective matters of pleasure and pain – these qualities being matters that can be referred to by purely factual statements devoid of value judgement.

Back to logic.

The thought that conclusions containing an 'ought' cannot be deduced from premises not containing an 'ought' is not itself a meta-ethical claim but a purely logical point for which matters of ethics present no special case. The same principle can be applied to all sorts of concepts, and not just ethical ones. For example, conclusions containing reference to grapefruits cannot be logically derived from premises that do not refer to grapefruits, but this does not mean that there is a fundamental, logical difference between facts about grapefruits and any other kind of fact. Ethics is logically autonomous, and this is the essence of the is/ought gap, but it shares this trait with many other kinds of discourse. Meta-ethical claims must be argued on different grounds.

See also

1.4 Validity and soundness
4.16 Thick/Thin concepts

Reading

*David Hume, *A Treatise of Human Nature* (1740), bk 3
*G. E. Moore, *Principia Ethica* (1903)

3.16 Leibniz's law of identity

The concept of things being 'identical' to one another in ordinary speech is ambiguous. We may confront two different things that are identical in all discernible respects, such as two cars fresh off the production line that are the same model, colour and so on. Or we may face one thing, identified in two ways, such as the morning star and the evening star, or Bill Gates and the founder of Microsoft. It is the latter kind of identity – where we identify two distinct terms with the same person or object – that is the strictest form of identity and is the subject of Leibniz's law. This philosophical tool is attributed to the German philosopher, Gottfried Wilhelm, Baron von Leibniz (1646–1716), as he first formulated it in his *Discourse on Metaphysics* (1686).

Leibniz's law states in simple terms what must be true if X and Y are identical in this strict sense. In its classic formulation it states that:

> X is identical with Y if and only if every property of X is a property of Y and every property of Y is a property of X.

A similar principle is known as the *principle of the 'identity of indiscernibles'*:

> If X and Y are absolutely indiscernible, then they are identical.

Notice, however, how this second formulation defines identity in terms of how things are conceived or grasped by the mind (if the mind can't discern a difference, then they aren't different), while the former defines identity according to the properties possessed by the object itself (if the objects have the same properties, then they are really one). Which, if either, of these formulations is to be preferred may imply different metaphysical and epistemological positions.

In any case, for most purposes the principles seem obvious. If, for example, it turns out that everything that is true of the murderer of Mai Loh is also true of Sam Smith, then it must be the case that Sam Smith is the murderer of Mai Loh.

Mind–brain example.

Passing the test of Leibniz's law, however, is not always that easy, and neither is it always clear what passing requires. This has been most evident in the philosophy of mind and the claim that mental states are identical with brain states. This has been widely disputed, for the reason that brain states – being physical states – by definition have only physical properties. Mental states, on the other hand, are said to have mental properties that just cannot be reduced to merely physical things. For example, one cannot describe the sensation of pain in purely physical terms. If this is granted, it is clear that, according to Leibniz's law, mental states cannot be identical with brain states, as the former possess properties the latter do not. French philosopher René Descartes's argument for a 'real' or metaphysical distinction between thinking substance (mind) and extended substance (body) hangs on a similar line of reasoning.

The debate thus moves on. It might be concluded that the relationship between mental states and brain states is not one of identity. It might be claimed that, contrary to appearances, brain states can and do have mental properties. Or further work may be done to clarify what the requirement for identity of all properties in Leibniz's law really entails. Though, however, the debate can be taken further, it is fair to say that no one really disputes the truth of Leibniz's law, only what its implications are.

Space and time.

A further point that needs to be stressed is that, when we talk of properties here, we must include spatio-temporal location. If Jane and Mary are physically identical and have the same thoughts and feelings, but Jane is in Hong Kong and Mary in New York, they cannot be identical. The time and place of X and Y must be the same if X and Y are to be identical.

Problems of personal identity.

Leibniz's law can be seen in action in recent discussions about personal identity. Many philosophers have argued that personal identity is determined by psychological connectedness and continuity: a future person, X, is the same person as a present person, Y, if they are psychologically connected and continuous with each other. Put crudely, X and Y are 'psychologically connected and continuous' if person X has the same kind of continuity of memory, intention and personality with person Y that a normal person has over time.

If this is true, then it would seem that people can survive teletransportation – the fictional mode of transport where my original body is destroyed but all the information about it is collected and sent to, say, Mars, where my body is recreated. If this process has the result that the person on Mars has the same kind of psychological relationship with me as I do with my past self, then psychological reductionists say that that person is me. In other words, if he remembers what I have done, shares my opinions, plans and personality, he is me.

Critics point to a counterexample: What if the machine malfunctions and creates two of me on Mars? In such a situation, it cannot be that both people on Mars are me, as a simple application of Leibniz's law shows. Call the person prior to teletransportation 'A' and the two people on Mars 'X' and 'Y'. If A is X and A is also Y, then it would have to be true that X is Y. This is because both X and Y would have to be identical in all respects to A, which means they must clearly also be identical to each other. But X cannot be identical with Y, because Leibniz's law states that if X = Y then X and Y must share the same properties. It is clear that if X cuts himself, Y has no scar, and that where X is, Y cannot also be. Therefore X has a property Y does not have, so they cannot be identical. And if X and Y are not identical with each other, they cannot both be identical with A.

Problem of change.

Leibniz's law also seems to raise Heraclitean questions. The pre-Socratic Greek philosopher, Heraclitus of Ephesus (*fl. c.*500 BCE), held that because it is continuously changing, one cannot step into the same river twice. But if temporal location is to be taken as a relevant property of things, then X at time T_1 is discernibly different from X at time T_2. But if X is discernibly different at the two different times, then it must be two different things – X and later non-X. Thence it follows that there is no personal identity over time. It would, therefore, seem then that one must be a different person at every moment – just as the eighteenth-century philosopher David Hume had implied. The problem, then, is to reconcile the cross-temporal non-identity apparently implied by Leibniz's law with the cross-temporal identity apparent through the psychological determinations of memory, intention, common sense, and so on.

These simple applications of Leibniz's law have not necessarily destroyed the view that personal identity is essentially about psychological continuity, but they do create problems that have required sophisticated responses.

See also

3.17 Masked man fallacy
4.17 Types/Tokens

Reading

Gottfried Wilhelm Leibniz, *Discourse on Metaphysics* (1686)
Gottfried Wilhelm Leibniz, *New Essays on Human Understanding* (1704), bk
  2, ch. 27

3.17 Masked man fallacy

Mohammed, a philosophy student, has just listened to a lecture about
Leibniz's law. This law, as he understands it, states that if X and Y are
identical, then what is true of X is true of Y.

That evening he goes to a masked ball. He believes his friend Tommy will
be there. He sees a masked man and wonders whether it could be Tommy.
Applying Leibniz's law, he concludes that it cannot be. Why is that? He
reasons, 'If the masked man is identical with Tommy, then what is true of
Tommy must be true of the masked man. I *know* who Tommy is but not
who the masked man is. Therefore it is not the case that what is true of
Tommy is true of the masked man. Therefore, they cannot be identical.' At
that point, the masked man takes off his mask to reveal that he is Tommy.
What went wrong?

Mohammed's mistake turned upon his use of a convenient but misleading shorthand for Leibniz's law: 'X and Y are identical if what is true of X is
true of Y.' A more proper formulation of the principle, however, is that 'X
and Y are identical if and only if they share all the same properties.'

On this version of the principle, in order to make the error Mohammed
has to accept that if he knows who Tommy is, but not who the masked man
is, then Tommy has a property – *being known by Mohammed* – that the masked
man does not.

The property of 'being known'.

But can being known by someone really count as a property of a thing? If so,
it would be a very odd one. For example, it would mean that Monica Lewinsky
could gain a property without having changed at all, simply in virtue of
someone coming to know who she is. What must it have been like to gain so
many properties virtually overnight?

A more attractive, alternative view is that what is known, thought or
believed about an object does not count as one of its properties. Tommy
may be the masked man because what Mohammed knows about him is

not actually a property of him. (On the other hand, one might try to save the claim that 'being known by' is a property of things by showing how Mohammed is guilty of the fallacy of equivocation. That is, one might try to show that his use of the word 'know' is semantically different in the sentences [1] 'I know who Tommy is,' and [2] 'I don't know who this masked man is.')

The masked man fallacy, then, might just seem to be a handy clarification of Leibniz's law, but it is much more. It also illustrates why it may be wrong to classify what we *know*, *think*, *believe* or even perhaps *perceive* of an object as a *property* of that object. This raises a whole nest of new issues about what exactly properties are.

Descartes example.

A noted example of the masked man fallacy appears in Descartes's argument that mind and body must be distinct substances. He reached this conclusion by a simple application of Leibniz's law. Consider first the properties of matter: it is spatial and temporal; has mass, size and solidity; and is divisible. Now, consider the properties of mind. It is not spatial. You can't touch it or measure its length. It has no mass or size. (How absurd it is to ask how much a thought weighs!) It isn't solid, and it is not divisible. Therefore, reasons Descartes, as mind and matter clearly have essentially different properties, they cannot be the same thing. Hence mind and matter must be two different substances. (This is the doctrine of mind–body dualism.)

One may resist this argument by appealing to the masked man fallacy. The fallacy shows that what we think, believe or perceive of something does not necessarily correspond to what the properties of that thing actually are. Certainly, mind does not *seem* (to us) to have mass, size or solidity; but does that necessarily mean it does not *in fact* possess those properties? Couldn't mind be like the masked man – when we observe it from a certain point of view (as a brain) we don't recognize it for what it is? Couldn't the physical stuff that is our brain still be mind? Spinoza in fact advanced a similar line of criticism against Descartes.

What the dualist needs to show is not just that mind does not *seem* to have physical properties, nor matter mental properties, but that there is a *real* distinction between two different substances. The dualist needs to show why the apparent distinction between minds and brains is not a product of the fact that we perceive brains and minds in different ways – or that we simply misunderstand what is meant by 'mind'. Or, perhaps the burden of proof rests with the challengers. Perhaps it is the critic who must show that the mind and body only *seem* to possess essentially different properties – that they are 'wearing masks'.

Perhaps answering these questions will depend on whether we take the viewpoint of the objective observer, looking on the brain, or the subject, thinking and feeling.

See also

3.16 Leibniz's law of identity
4.17 Types/Tokens

Reading

*René Descartes, *Meditations on First Philosophy* (1641), Meditation 6
Benedictus Spinoza, *Principles of Descartes's Philosophy* (1663)
Gottfried Wilhelm Leibniz, *Discourse on Metaphysics* (1686)

3.18 Ockham's Razor

The Pre-Socratics' attempt to reduce the world's diverse phenomena to a single basis or *archē* shows that in a sense the principle known as Ockham's Razor is as old as philosophy. Named after the medieval monk William of Ockham (1285–1349), this fundamental rule of philosophical thinking holds that entities should not be multiplied beyond necessity. In other words, philosophical and scientific theories should posit the existence of as few types of entities as possible. A second formulation of the Razor is broader, focusing not just on the number of entities, but the overall economy of an explanation: where two competing theories can both adequately explain a given phenomenon, the simpler of them is to be preferred. Hence Okham's Razor is also known as the principle of simplicity. Ockham himself formulated the principle in various ways, among them 'Plurality is not to be assumed without necessity.'

Ockham's Razor has had so many applications in philosophy that it is often not mentioned explicitly. Ockham himself used it to dispense with the 'ideas in the mind of the Creator' that some philosophers believed were necessary corollaries of objects in the world. He argued that the corresponding entities in the world could sustain their own existence quite happily. Although often viewed as a 'common sense' theory, Ockham himself used the Razor to argue that there is no need to posit the existence of motion since a simpler explanation is that things just reappear in a different place. This hardly provides the best advertisement for the tool's value.

Principle of method.

Ockham's Razor is not a metaphysical claim about the ultimate simplicity of the universe but rather a useful rule of thumb or working method. The fact that on occasion a more complex explanation is better is therefore no use as an objection to the general usefulness of the principle. At the very least, it is surely wise to look at the simplest explanation first before considering more fanciful alternatives. Where, for example, we have five points on a graph, which can be joined by a straight line, those points could alternatively be joined by an infinite number of squiggly lines. It is, however, accepted best practice to assume that the points have a linear relationship, at least until new data provides points outside the straight line.

Metaphysical principle.

However, some philosophers have taken the Razor further, using it not just as a methodological procedure, but to justify more concrete conclusions about the existence or role of entities. For example, some behaviourists in the philosophy of mind argue that our language and behaviour can be explained without recourse to first-person accounts of subjective mental states – the way thoughts, feelings and sensations feel or appear to those who have them. So, Ockham's Razor in hand, they deny these subjective states' existence. This explanation is simpler than the messy alternatives that try to reconcile physical actions and brain states with non-physical subjective states. Critics have said that the behaviourist explanation is only plausible if one 'feigns anaesthesia' – in other words, pretends to oneself that one doesn't have any feelings or sensations.

While it may be going too far to claim that subjective mental states do not exist, more moderate behaviourists argue that they have no role to play in explaining our actions. The way things appear and feel to us is merely a by-product or 'epiphenomenon' of the physical processes that cause us to act. In this instance, the Razor is not used to deny the existence of certain entities or states, but to distinguish between those that have a role in explanations and those that do not. In another example of this use of the Razor it is common to argue that, although God's non-existence cannot be proved, there is no need to take him into account when we consider the way in which the natural world and human beings have come to be as they are.

Simplicity vs. completeness.

The behaviourist example suggests a very important qualification. A simpler theory should not be a less complete one. A complete explanation will explain all the relevant phenomena. In the behaviourist case much of the relevant phenomena, such as human speech and behaviour, is explained. However, their simpler account of the mental does not explain the phenomenon of the subjective nature of mental states such as imagining or feeling pain. These demand explanation even if they are found not to play a role in behaviour. The only alternative is to deny the reality of these phenomena, in which case it needs to be shown why we are wrong to suppose they exist in the first place.

Implicit in Ockham's principle is the subclause 'all other things being equal'. One should obviously not prefer a simpler explanation if it is less complete, or less in accordance with other accepted theories, than a more complex one. The principle is not about favouring simplicity for simplicity's sake.

See also

3.5 *Ceteris paribus*
3.10 Error theory
3.26 Saving the phenomena

Reading

William of Ockham, *Summa totius logicae* (1488)
William of Ockham, *Summulae in libros physicorum* (1494)

3.19 Paradoxes

People who know little about philosophy but wish to appear philosophical are extremely fond of paradoxes. They are apt to point out 'paradoxes of the human condition' such as 'You don't know what you've got until it is gone.' They might utter profound-sounding but empty 'paradoxes' such as 'The only true knowledge is ignorance.' Sometimes it seems as though to observe that something is paradoxical is equivalent to doing philosophy.

Paradoxes are important in Western philosophy, but not because they somehow express deep truths. 'Paradox' means something quite specific in philosophy, something that is generally not an enigmatic or contradictory assertion.

Paradox type 1: when reason contradicts experience.

The word 'paradox' derives from the Greek, which may be translated as 'contrary to belief'. The first type of paradox we wish to look at, then, is generated when, using apparently flawless reasoning from apparently true premises, a conclusion is generated that contradicts or flies in the face of what other common reasoning or experience tells us.

Classics of this type are the paradoxes developed by Zeno of Elea (*c.*470 BCE) to advance the doctrines of his master Parmenides (*fl. c.*480 BCE). Consider this one: Imagine Achilles races a tortoise and gives the tortoise a head start. The tortoise is slow, but it moves at a constant speed. Now, in the time it takes for Achilles to get to the point from which the tortoise started, the tortoise will have moved forward and will now be at another point (call it A). In the time it subsequently takes Achilles to get to A, the tortoise will have moved forward a little more, and will be at point B. And in the time it now takes Achilles to get to point B, the tortoise will have moved on to point C. And so on. So it seems that Achilles cannot overtake the tortoise.

This is a paradox because there seems to be nothing wrong with our reasoning but we know that, contrary to the conclusion, Achilles would overtake the tortoise. So it seems we either have to accept that our reasoning is wrong (even though we can't see why) or accept that overtaking is impossible (even though it seems that it is). Both options defy experience and reasoning – hence a paradox.

Paradox type 2: when reason itself leads to a contradiction.

Here's a puzzling claim: 'This statement is false.' The paradox is generated here when we ask whether this sentence is true or false. If it is true, then it is false. But if it is false, it is true! (Another famous example is the liar's paradox, which may take the form 'Everything I say is a lie.') Given that a sentence cannot be both true and false, we find ourselves faced with a paradox. There seems nothing about the sentence to suggest it is ill-formed, but apply some simple reasoning to it and you get strange and perhaps contradictory conclusions (it is true if false and false if true).

Another famous paradox of type 2 is known as Russell's Paradox. It points to a conceptual problem noticed first by Bertrand Russell that apparently subverts what's often called in set theory the axiom of inclusion. According to this axiom, everything is a member of some set (e.g. the set of all red things); even sets are members of sets (e.g. the set of all sets that have more than three members – which is also, interestingly a member of itself). What Russell noticed is that there seems to be a specifiable set whose categorization is paradoxical: namely, 'the set of all sets that don't have themselves as members'. If this set *is* a member of itself, then it is *not* a member of itself. But if it is *not* a member of itself, then it *is* a member of itself! The set theorists are still reeling.

Paradox type 3: when experience contradicts reason.

The history of philosophy includes yet another use of paradox. Kierkegaard argued that the rationalistic aspirations of much of modern philosophy – especially those of Hegel – crash on the shoals of the Christian doctrine of the incarnation. According to Christian doctrine Jesus Christ was/is simultaneously the eternal, all-powerful, all-knowing God *and* a mortal, finite, limited man. Logically, according to Kierkegaard, the very idea is absurd, self-contradictory and paradoxical. It is a condition that reason and systematic philosophy cannot grasp. This, however, is, according to Kierkegaard, the very strength of the doctrine, for in reflecting on the incarnation, we can come to see not only the exceedingly limited quality of reason and system but also the power of faith. One cannot, therefore, reason one's way into being a Christian; one can only do so by making an existential 'leap of faith'.

The value of paradoxes.

Why are paradoxes so interesting to philosophers? It is not usually because we take them to reveal something amazing about reality or logic we didn't know before. Few people think that the lessons of the paradoxes above, for example, are that overtaking is impossible and that sentences can be true and false at the same time. Rather, the interest in paradoxes lies in what they reveal about the nature and limits of reasoning. We are forced to examine the arguments and premises that generate the paradoxes because that is the only way to solve them. Given that both premises and reasoning seem flawless, if we do this successfully we will learn that something apparently obvious is in fact profoundly confusing. It may be that an apparently straightforward premise contains a hidden ambiguity or contradiction. It may be that an apparently valid piece of deduction may seem to be invalid or malformed. Or we may find that certain forms of argument do not work with certain types of sentence. For example, perhaps we cannot do classical logic with vague concepts. We may even come to see the limited nature of reasoning itself. The power of paradoxes, then, is this: they force us to scrutinize what seems so obviously right. That in itself is pretty strong stuff.

See also

1.4 Validity and soundness
1.12 Tautologies, self-contradictions and the law of non-contradiction.
3.27 Self-defeating arguments

Reading

Nicholas Rescher, *Paradoxes: Their Roots, Range, and Resolution* (2001)
Wesley C. Salmon, ed., *Zeno's Paradoxes* (1970, 2001)
R. M. Sainsbury, *Paradoxes* (1988, 1995)

3.20 Partners in guilt

Kant once wrote that one should always treat persons as ends, never as means. Many people have agreed with him. Further, they have invoked this principle in arguments against their opponents. But in doing so they may have opened themselves up to the objection that they are 'partners in guilt'. To see why, consider the following, highly simplified philosophical exchange.

Deontologists believe that actions are right or wrong, regardless of their consequences, whereas consequentialists, as their name implies, believe that the consequences of an action determine whether it is right or wrong. It is often held up as a criticism against consequentialists that their principles permit unacceptable wrongdoing. For example, what if it were possible, for a bizarre set of reasons, to save the lives of ten innocent people by murdering just one innocent person? Because the consequences of this one murder are that one innocent person dies, and the consequences of not murdering are that ten innocent people die, many consequentialists would say that the morally right action is to murder the innocent individual.

Some deontologists object that this murder contravenes Kant's principle: what we would be doing is using this innocent individual as merely a means to a greater good. In murdering her, we are not respecting her life as an end in itself.

However, the consequentialist may try to turn this objection against the deontologist. If we refuse to kill this innocent person, then are we not treating the lives of the ten innocent people who die as means rather than ends? We are not respecting their lives as valuable in themselves, but treating them as mere means to preserving our own moral integrity. Isn't the way to follow Kant's injunction to consider all the parties involved equally and see what benefits the most, considering all the lives involved as valuable in themselves?

Strengths and weaknesses of the tool.

The consequentialist is using the partners in guilt move as a *defence* against attack. This means deflating the objection advanced and showing that it is a criticism that can equally be used against the attacker: 'If your criticism is a good one, then we are *both* in on the wrongdoing.' When it works, this is clearly a powerful way of neutralizing objections.

However, the technique does involve risks. By turning the criticism back on the critic, one might show that the criticism is empty, in that it could be made of anyone. If, according to the criticism, everyone is wrong, then there is no such thing as being right. But it might equally show not that you're right but that *both* sides are guilty of a mistake. If you are as wrong as I am, that does not make me right.

In our example, the partners-in-guilt move is played effectively because it makes the critic's position look weaker. In other words, the consequentialist tries to show that, in fact, his or her view looks better not only on its own terms *but even on the critic's* (Kantian) *terms*. This is not so much a case of both parties being partners in guilt, but of turning the tables so that the accuser becomes the accused.

See also

1.6 Consistency
3.27 Self-defeating arguments

Reading

David Brink, *Moral Reasoning and the Foundations of Ethics* (1989)
Christine M. Korsgaard, 'Skepticism about Practical Reason', in idem, *Creating the Kingdom of Ends* (1996)

3.21 Principle of charity

Imagine you are trekking through a foreign country and do not speak its language. It is a very hot day, and coming across a calm river shaded by trees you decide to stop for a cooling swim. A local soon joins you and seems to find the water as agreeable as you do. There may be other, less obvious reasons for her delight than finding a retreat from the sun. Perhaps the river is regarded as holy in her country, and she is visiting it at the end of a long pilgrimage, or perhaps she is performing a kind of baptism, or thinks that immersion in its waters will result in a healthy harvest for her crops. Under the conditions as you know them, however, you will probably assume that she has the same motives as yourself.

Now, if the woman had instead jumped into the cool water and immediately climbed out muttering what you have picked up as a few of the local curses, you would not normally assume that the woman did not like cooling herself down on hot days. Imagine that she explains (or appears to explain) that she had believed 'S' about the water. From your position of ignorance, S could mean just about anything; but as a reasonable person, you might fancy that she had been expecting a hot spring in which to bathe, or that she had thought the water was safe before spotting a crocodile on the far bank. In being so reasonable, you would be obeying the principle of charity.

The main point.

The 'principle of charity' states that interpreters should seek to maximize the rationality of others' arguments and claims by rendering them in the strongest way reasonable. In other words, when there are different translations that could reasonably well explain an individual's speech or behaviour, the one that should be chosen above the others is (*ceteris paribus*) the one that renders it most rational under the relevant circumstances. These circumstances might include the physical backdrop to the case, the subject's wider set of beliefs or, in the exegesis of a philosophical text, other writings by the thinker in question. Accusations of such logical vices as bias, prejudice and blatant self-contradiction should, if possible, be resisted unless evidence compels them. Again, the principle of charity demands that another's position or behaviour be portrayed in the best possible light.

Judicious use of the principle certainly keeps things simple, but in our example we may have had a further reason to discount the more fanciful interpretations of the local's behaviour. Unless we take a well-grounded alternative view of her country, we will be wary of imputing beliefs to the local person that we would ourselves hold to be false. The typical Westerner does not believe that a farmer can make her crops grow faster by bathing in a certain river, no matter how holy it is. The farmer may, of course, turn out to hold that belief nonetheless, but we would do well to regard the translation as at best provisional until we have acquired a mastery of the farmer's language. Similarly, we will rule out translations that cast her statements as what we would consider to be biased, prejudiced, circular or meaningless or as blatant self-contradictions, even though we may later find that these vices riddle her speech.

One might say that according to the principle of charity, others' arguments are to be presumed strong, their views cogent, and their behaviour sensible until shown to be otherwise.

Problem of interpretive imperialism.

The sentiments that underpin the principle of charity might begin to seem familiar at this point. There are, however, many indigenous peoples who might regard 'charity' as a misnomer. The principle seems to require the belief that all human beings share the same basic interests and desires, and this has been the assumption of many an imperialist. What counts as 'the best possible light' may, as a matter of fact, vary among cultures, and who is to say which view is to be preferred? On the other hand, one might argue that the flaw of the imperialists was in not pressing the principle of charity far enough or in having a mistaken view of 'the best possible light'.

There is, for example, more than one way of respecting the dead. If one came across a tribe that marked the passing of a loved one with cheerful music and dancing, it might be celebrating the deceased's entry into heaven rather than showing how glad its people are to see the back of him. Before one knew the facts, it would certainly betray a lack of imagination and a less than generous comportment to dismiss the tribe's behaviour as vicious or obnoxious.

Avoids straw men.

Indeed, forgoing the principle of charity not only exposes one to these sorts of moral and political charges; it also sets one up to commit a logical error called the straw man fallacy – criticizing a silly caricature of another's position rather than the position itself. Moreover, keep in mind that it's generally a good idea to cast the arguments of one's opponents in the strongest possible light, because if one can defeat the strong version of their argument, then one can certainly defeat weaker versions. Therefore, there seem to be not only moral and political reasons but also logical considerations for embracing the philosophical tool known as the principle of charity.

Plato example.

Similar considerations should be employed when approaching philosophical texts. In his dialogue, the *Republic*, Plato speaks of such qualities as large and small, heavy and light as 'contraries' and says that it is characteristic of the objects we perceive in the ordinary world to present contrary appearances, sometimes simultaneously. There is then a problem in that the nature of sensible objects is sometimes indeterminate and even apparently self-contradictory – both a thing and at the same time *not* that thing. Modern philosophers are wont to object that, in fact, these terms are not strictly speaking contrary but relational. That is, it's not that one object exhibits the property 'largeness' and another 'smallness', but that one is 'larger than' the other, and its fellow 'smaller than' the other.

Critics then argue that if Plato had recognized this fact, he would have realized that there is no contrariety involved, because being larger than another thing is not also contrary to being smaller than another. Certain decidedly uncharitable commentators, citing additional evidence from another dialogue, the *Phaedo*, have gone on to claim that Plato believed that an object could be essentially 'equal' without at the same time being equal to any other object.

If, however, one were to employ the principle of charity in this case, then rather than trying to interpret Plato's arguments in such a way as to make them as implausible as possible, we would instead attempt to maximize their rationality – to interpret them in the way that makes them most, not least, reasonable. Approaching the arguments with this charitable attitude, we might note that Plato, elsewhere in his works, shows a perfectly lucid familiarity with such relational concepts as 'father', 'brother', 'master' and 'slave' (in, e.g., the *Symposium* and the *Parmenides*). Plato may have been mistaken in dismissing the role of relations in favour of simple properties in rendering the nature of objects in the world, but he was not ignorant of the possibility – even though that impression may be given by the passages in question (*Republic* 479a–b and 523e–524a). Elsewhere in the *Republic* (523e–524a) Plato makes clear that when we can ascribe what could be called a 'relational quality' to an object, we can do so without thinking of that quality as relational. When we say, for example, that a pillow is soft, we are not at that time also thinking of some marble slab that it is softer than. Plato's critics, then, may be guilty of attacking a straw man and not the real Plato.

The principle of charity remains, then, a mere rule of thumb that may sometimes lead one to make mistakes. But it is still grounded in common sense, which demands some constraint on the kind of translations we may permit ourselves to proffer at the outset, and it helps us to avoid certain argumentative missteps. As Quine put it, 'one's interlocutor's silliness, beyond a certain point, is less likely than bad translation'.

See also

3.18 Ockham's Razor
3.5 *Ceteris paribus*

Reading

Donald Davidson, *Inquiries into Truth and Interpretation* (1984)

3.22 Question-begging

Perhaps the most famous quotation in philosophy is Descartes's 'I think, therefore I am.' At first sight, this seems about as unobjectionable a piece of reasoning as one could imagine. However, some have argued that Descartes's argument fails because it begs the question. How is this so?

To beg the question is in some way to assume in your argument precisely what you are trying to prove by it. A flagrant example would be someone who wants to show that spanking a child is wrong because violence against children is wrong:

1.   Violence against children is wrong.
2.   Spanking is violence against children. [Assumption]
3.   Therefore, spanking is wrong.

This argument begs the question because it assumes something crucial that's a matter of contention. Someone who thinks spanking is sometimes permissible is unlikely to regard it as a form of violence, at least not in all cases. Simply assuming that spanking is a form of violence, then, will hardly produce a convincing argument. It is the sort of argument that preaches only to those already converted.

Descartes example.

How does Descartes's argument (at least as it is commonly rendered) beg the question? We can perhaps see how by setting out the argument on two lines.

I think
Therefore I am

What you should notice here is that, in the first line, Descartes says, 'I think'. (He might, alternatively, have said, 'There is thought'.) Now, in using 'I' he is arguably already assuming that he exists. Hence what he goes on to deduce – I am – is already assumed in the premises. Therefore the argument begs the question.

Interestingly, Descartes may have been aware of this. In his *Meditations*, he doesn't say, 'I think, therefore I am,' but 'I am; I exist.' This is not presented in the form of an argument. Rather it is an incontrovertible intuition. It is not that one can deduce that one exists from the fact that one thinks; it is rather that it is impossible to think without being aware that one exists.

If an argument begs the question it quite clearly fails. Generally, the point of an argument is that it should give reasons to accept its conclusion. But if that conclusion is assumed by the reason offered, those reasons *provide no independent support* for the conclusion. The argument should persuade only those who already share the assumptions – in other words, those who already agree with the conclusion!

It should be noted that, as with so many philosophical terms and concepts, there are popular uses of this expression that are importantly different. In everyday English, people often say, 'That begs the question,' meaning 'that leads to a further question'. For example, someone might say that we need to cut carbon dioxide emissions to reduce global warming, and someone else might reply, 'That begs the question: what should we do if we are not successful in cutting carbon dioxide emissions?' Whether or not this is acceptable usage or not is a question that vexes linguists and grammarians. Whatever they decide, it is not the philosophical usage and should be clearly distinguished from it.

See also

1.1 Arguments, premises and conclusions
1.2 Deduction
3.6 Circularity
4.7 Entailment/Implication

Reading

*René Descartes, *The Discourse on Method* (1637)
*Patrick J. Hurley, *A Concise Introduction to Logic*, 7th edn (2000)

3.23 Reductios

Hollywood loves what it calls 'high concept comedies'. There's an element of double-speak here, because by high concept they do not mean anything highbrow or intellectual. Rather, a high-concept comedy is one where the whole film springs from a simple, comic premise. The whole film can then be captured in a single sentence with the suffix 'with hilarious consequences' appended. So for example, 'man dresses up as a woman so he can work as housekeeper in his ex-wife's home and see his kids, with hilarious consequences'. Or, 'cast of science fiction TV series are mistaken by aliens for real intergalactic heroes, with hilarious consequences'.

High-concept comedies share something in common with a form of philosophical argument known as *reductio ad absurdum*. The comedies start from premises that are possible or plausible; the philosopher starts with premises held by those whose position they undermine. The high-concept comedy then follows through the logical consequences of that premise to its (we hope) hilarious conclusions; the philosopher follows through the logic of the premises to their absurd conclusion. The comedy aims to entertain; the philosopher hopes to show that, if the premises lead to absurd consequences, the premises must be wrong.

A powerful tool.

Plato was a master of the *reductio ad absurdum*. In book 1 of his *Republic*, for example, his protagonist, Socrates, employs the technique in his discussion of justice. On one occasion, he is considering the view that justice is repaying debts. He quite easily shows that the logical consequence of this view is that it is just to return weapons one owes to a madman, even though we know he'd use them to kill people. This can't be what justice is, he argues. Therefore the original premise that led to the conclusion – that justice is repaying debts – must be false (*Republic* 331e–332a).

The technique is particularly powerful because it allows us, for the purpose of argument, to grant for a moment what our opponent believes. We say, 'Let's suppose you are right. What would be the consequences?' If we can then show that the consequences are absurd, we can force the opponent to admit something is wrong in his or her position: 'If you believe X, you must believe Y. Yet Y is absurd. So, do you really believe X?'

In our example, Socrates is careful not to read too much into his first strike. He employs the principle of charity and assumes that his opponent couldn't possibly mean by 'justice is the repaying of a debt' that one should return weapons to a madman. So he then goes on to interpret the principle in a way that doesn't lead to this absurd conclusion. This is a good example of how a reductio can encourage us not to abandon a position, but to refine it.

Complexities.

Reductios are very commonly used, but they are not unproblematic. The core problem is this: How do we decide when to bite the bullet and accept the 'absurd' consequence of our position, and when do we abandon or modify the position? For instance, does Socrates' argument really show that justice is not the repaying of a debt or that, contrary to our initial intuitions, it is just to return weapons to enemies and madmen? The problem here is that we seem to have to rely on our intuitions to decide whether the consequence is absurd or just surprising.

The problem is less acute if the consequence is a logical contradiction – this subspecies of reductios is called *proof by contradiction* (or *reductio ad impossibile*). If a set of premises has the logical consequence that round objects are square, that would show decisively that the premises are flawed. But reductios usually do not work in this way. It is not a contradiction to say it is just to return weapons to madmen; it is merely counter-intuitive.

Reductios are not usually conclusive, except in the case of proof by contradiction. Rather, they offer a *choice*: accept the consequence, no matter how absurd it seems, or reject the premises. That's a hard choice, but it is not strictly speaking a refutation.

See also

1.8 Refutations
3.21 Principle of charity
6.6 Self-evident truths

Reading

*Benson Mates, *Elementary Logic* (1972)

3.24 Redundancy

The great French mathematician and astronomer Laplace (1749–1827) did some ground-breaking work on the movement of celestial bodies, using Newtonian mechanics. There is a story, possibly apocryphal, that Laplace presented his work to Napoleon, who asked him where God fitted in. Laplace's reply was 'I had no need for that hypothesis.'

Laplace's observation is a clear example of redundancy. God had no place in his account of the movement of the planets, not because he had proved God does not exist, nor that God does not have certain powers, but simply because there was no place for God in the system – God was redundant because the explanation was complete without him.

Redundancy vs. refutation.

When we want to argue against something, we often look for refutations. We want conclusive arguments that the position we are opposing is false, or the entity we are denying exists does not exist. But often making a concept or entity redundant is as effective a way of removing it from the discourse. If we can show there is no reason to posit the existence of something and that our explanations are complete without it, we take away any motivation to believe in its existence.

A classic example of an attempt to use redundancy in this way comes in Bishop George Berkeley's (1685–1753) response to John Locke. Locke argued that objects have primary and secondary qualities. Essentially, secondary qualities are sense-dependent features like colour and smell. These are properties an object has only because the perceivers of those objects have a particular way of sensing them. Primary qualities, on the other hand, are the properties objects have independently of how they are perceived. These qualities – such as mass, size and shape – do not change according to the different senses of beings who perceive them.

Berkeley's argument against Locke was not to show directly that objects do not have any primary qualities, but to show that they were utterly redundant. Berkeley argued that what Locke called primary qualities were as sense-dependent as secondary qualities. We do not need to worry here about how he did this, or whether he was successful. To see his strategy, we just need to see where that leaves primary qualities if he was successful. Note that he hasn't shown there are no primary qualities. All he has shown is that all the primary qualities Locke has identified are, in fact, secondary qualities. This now leaves the idea of primary qualities redundant. For all we know, there may be some, but if all the properties of objects of which we are aware are secondary qualities, there is simply no work left for primary qualities to do.

That should be sufficient to consign the whole idea of primary qualities to the dustbin. If there is no longer a role for primary qualities and the explanation of the properties of objects is complete without them, why persist in asserting that they exist? Their whole *raison d'être* has been removed, and so they too must be removed.

Of course, it is highly debatable whether Berkeley succeeded in his argument. Though he attempted to show primary qualities were redundant, we should not assume he actually did so. Nevertheless, his strategy is instructive even if it failed, for it shows that you can do with redundancy many of the same things you can do with refutation.

See also

1.8 Refutation

Reading

*George Berkeley, *The Principles of Human Knowledge* (1710)

3.25 Regresses

Philosophers have on occasion been known to start behaving like children when the argument starts to slip away from them, but this is not what is generally meant by saying an argument leads to a *regress*. A regress is a far more serious flaw, though a far less entertaining one.

The idea of a regress, and why it is problematic, is captured in the old idea that the world sits on the back of an elephant. The question now arises, what is the elephant standing on? If it is another elephant, what is that elephant standing on? Another world? But then what is supporting the world? Yet another elephant? And so on. The explanation always requires the postulating of some other entity, and this process has no end. Therefore, the explanation fails.

Fodor example.

The philosopher of language Jerry Fodor (1935–) has had the allegation of regress directed at his language of thought hypothesis. Put rather crudely, Fodor argues that one cannot learn a language unless one already knows a language that is capable of expressing everything in the language we are learning. Put slightly differently, Fodor claims we need to possess an inner language – a language of thought – 'as powerful as any language we can learn'.

Some have smelled a regress here. Fodor says we need already to have a language of thought before we can acquire another language, such as English. But how do we acquire our language of thought? According to Fodor, to learn any language we need already to possess a language at least as powerful. That means that, surely, we can learn the language of thought only if we already know another language, call it the pre-language of thought. But how do we learn this language? We would surely need already to know a prior language . . .

This is an example of an *infinite regress*. Such a regress occurs when the logic of a position requires one to postulate an entity or process prior to that position; but then this entity or process itself, by the same logic, requires the postulating of a further prior entity or process, and so on, *ad infinitum*. Such a regress is extremely damaging for at least two reasons.

First, because it multiplies entities or processes infinitely, it leads to highly implausible theories. We might grant Fodor one language of thought, but the idea that there must be an infinite number of languages of thought nesting inside the mind is too preposterous.

Second, when there is a regress the intended explanation is *deferred* rather than *offered*. The language of thought hypothesis, for example, is supposed to explain how we acquire language. But, if the hypothesis does lead to a regress, we do not, in fact, ever explain how we get our first language. We're just told that for any particular language, we must already have learned a prior one to acquire it. It does not explain how we acquired the first language in the first place.

Not a slippery slope.

A regress need not be infinite. It may only push back the final explanation one, two or any *finite* number of steps. Indeed, Fodor would argue that his regress is not infinite at all. Certainly the thesis that to learn any language requires a prior language of thought means that the explanation of how we acquire language in the first place is pushed back from the question of how we acquire our native tongue to how we acquire the language of thought. But Fodor would argue that we are not forced off on an infinite regress by this. Because the language of thought is not learned but is hard-wired into our brains at birth (it is 'innate'), the question of how we learn the language of thought does not arise. We do not need to learn it; we are born with it, so the regress stops there.

The question for Fodor is whether or not this genuinely halts the regress or whether he has just strategically placed another philosophical elephant.

See also

3.18 Ockham's Razor
6.1 Basic beliefs

Reading

Jerry Fodor, *The Language of Thought* (1975)
Sextus Empiricus, *Outlines of Pyrrhonism* (*c.*200 CE), bk 1, ch. 15

3.26 Saving the phenomena

When Daniel Dennett wrote the ambitiously titled *Consciousness Explained*, his critics complained that the book did not appear to mention consciousness as we know it very often and that, as a result, he had simply 'explained consciousness away'.

Dennett was being accused of breaking a cardinal rule of philosophy: that one must always 'save the phenomena'. Whatever else a philosophical explanation might do, it must account for the way things 'seem like' to us. This principle presents us with a powerful tool of criticism.

The critical point.

A theory of ethics, for example, is inadequate if it cannot account for our experience of moral behaviour and judgement. A theory of perception is inadequate if it cannot account for our ordinary experiencing of sights and sounds. Any philosophical doctrine that seeks to deny these phenomena will be fighting a losing battle. The conclusions we draw from our experience can be debated, but the very event of that experience must not be sacrificed or ignored for the sake of theoretical interest. To paraphrase the physicist Richard Feynman: if your conclusions contradict common sense, then so much for common sense; if they conflict with received philosophical opinion, then too bad for received opinion; but if they should deny the very facts of our experience, then you must consign your conclusions to the flames.

The demands of explanation.

The necessity of saving the phenomena becomes obvious for another reason if we consider the relationship of an explanation with what it explains – what philosophers technically call its '*explanandum*'. In order for there to be an explanandum in the first place, there must be some phenomenon that can be 'picked out' or 'individuated' in our experience and then explained. But if an explanation does not account for the existence of the explanandum, or the possibility of our picking it out, then it cannot really have explained it at all.

In the case of ethics, one might start with twinges of conscience, feelings of compassion and tugs of commitment, and then go on to formulate a moral theory. But if that theory, in its final reckoning, finds no place for these experiences for which it was initially produced, then we may be left wondering just in what way it can be said to be a moral theory at all.

Limitations of the critical point.

Sometimes, however, the accusation that phenomena have not been saved rings hollow. We can see from Dennett's case that failing to mention the phenomena is not the same as failing to save them (though whether he fails to save the phenomena for other reasons is a different matter). Dennett responded to his critics by arguing that if an explanation is to live up to its name, the phenomenon it explains cannot rightly appear in its full glory within the framing of that explanation. His point is a strong one. It would be as if one were to go about solving an equation for x and then claim to have succeeded, though the value x remained on both sides of the equation.

Another illustration he uses is to imagine a box diagram that explains consciousness. If the explanation therein were complete, one would certainly hope not to find a box buried somewhere within it labelled 'consciousness'. If there were such a box, then we might as well dispense with all the other boxes in the diagram as superfluous. Needless to say, if the box that then remained contained nothing but the phenomenon of consciousness, then the diagram would provide no explanation to speak of.

Levels of explanation.

Whether or not one finds Dennett's arguments convincing, one can allow that there are different levels of explanation. An aspect of a phenomenon apparent at one level might not be apparent at another. The liquidity of water is not apparent in its microstructure, but that does not mean that the description of water as H_2O is inadequate or mistaken, or that chemists have failed to save the phenomena. There is no denial of the phenomena here, because to ascribe a chemical structure to water is not to deny water's liquidity – liquidity not being a property of individual atoms. Once we have described that chemical structure, we can move to showing how a large body of such atoms becomes a liquid at certain temperatures. As long as one's theory can account for the move from microstructure to macrostructure, or from explanation to explanandum, the phenomena are saved and the explanation has passed first base.

Similarly, even the ancient Greek philosophers Parmenides's and Plato's claim that the sensible world is in a sense illusory is not a case of failing to save the phenomena. Explaining that phenomena are illusory is an explanation of those phenomena.

See also

2.8 Reduction
3.10 Error theory

Reading

*Daniel C. Dennett, *Consciousness Explained* (1993)
Bas van Frassen, *The Scientific Image* (1980)
Maurice Merleau-Ponty, *The Phenomenology of Perception* (1962)

3.27 Self-defeating arguments

Shooting yourself in the foot. Being hoisted by your own petard. Scoring an own goal. There are many colourful ways of describing acts of accidental self-destruction. Unfortunately, in philosophy we're stuck with the prosaic term 'self-defeating argument'.

A self-defeating argument is an argument that, if taken to be sound, shows itself to be unsound. The term is often used for positions or theses as well as arguments where, if one takes the principle proposed to be true, it undermines itself by its own logic. Such cases are more accurately described as self-defeating positions.

Examples.

One famous example of a self-defeating position is crude relativism. A crude relativism holds that no statement is universally true, for everyone at all times and places. But if this were true, then that principle itself would not be true for everyone at all times and places. But the principle is claimed to be true for everyone at all times and places. To assert the principle, then, is simultaneously to deny it. The position is thus self-defeating.

Another famous example is a simple version of verificationism, which states that only statements that are verifiable by sense-experience are meaningful – all others are nonsense. But if we apply this principle to itself, we'll see that the principle itself is not verifiable by sense experience. Hence the principle itself must be nonsense. So, if we take the principle to be true, we find that the principle is undermined by itself.

Alvin Plantinga (1932–) has recently attacked purely naturalistic evolutionary theory (which regards the evolutionary process as purely natural and without intelligent guidance or purpose) as being self-defeating. Roughly, Plantinga holds that naturalistic evolutionary theory holds that beliefs develop in humans only through their helping individual humans adapt to their environments and pass on genetic material. But while there is only true belief on any topic there are many false beliefs (for the sake of argument, let's say 99) that also accomplish the purposes of adaptation and survival. Therefore, if our beliefs are the result of purely naturalistic evolutionary processes, we face a larger probability that they are false (here 99 per cent) than that they are true (1 per cent). Hence, on the basis of the premises of evolutionary theory, all of our beliefs are probably false. But naturalistic evolutionary theory is itself a human belief. Therefore, on its own terms, naturalistic evolutionary theory is probably false and self-defeating. (If you don't like the conclusion of Plantinga's argument, we suggest examining the assumptions about truth that shore it up.)

Spotting a self-defeating argument is a bit like witnessing something spontaneously combust. It is so devastating because there is little room to disagree with a criticism if that criticism is based precisely on one's own central claims. What may be surprising is how common self-defeating arguments are.

Commonplace in philosophy.

An analogy may help us to understand why philosophy is so vulnerable to this. Imagine you run a club and you need to make a set of rules that will determine who is allowed to join. In some clubs these rules will be very clear, since membership will depend on something straightforward, like being an alumnus of a particular university or a resident in a certain area. But some clubs have memberships that are harder to define. Think of a writers' club, for instance. If you exclude unpublished writers, you may be excluding talented and dedicated bona fide writers. But if you let in unpublished writers, you'll find that perhaps too many people can claim to qualify. When you try to come up with a subtle, carefully worked-out rule that tries to get over these difficulties, you might well find yourself inadvertently coming up with a rule that technically speaking makes you ineligible for membership.

Philosophers don't make rules for club membership, but they do try to make rules for what falls under a particular concept. In our examples above, these are rules for what should count as meaningful or true. It is philosophy's business to tackle difficult concepts, and so, like the club that has unclear criteria for membership, there is an inherent risk of coming up with rules that can be turned against themselves. The fact that self-defeating arguments keep on popping up in philosophy is not a sign of the stupidity of philosophers, but of the intrinsically difficult job they try to engage in.

See also

3.19 Paradoxes
3.20 Partners in guilt
4.2 Absolute/Relative

Reading

Alvin Plantinga, *Warrant* (1992)
*A. J. Ayer (1910-89), *Language, Truth and Logic* (1936)
Theodore Schick, Jr, and Lewis Vaughn, *How to Think about Weird Things: Critical Thinking for a New Age*, 3rd edn (2002)

3.28 Sufficient reason

Anyone who takes up philosophy for any length of time will at some point meet at least one person who finds the whole idea of philosophy baffling. Quite often, this bemusement is directed at the philosophical impulse to explain everything. Sometimes it seems that philosophers are like children who can't stop asking, 'Why? Why? Why?' Exasperated non-philosophers are likely to say something like 'Not everything can be explained,' surprised that you have failed to recognize this basic truth about the universe.

It is important to see the truth in this sentiment, but also to see how a proper understanding of the philosophical pursuit of explanations accommodates this truth. One can do this by considering a very simple principle set out by Leibniz – the *principle of sufficient reason*: 'There can be found no fact that is true or existent, or any true proposition, without there being a sufficient reason for its being and not otherwise, although we cannot know these reasons in most cases' (*Monadology* 32). Or a bit more pretentiously, following Schopenhauer: '*Nihil est sine ratione cur potius sit quam non sit*' (Nothing is without a reason for why it is rather than is not).

This principle succinctly captures the philosophical attitude to explanation. It also alludes to a basic question that is liable to strike us all from time to time and which has motivated a great deal of philosophy. Why, after all, is there something rather than nothing?

Sometimes the very fact that anything at all exists seems astonishing, and it seems as though there simply must be a reason for it all. Moreover, properly understood the principle also contains within it the riposte to the critic who thinks philosophers try to explain too much.

It is worth focusing on the last clause of Leibniz's formulation: 'although we cannot know these in most cases'. Leibniz accepts that we often do not know what reasons there are. But this is not the same as saying there are no reasons. For example, for the millennia before Albert Einstein's general theory of relativity people had no idea, or had wrong ideas, why gravity pulled objects to the Earth. But pre-Einsteinian scientists and philosophers still believed, correctly, that there was some reason why gravity worked. One can accept that there are reasons for the world being the way it is while also accepting that one hasn't a clue what those reasons are.

Schopenhauer's fourfold.

German philosopher Arthur Schopenhauer (1788–1860) delineated four categories of sufficient reason in the world. Note how it is possible for us to have a pretty good idea of the sufficient reasons of one category but not another.

1. Sufficient reason for becoming.
2. Sufficient reason for knowing.
3. Sufficient reason for being.
4. Sufficient reason for acting.

Reasons and causes.

Whether or not Schopenhauer's list is exhaustive, the general principle states, in short, that there must always be a reason for everything. This may not be the same as saying there must always be a cause (a mistake Schopenhauer accuses Spinoza of making). There is a lengthy debate about what kind of reasons are not ultimately explicable in terms of causes. For our purposes here, however, we need only note that the principle of sufficient reason itself does not presuppose that all explanations will be causal explanations. This makes the principle stronger, since it leaves open the kind of explanation that could be a sufficient reason and so does not commit itself to any particular view of what ultimate explanations are like.

Hume's doubts.

It is worth pointing out that not all philosophers agree with the principle of sufficient reason. The principle is often considered a central feature of rationalism, but when you think about it, the very idea seems to be a pretty remarkable assumption. How on Earth could you ever possibly prove whether or not it is true? Is it anything more than an article of faith or metaphysical speculation? In attacking the doctrine of causation developed by rationalists like Samuel Clarke (1675–1729) and Descartes (who held that causes are reasons), Hume came to regard the principle as rationally baseless. In his famous *Treatise* Hume writes, 'The separation . . . of the idea of a cause from that of a beginning of existence is plainly possible . . . and consequently the actual separation of these objects is so far possible, that it implies no contradiction nor absurdity; and is therefore incapable of being refuted by any reasoning from mere ideas; with which 'tis impossible to demonstrate the necessity of a cause' (*A Treatise of Human Nature*, bk 1, pt 3, §3). In other words, you can't prove that there's a reason for the way causes hook up with effects. Hume's argument radically changed the way we think about science by calling into question the extent to which we can give reasons for the way nature operates. Many subsequent philosophers have agreed with him.

In any case, seeing the principle of sufficient reason in its proper light will help dispel the illusion that philosophers cannot accept uncertainty or are dogmatic about what kinds of explanations we need. Philosophers are well aware of the difficulties of the principle. If it has any value, however, it is as a useful stimulus to investigation. Where people have looked for reasons and found them, they have better understood their world and been in a better position to manipulate it. No one has ever understood anything better by assuming that there is no reason for why it is the way it is. Even philosophical sceptics emphasize the importance of remaining open and searching. Perhaps this answer, then, weak in some respects though it is, also goes some way to correcting the myth that the reasons a philosopher cites must always be conclusive.

See also

1.3 Induction
1.4 Validity and soundness
2.2 Hypothetico-deductive method
4.1 A priori / A posteriori
4.7 Entailment/Implication

Reading

*David Hume, *A Treatise of Human Nature* (1739–40), bk 1, pt 3, §3
Gottfried Wilhelm, Baron von Leibniz, *Monadology* (1714)
Arthur Schopenhauer, *The Fourfold Root of the Principle of Sufficient Reason* (1813, 1847)

3.29 Testability

A common indicator of what someone most fears is what that person says he or she is most fervently opposed to. If this is true of philosophy, then in the modern era it is arguable that philosophy has been most afraid of sophistry: nonsense masquerading as sophisticated thought. Ever since Berkeley argued that we should abandon philosophical conceptions of material substance not because they're false but because they're literally *meaningless*, philosophers have been engaged in an ongoing purge from their discipline of all perceived nonsense – or what Wittgenstein described as *unsinnig*.

This fear that philosophy is contaminated with meaningless nonsense that stands in the way of fruitful reflection peaked in the early part of the twentieth century. The logical positivists and their successors in what became known as analytical philosophy attempted to purge the nonsense by coming up with simple rules that would enable us to sort the cogent wheat from the empty chaff.

One such rule was the verification principle of meaning, a principle particularly well developed by Alfred Jules Ayer (1910–89). The principle appeared in various forms. It may be roughly stated as: *only propositions that can be verified by reference to sensation are meaningful.*

All others are not merely false, but literally meaningless. So, for example, the idea that there is an invisible, intangible pink elephant in this room is meaningless, since there is no way, even in principle, that this claim could be verified by sense experience, as anything intangible is by definition unexperiencable. On this view, much of metaphysics, theology and ethics is meaningless and should be cast off by philosophy.

Verificationism *as a principle of meaning* failed because no one could come up with a formulation that didn't exclude what it was supposed to permit, or permit what it was supposed to exclude. More fatally, since the principle itself could not be verified by sense experience, it appeared to be nonsense by its own criterion. This, however, wasn't simply a problem with semantics. It also affected the philosophy of science.

Testability and science.

Philosophers of science have undertaken to articulate the properties of good explanations, especially with regard to scientific theories. Testability is among the most important of those properties. For example, the hypothesis that everything in the universe doubles in size every night at midnight is untestable (because the standards of measurements would also double) and hence cannot be part of a solid theory. Only testable theories can be good theories. Rejecting speculative, untestable hypotheses, Isaac Newton is said to have proclaimed, 'I feign no hypotheses' – *hypotheses non fingo*.

Or, as more recently, Imre Lakatos might have said, 'Testability is a property of good explanations and good scientific theories.'

But if this is so, the verification principle seems a poor way of conceptualizing testability. Most importantly, it is impossible to verify scientific laws of nature. Scientific laws (e.g. $E = mc^2$) make logically universal claims – claims about *all* instances of certain phenomena across the entire universe, past, present and future. But no one can verify such claims.

Falsifiability to the rescue?

In verification's footsteps came *falsification*, Karl Popper's thesis that it was the fact that a scientific generalization could be falsified that made it (in Popper's original formulations) a good scientific hypothesis. Paraphrasing Popper, one might put it this way: science advances by making conjectures (hypotheses), which are tested and perhaps refuted; if refuted, they are replaced by further conjectures until conjectures are found that are not refuted by the tests.

Universal claims such as scientific laws can be easily falsified. To falsify the claim that 'all comets travel in elliptical orbits', one only need find a single comet that does not travel in an elliptical orbit. In science this process of conjecture and refutation goes on and on, perhaps *ad infinitum*. The problem with falsification and science, however, is that it fails to work with logically particular claims such as 'some swans are purple'. Examining a million swans and finding no purple animals among them does not falsify the statement, since there might possibly still be a purple one out there.

Relation of the two principles.

Verification and falsification are not two sides of one coin. The verificationists like Ayer wanted their principle to apply to all philosophy, indeed all discourse, whereas Popper saw falsification as a method distinctive to science. But what verification and falsification have in common is the idea that a proposition has *somehow to be testable* to be part of a good theory. Whether that test must be able to verify or falsify the proposition – or perhaps both – is a matter of dispute, but the core claim is the broader one about testability. (In practice, science uses both verification and falsification.)

Testability and holism.

A good deal of more recent philosophy – including work by figures like Wittgenstein, Quine and Kuhn – have shown that testing for the most part makes sense only within an already accepted body of concepts, beliefs and practices. From this point of view the process of testing doesn't settle everything and won't resolve crucial questions that may arise among people.

Yet, the general idea that testability is important has, at least in a tacit form, proved to be remarkably durable, although its scope seems questionable. While, for example, testability may be vital for scientific hypotheses, the idea that ethics, for example, is (or should be) testable seems less clear. And, as the holists argue, testability won't bring disputes to an end or uniformity to belief. The challenge, however, first set down by the verificationists is a valuable one. In effect, it challenges us to ask, 'If you're not saying something that can be tested against experience, what are you saying, how is it meaningful, and is it really a justifiable part of a strong theory?' There are many adequate answers to these questions, but a failure to find them should make us consider whether or not our deepest philosophical fear has come to pass, and whether we are engaging in sophistry after all.

See also

1.3 Induction
2.1 Abduction
2.2 Hypothetico-deductive method
3.14 Hume's Fork

Reading

*A. J. Ayer, *Language, Truth, and Logic* (1936)
*Karl Popper, *Conjectures and Refutations* (1963)
Imre Lakatos, *The Methodology of Scientific Research Programs: Philosophical Papers* (1978), vol. 1

chapter 4
Tools for Conceptual Distinctions

4.1 A priori / A posteriori

When I was taught geometry at school, I remember a stage when I puzzled over the claim that internal angles of a triangle always added up to 180°. For a while, what bothered me was that I couldn't see how one could be entirely sure about this. Isn't it possible that one could, one day, find a triangle, measure its internal angles and discover that the angles added up to only 179°, or a copious 182°?

What I hadn't yet realized was that the claim that the internal angles of a triangle add up to 180° is an a priori claim. That is to say, according to many philosophers, it can be known to be true independently of (or prior to) particular experiences. I was thinking of geometry as if it were a branch of a posteriori knowledge, where we only know if something is true or false by reference to relevant, past (posterior) experiences.

A priori knowledge.

Why are geometric claims like this thought of as a priori? The reason is that the objects of geometry – triangles, squares, and so on – are not, in a sense, objects in the 'real world'. A triangle in the real world is never quite a perfect geometric triangle, though it may resemble it closely enough for us to act as though it is. For a start, we live in a three-dimensional world, whereas shapes like triangle and squares are purely two dimensional.

Because of this, the properties of triangles in *general* can be known without any reference to particular experiences of the world, such as measurements of *particular* triangles. We don't have to examine actual triangles; we need only to think of what it is for something to be a triangle, and, given the definitions we use, their properties can be derived by reason alone. (It may be, however, as Kant argues, that we can know this about triangles as well as other bits of a priori knowledge because we have the capacity for experience *in general*.)

Origin vs. method of proof.

The distinction appears clear but the waters can become muddied, sometimes unnecessarily and sometimes because of some serious further reflections.

Unnecessary muddying occurs when one misunderstands what is meant by 'knowledge independent of experience'. If you are tempted to say that we know only what triangles are because of experience, since we were taught about them at school, you have misunderstood the sense in which geometry is a priori. The means by which we come to find out about things like geometry, mathematics and pure logic (all of which are branches of a priori knowledge) is through experience. But what makes something a priori is not the means by which it came to be known, but the means by which it can be shown to be true or false. We may need experience to furnish ourselves with the concept of triangle, but once we have that concept, we don't need to refer to experience to determine what the properties of triangles are. A priori knowledge is thus distinguished by its method of proof, not by how we came to acquire it.

A posteriori knowledge.

When we turn to things like hurricanes, however, much of our knowledge is a posteriori. We cannot hope to discover many factual things about hurricanes by simply attending to the concept of hurricane or the meaning of the word 'hurricane'. We have to see what actual hurricanes are like and learn from that. Consider the following claims about hurricanes:

1.   All hurricanes are storms.
2.   By definition, all hurricanes have winds exceeding 85 mph.
3.   The behaviour of hurricanes is governed by natural law.
4.   The average wind speed recorded in hurricanes is 125 mph.

Sentences 1 and 2 might be considered true by definition and hence not a posteriori but things that can be known about hurricanes without actually examining any. In order to know whether or not they are true, one need only know the definition of 'hurricane'. Sentence 3 might be thought of as a claim based upon our a priori knowledge that all natural phenomena are governed by natural laws, but this knowledge is more plausibly categorized as a posteriori. Sentence 4, however, requires actual measurement of particular hurricanes and is therefore definitely an a posteriori claim.

Historical importance.

But what use is this distinction? Over the course of philosophical history, thinkers have disagreed about how much of our knowledge is a priori and how much is a posteriori. The distinction is a useful tool, therefore, in comparing and coming to grips with various philosophers' epistemological positions.

Rationalists such as Leibniz, Alexander Baumgarten (1714–62), and Descartes as well as empiricists like Hume understood all true a priori judgements to be analytic and all true a posteriori judgements to be synthetic (see 4.3). They disagreed, however, about what parts of knowledge fall into which category. The a priori / a posteriori distinction gives a quick way to show this, as well as to describe Kant's new wrinkle.

1. All experienced events have causes.
    a. Descartes: analytic a priori
    b. Hume: synthetic a posteriori
    c. Kant: synthetic a priori

2. $7 + 5 = 12$
    a. Descartes and Hume: analytic a priori
    b. Kant: synthetic a priori

3. Paris is the capital of France
    a. Leibniz: analytic a priori
    b. Descartes, Hume, Kant: synthetic a posteriori

The debate rages on today in new forms, particularly in the debate over naturalism, which may be thought of as the project of trying to base philosophy in the methods and data supplied by the natural sciences. The fact that this form of radical empiricism is resisted by many who would not consider themselves rationalists shows that the question of where to draw the line between the a priori and the a posteriori is a live and difficult question.

Critique of the distinction.

The distinction between a priori and a posteriori knowledge has come under attack, and the general thrust of recent philosophy has either been to construe all knowledge as a posteriori or to look for a third way of understanding what is called knowledge. Just as Quine attacked the synthetic/analytic distinction, he also claimed there was no such thing as a priori knowledge by arguing that all knowledge claims are in principle revisable in the light of experience (see 4.3).

See also

4.3 Analytic/Synthetic
4.10 Necessary/Contingent

Reading

Immanuel Kant, *Critique of Pure Reason* (1781)
W. V. O. Quine, 'Two Dogmas of Empiricism', in idem, *From a Logical Point of View* (1980)
Paul K. Moser, *A Priori Knowledge* (1987)

4.2 Absolute/Relative

In 1996 the physicist Alan Sokal published a paper 'Trangressing the Boundaries: Towards a Hermeneutics of Quantum Gravity' in the journal *Social Text*. However, the article was a spoof, a deliberate piece of nonsense and confusion designed to show how a sloppy relativism had pervaded American humanities and social sciences, and how scientific ideas were being misused by people who didn't understand them. Sokal had blinded the journal's editors by a combination of science and relativist philosophy.

The two targets for Sokal's spoof are closely linked, since the whole distinction between the absolute and the relative only came to the fore in intellectual life because of science. It was Einstein's work on time and space, and controversies over the meaning of certain findings in quantum mechanics, that more than anything threatened an absolute scientific conception of the world.

Two views of time.

The common-sense view of time is that time is absolute. What this means is that there is one standard, imaginary clock, that tells the time throughout the universe. When it is six o' clock in New York it is also 12 noon Greenwich meantime, and so it is also 12 noon GMT everywhere else in the universe. If I clap my hands at 12 noon GMT, it is possible for someone else on Alpha Centauri also to clap his or her hands at 12 noon GMT and our hand-clappings will be simultaneous for everyone everywhere. This was Isaac Newton's position.

With his theory of 'special relativity' (1905), Albert Einstein (1879–1955) claimed that this common-sense view is wrong (and his view is now universally accepted among physicists). Rather than an absolute time – one clock that can be used to time all events in the universe – time is relative. That is to say, what the time is depends on how fast one is moving relative to the speed of light and another frame of reference (or point of view). To answer the question 'When?' you also need to know 'how fast'. Strange as it seems, two events on opposites sides of the galaxy may therefore be simultaneous from one frame of reference but not from another – and we cannot privilege one point of view over the other. Both are right – relative to their own points of view.

There is no clearer paradigm for the absolute/relative distinction than Einstein's work on space and time. It makes clear how the absolute requires a single standard that holds good in all places and all times, while the relative implies a standard that is context dependent. All other proper uses of the absolute/relative distinction follow this pattern.

Application: ethics and social science.

In ethics, for example, an absolute conception is that standards of right and wrong hold good for all people and all times – perhaps, for example, because they are determined by God, or reason, or fixed by nature. If killing innocent beings is wrong, then it is wrong whether you're a twentieth-century Manhattanite, a Roman legionnaire or a Vesuvian prince. An ethical relativist, on the other hand, will say that what is right or wrong depends on where you are, when you're there, or maybe even who you are. One reason relativists hold this position is that they regard standards of right and wrong to be dependent upon or internal to particular societies, specific situations, or individual lives. Outside these, standards of right and wrong, good and bad, beautiful and ugly are simply inapplicable.

The absolute/relative distinction can also be used in other contexts. Economists, sociologists and political philosophers, for example, are concerned with the idea of poverty. Like ethical standards, poverty can have an absolute or relative sense. Absolute poverty will be defined so that one standard can be used, in modern-day Berlin and Calcutta, as well as first-century Rome and Jerusalem, to determine whether a person is poor or not. A relative conception of poverty, on the other hand, will allow for the possibility that someone with a flat and a television in Paris could be considered poor, even though he or she would, with that same amount of wealth, not be poor if transplanted directly to the Sudan.

Two cautions.

When using the absolute/relative distinction, two cautions should be remembered. To describe something as relative is not, as these examples make clear, to say that there are no standards by which to make judgements, or that 'anything goes'. It is merely to say there are no *universal* standards. It cannot be assumed (though it is often argued) that to abandon an absolute standard is to be left with no standards at all. Rather, relativism means that there may be multiple standards, none universally superior to the others.

Second, it is not always a case of choosing either an absolute standard or a relative one. Sometimes, it is just a matter of being clear which is being employed. So, for instance, one can have both a relative and an absolute conception of poverty but use them for different purposes. Here, what is important is being clear about which standard is being used, not making an either/or choice between them.

Political import.

The multiplicity of standards, none superior to the others, may be thought of as a type of equality. Because of this, people with democratic and left-leaning political sympathies (i.e. for whom political and social equality are important) have often found relativism attractive. Conservatives who feel more comfortable with social and political hierarchies often appeal to absolutes that privilege one set of claims, practices and standards above others. However, one needs to be careful not to allow one's political leanings to cloud one's judgement on this issue, nor to assume that absolutism is always conservative and relativism the natural home of the left.

See also

4.10 Necessary/Contingent
4.12 Objective/Subjective

Reading

*Alan Sokal and Jean Bricmont, *Intellectual Impostures* (1998)
Isaac Newton, *Philosophiae Naturalis Principia Mathematica* (1687)
Albert Einstein, 'On the Electrodynamics of Moving Bodies', in A. Einstein, Hendrik A. Lorentz, Hermann Minkowski and H. Weyl, *The Principle of Relativity* (1923)

4.3 Analytic/Synthetic

Like many philosophical concepts, the analytic/synthetic distinction at first appears crystal clear but then becomes more and more unclear until one wonders whether it serves a useful purpose at all.

The distinction was introduced by Immanuel Kant. An *analytic* judgement, in Kant's terminology, is one that does not add anything to what is included in the concept. It is often defined in terms of the relationship between subject (the thing the sentence is about) and predicate (what is said about the thing the sentence is about). For example, in the sentence 'Snow is white,' 'snow' is the subject and 'white' the predicate. In these terms, an analytic judgement may be formulated as a sentence where the meaning of the predicate is wholly contained in the subject. Hence the judgement simply unpacks or analyses the subject to yield the predicate. For example:

1. All bachelors are unmarried men.
2. All barns are structures.

In both cases, the predicates (unmarried men and structures) are already 'there' in the subjects (bachelors and barns). In Kant's terms, the judgements as a whole do not go beyond what is already contained in the concepts that are the subject of the judgements (bachelor and barns).

This sort of analysis may also be construed in argument form. For example, if I think that Charles is a bachelor and I then conclude he is not married, I have made an analytic judgement, since in saying he is not married I have said nothing that is not already contained in the thought that he is a bachelor.

If, however, I think that something is water and I judge that this liquid boils at 100 °C, I am making a *synthetic* judgement, since nothing in the mere thought that something is water can tell me what its boiling point is. (Leibniz, to the contrary, held that all true judgements about things are analytic. A complete concept of a thing contains all its properties.) The judgement about the boiling point of water goes beyond what is contained in the concept of water, whereas the judgement that a bachelor is unmarried does not go beyond what is already contained in the concept bachelor. In other words, the predicate adds something to the subject. Hence the following claims are synthetic:

1. The average lifespan of Scottish bachelors is 70 years.
2. The barn on Hugo's horse farm is white.

That may seem clear enough. But things soon become more difficult.

Psychology or logic?

First of all, Kant's definition can appear to depend on the psychology of the thinker rather than the logic or meaning of the concept. This is made clear by Kant's claim that $7 + 5 = 12$ is a synthetic judgement. The idea of '12' seems to be already contained in the idea of '7 + 5'. But psychologically, one can have the idea of '7 + 5' without having the idea of '12'. This is even plainer in larger sums, where one can have the idea of $1,789 + 7,457$ without having the idea that the sum of the two numbers is 9,246, even though the sum contains all that is logically required to determine the answer.

Much then depends on how we unpack Kant's idea that synthetic judgements go beyond a concept. We can understand this logically or psychologically, but also semantically – in terms of what the words mean. Sometimes analytic statements are said to be those that are true in virtue of the meanings of the words, regardless of what the speaker understands by them. So 'a bachelor is an unmarried man' is analytic, not because a speaker already *knows* that 'bachelor' means 'unmarried man' (indeed he or she may well not know this), but just because 'bachelor' objectively means 'unmarried man' (whether he or she knows it or not).

The existence of these subtly different uses of analytic and synthetic is confusing. For this reason it is advisable never to appeal to the distinction without making it clear what you take the distinction to mean.

These are important points, since they mark the difference between the synthetic/analytic distinction and the a priori / a posteriori distinction. The a priori / a posteriori distinction is concerned with whether any reference to experience is required in order to legitimate the judgements. The analytic/ synthetic distinction is concerned with whether thinkers add anything to concepts when they formulate their judgements, thereby possibly expanding rather than simply elaborating upon their knowledge.

Quine and containment.

Quine pointed out in his famous essay 'Two Dogmas of Empiricism' (1951) that it seems impossible to define adequately just what is meant by the metaphor 'contain', which is found in the idea that in analytic judgements the predicate is contained in the subject. Just how does one concept 'contain' the meaning of another? It seems that this can't be spelled out in any general way that keeps the scope of the concept clearly defined. On the other hand, surely there must be a distinction between simply explaining the meaning of a concept and connecting new information to it. (A similar problem faces the concept of 'entailment'.)

The analytic/synthetic distinction may seem simple, but it opens up some difficult and fundamental issues in philosophy.

See also

4.1 A priori / A posteriori
4.7 Entailment/Implication
4.10 Necessary/Contingent

Reading

Immanuel Kant, *Critique of Pure Reason* (1781)
W. V. O. Quine, 'Two Dogmas of Empiricism', in idem, *From a Logical Point of View* (1980)
H. P. Grice and Peter F. Strawson, 'In Defence of a Dogma', *Philosophical Review* (1956)

4.4 Categorical/Modal

Critics of philosophy in the English-speaking world sometimes protest that it is too in thrall to logic, and one of the problems with logic is that it just doesn't capture the complexity of the world. The critics are right and wrong.

The critics are right that general logic's 'categorical' rendering of truth fails to capture many of the subtleties of our epistemic life. For general logic the truth or falsehood of sentences can be expressed by it in just two, simple 'categorical' ways – true or false. But consider all the different kinds of true propositions there are:

Some are true at certain times but not others: 'The sun is shining.'
Some are certainly true: 'Something exists.'
Some are known to be true: 'The uranium atom can be divided.'
Some are possibly true (though also possibly false): 'The Conservative Party will win the next election.'
Some are necessarily true: '1 + 1 = 2.'
Some are believed to be true (but perhaps are not really true): 'The husband of Jocasta is not the killer of Laius – according to Oedipus.'

But although critics are right that these elaborations on truth are not accommodated by classical logic, they are wrong to see philosophy as a whole as being impoverished by it. First of all, it just isn't the case that all philosophy is done within the confines of classical logic. Second, even logicians are aware of this issue and have developed what is known as modal logic to deal with them. Modal logics attempt to accommodate various 'modalities', such as those listed above: this includes *temporal modality* (it is true at such and such a time), *logical modality* (it is necessarily true), *epistemic modality* (it is certainly true; it is known to be true), and *intensional logics* (it is believed to be true). Such modal propositions contrast with the simple categorical propositions of the form 'it is true' or 'it is false'.

Modal logic itself is a specialized area of philosophy. The important lesson for the majority who don't study it is simply to remember that when we say 'X is true,' we usually adopt the categorical form, even though a more complete or accurate expression of the proposition might be in a modal form. The challenge is to be able to recognize whether a proposition should be understood as true categorically or modally and, if the later, what sort of modality applies.

Note that sometimes the term 'modal logic' is used to describe logics that incorporate the concepts of 'possibility' and 'necessity' but not the others listed above.

See also

4.8 Essence/Accident
4.10 Necessary/Contingent

Reading

G. Hughes and M. Cresswell, *A New Introduction to Modal Logic* (1996)
Richard Patterson, *Aristotle's Modal Logic* (1995)
Nicholas Rescher and A. Urquhart, *Temporal Logic* (1971)

4.5 Conditional/Biconditional

Chas Chaplin told Dirk Dorking that if he (Chas) got promoted, he would stand in the middle of Oxford city centre and sing 'Nessun Dorma' wearing a rabbit costume. So when one day Dirk was passing through the centre of Oxford and heard the distinctive dulcet tones of Chas's rendition of the Puccini aria coming from a man in a rabbit suit, who on closer inspection indeed turned out to be Chas, he went up to him and congratulated him on his promotion.

'Promotion?' replied Chas. 'You're kidding! I've been sacked and now I'm busking for a living.'

Dirk's mistake is an understandable one, and it rests on a confusion between two uses of the word 'if' in our ordinary language, which in philosophical parlance are the conditional and biconditional. The conditional is a simple 'if', whereas the biconditional means 'if and only if' ('iff'). The difference is crucial. Consider the difference between these two propositions:

1. If I get promoted, I'll do the bunny singing thing.
2. Iff (if and only if) I get promoted, I'll do the bunny singing thing.

In each case, we can divide the propositions into two parts:

The *antecedent* – the part immediately following the if or iff ('I get promoted')
The *consequent* – what follows if the antecedent is true ('I'll do the bunny singing thing').

If 2 above is true and you see Chas doing the bunny singing thing, you can deduce that he has been promoted. This is because in a biconditional statement the consequent is only true if the antecedent is true. Because it is 'if *and only if*', the consequent will not be true unless the antecedent is. So you know that if the consequent is true, the antecedent must also be true, because that is the only circumstance under which the consequent could be true.

In an ordinary conditional, however, this does not follow. Chas did not say he would do his bunny singing thing if *and only if* he got promoted. The possibility that the consequent could be true *for some reason other than being promoted* remained open.

A clear example of this is when my friend says, 'If I win the lottery I'm going to take a long holiday in the Bahamas.' My friend doesn't mean that she will go on a long holiday in the Bahamas *only if* she wins the lottery. If she inherits a large sum of money, or wins it in another way, for instance, she will also take that trip. Therefore, if someone says, 'If I win the lottery, I'm going to have a long holiday in the Bahamas' and you find out he or she are on such a holiday, you can't be sure it is because of winning the lottery.

A fallacy.

This mistake – taking the antecedent to be true in a conditional, because the consequent is true – is a fallacy known as 'affirming the consequent'. It is a very simple mistake to make, since in everyday English, we distinguish between conditionals and biconditionals implicitly, by context, rather than by explicit stipulation. Therefore it is easy to take an 'if' to mean 'if and only if' or even just plain 'only if' when, in fact, it should be read as a simple 'if'.

The way to avoid this kind of mistake is, in one's reading and listening, always to check to see whether an 'if' is being used as a conditional or a biconditional, and in one's own writing, explicitly to use 'iff' or 'if and only if' when one intends a biconditional. That way, one won't jump to conclusions when one sees grown men in rabbit costumes singing opera.

See also

Reading

*Patrick J. Hurley, *A Concise Introduction to Logic*, 7th edn (2000)
Irving M. Copi, *Introduction to Logic*, 10th edn (1998)
D. Edgington, 'On Conditionals', *Mind* 104 (1995)

4.6 Defeasible/Indefeasible

In the debate over the death penalty, people often point to a crucial difference between a death sentence and a sentence to a penal term. In judging a person guilty, the law allows for the fact that if evidence comes to light later that questions the verdict the verdict can be reconsidered and, if necessary, the punishment rescinded. However, if the death penalty is carried out, this option is removed. The punishment cannot be rescinded because it is irreversible.

Opponents of the death penalty use this fact in their arguments against capital punishment. To use philosophical language, the crux of their case is that any judgement of guilt or evidence given by a court is defeasible. That is to say, the possibility – however remote – always remains open that the judgement will be revised in the light of new or unconsidered evidence. Given that such judgements are defeasible, it is therefore inappropriate to sentence someone to a punishment that cannot be rescinded. Such a course of action could only be justified if court judgements were indefeasible. (A related philosophical term, 'corrigible', which means 'correctible', is often used in a way very much like 'defeasible'. The terms 'corrigible' and 'corrigibility' have been popularized by the pragmatists.)

Defeasibility and knowledge.

The debate over which claims are defeasible and which are indefeasible is a long-running one in philosophy. It is a central feature of the debate over the status of knowledge. Some have argued that any claim to knowledge must be a claim to know something indefeasible. To know something is to believe something to be true that is in fact true. If something is true, it cannot turn out later to be false. So, to have knowledge is to possess the truth, and since the truth can't change, knowledge is indefeasible.

Opponents of this view argue that such a criterion for knowledge is too strict. If knowledge must be indefeasible, then we just can't have knowledge very often, if at all. Hume, for instance, would have argued (though he wouldn't have used these terms) that only simple truths of mathematics and geometry are even in theory indefeasible – though in practice mathematical and geometric inferences remain defeasible. Any fact about the world is always open to revision in the light of sufficient contrary experience, and even in mathematics people are prone to make errors. In this century, semantic holists such as W. V. O. Quine have argued that even theoretical judgements such as '1 + 1 = 2' are defeasible, since we cannot rule out some new fact coming to light that would make us revise this claim.

The defeasible/indefeasible distinction is particularly useful now that the a priori / a posteriori distinction has been problematized (see 4.1). It is very useful to be able to distinguish between those claims that one believes to be in some sense provisional and those that are established. It is, however, somewhat old-fashioned to believe that a priori claims are all indefeasible and a posteriori defeasible. The defeasible/indefeasible distinction allows us to separate questions about the actual grounds of beliefs – experience or reason – from questions concerning whether or not those beliefs are in principle open to objection or not.

See also

1.11 Certainty and probability
2.1 Abduction
3.29 Testability
4.1 A priori / A posteriori
4.3 Analytic/Synthetic

Reading

George S. Pappas and Marshall Swain, *Essays on Knowledge and Justification* (1978)
Keith Lehrer, *Theory of Knowledge* (1990), vol. 1
G. P. Baker, 'Defeasibility and Meaning', in *Law, Morality, and Society*, ed. P. M. S. Hacker and J. Raz (1977)

4.7 Entailment/Implication

The relation between the everyday and philosophical uses of the terms 'implication' and 'entailment' is akin to the relation between splashes of paint on a wall and a work of abstract art: one may be more consciously ordered than the other, but both are messy and hard to get a handle on.

Entailment.

Entailment is the simpler of the two. Generally philosophers will say that a conclusion is entailed by an argument's premises if the inference is a formally valid deduction (see 1.4). You may not, however, be surprised to learn that things get a bit more complicated for logicians. Logicians have found that paradoxes arise if entailment is formalized in certain ways. But let's leave that topic to the logicians, as this is a particularly complicated issue.

Sometimes, however, logicians use 'entailment' in a rather different way. They use it to refer to a connection of *content* beyond what philosophers call 'truth-functionality'. That is, from the point of view of standard propositional logic, the relation in an argument (and in certain types of conditional) between the conclusion and the premises (or between the antecedent and consequent) is based only on the truth of each. The trouble is that sometimes two sentences may be true but unconnected, and this leads to rather odd things, logically speaking. For example:

1.   If green is a colour, iron is an element.
2.   Green is a colour.
3.   Therefore, iron is an element.

In standard propositional logic, the preceding argument is technically sound. (Its form is called *modus ponens*, the way of affirmation.) But the trouble is that there's no real connection between 'green is a colour' and 'iron is an element' – other than their both being true. *Relevance logic* would demand more of the first premise. In order to say that a conclusion not only formally follows from its premises but is also *entailed* by them, relevance theorists demand some additional connection. Consider how differently the concepts are connected in this argument:

1.   If green is a colour, then it is visible to the human eye.
2.   Green is a colour.
3.   Therefore, it is visible to the human eye.

Since there's an internal connection between colour and visibility, here the conclusion would count in relevance logic (as well as in standard logic) as being entailed by the conclusion.

Implication.

Implication contrasts with entailment in being a broader concept that includes not only various kinds of logical relations but also cases where one idea connects to another in other ways. We might say that an implication is a property of *any true conditional* statement – statements of the form 'If X, then Y.' (Note that arguments can be cast as conditional statements where *if* the premises are true, *then* the conclusion is also true.)

For example, 'If I stand in the rain without an umbrella or other protective covering, I will get wet' is a true conditional statement. This means I can say that 'standing in the rain without an umbrella or other protective covering' implies 'getting wet'. But this is not because 'I will get wet' is the conclusion of a valid argument of which 'if I stand in the rain' is the sole premise. It is just that we see in the statement that getting wet is intrinsically connected to being unprotected in the rain. Here the consequent is implied by the antecedent because of a kind of causal connection, but there may be other reasons one idea connects to or follows from another.

Of course, implications like this may serve as the basis of an argument – that is, a case of entailment. Consider the following:

1.   If I stand in the rain without an umbrella or other protective covering, I will get wet.
2.   I'm standing in the rain without an umbrella or other protective covering.
3.   Therefore: I will get wet.

And perhaps one could argue that we recognize implications just because they can be used in entailment. What's important to see, however, is that sentence 1, by itself, presents *not* an argument but only an implication; premise 2 and the conclusion are required to formulate an argument.

Good advice.

The problem with the distinction as set out is that it is all much, much messier than this. So much messier, in fact, that any attempt to tidy it up in a text such as this is bound to result in either an incongruously bloated entry or utter confusion. For instance, philosophers have noticed that implication comes in various guises: such as material implication, formal implication, Rudolf Carnap's (1891–1970) theory of L-implication and Clarence Irving

Lewis's (1883–1964) conception of strict implication (which is also sometimes known as entailment).

However, there are several useful lessons that can be taken from this brief discussion. The first is to avoid using the terms 'implication' and 'entailment' if an alternative, clearer way of expressing what you want to say is available. Talk about a 'valid deduction' or a 'true conditional', not about entailment and implication.

The second lesson is that the simplistic distinction set out is a decent rule of thumb. If you restrict your use of 'entailment' to valid deductions and your use of 'implication' to true conditionals, you won't go far wrong. All you'll be doing is using two general terms that also have other, more specific meanings, and you will, on some occasions, be using one where the other will also do. In neither case will you be wrong.

See also

1.2 Deduction
1.4 Validity and soundness
4.5 Conditional/Biconditional

Reading

C. I. Lewis, 'The Calculus of Strict Implication', *Mind* 23 (1914)
J. M. Dunn, 'Relevance Logic and Entailment', in *Handbook of Philosophical Logic: Alternatives to Classical Logic*, ed. D. Gabbay and F. Guenthner (1986)
Stephen Read, *Relevant Logic* (1988)

4.8 Essence/Accident

The singer and actress Madonna is well known for her continual self-reinvention. In her career she has changed image from hip Brooklyn girl, through dominatrix, sexual-religious icon, and sophisticate and cowgirl, to name but a few of her personae.

In Aristotle's terminology, all these changes have been mere accidents. This does not mean that the changes have not been planned – indeed, Madonna's success is in all likelihood the result of very clever planning. For Aristotelians, *accident* has a different meaning.

An *accident* is a property of something that is not essential to that thing –

that, in other words, can be changed without utterly destroying what the thing is. (Later thinkers also called such properties 'attributes' and 'modes'.)

The *essence* of a thing is what makes something what it is; to formulate a thing's essence therefore is to define it.

An essence therefore remains in place just as long as the thing it defines remains in existence. Accidents, on the other hand, can come and go. This is why Aristotle related the essence of a thing to what he called its *substance* (*ousia* in Greek) – what substands (*hypokeimenon*) or stands under change. For Aristotle, following but modifying his teacher Plato, the substance of a thing is most basically its *form* (*eidos*). So, in these terms, Madonna's accidents include her styles, public personae, haircuts and colours, while her essence is that she is a human. Throughout all those costume changes, she's remained a human; and if essence is particular, she has remained this human we call 'Madonna'. (Most philosophers in the Aristotelian and Platonic traditions have thought that essence is not particular but universal.)

Historical modifications.

The contrast appears in differing forms throughout the history of philosophy. Aristotelian natural science may be tersely described as the attempt to determine the essential features of natural entities. (Modern natural science, by contrast, centres less on determining essences than on formulating laws describing the way natural phenomena behave.) We also see this search in Descartes's famous *Meditations on First Philosophy*, where he reflects on a piece of wax in an effort to determine the essence of the material world. Like an Aristotelian, Descartes examines what changes and what does not in the wax as it melts. He concludes that the shape, smell, texture and hardness of wax are all accidental properties, whereas its essence is that it is an extended, flexible and changeable thing (*res extensa*). Descartes goes on to consider himself, and concludes that his entire body is not essential to what he is and that his essence is that of a purely thinking thing (*res cogitans*).

In Descartes we can see traces of a common variant on Aristotle's distinction. Descartes's view seems close to the view that essence defines the substance of which the thing is made. On the scholastic or Aristotelian model, accidents are those features of a thing that can have no existence independent of substance, but that are not substances themselves. Colour, for example, is an accident, since it is not a substance but is a property of substances. (Colour can't exist independently but must always be the colour of something.)

Descartes's radical change in looking at these issues was to demand that what's of first importance in determining substances, essences and accidents is how we think about them. Hence for Descartes and Spinoza, as well as for a great deal of philosophy after them, what is substantial is what we must, when our thinking is clear and rational, *conceive* as existing independently. For example, in Meditation 6 of his famous *Meditations*, Descartes determines that the mind and the body are really distinct from one another because he can clearly and distinctly conceive of the one without the other.

Thinkers from Kant to Hegel to Wittgenstein to Husserl to Heidegger to Derrida have in various ways inherited this method but modified it in various ways – most recently by looking at the way *language*, rather than thought, structures the way we understand what things are.

Metaphysically speaking, most philosophers today reject the idea of essences – at least on the ancient model. Substance doctrines largely crashed upon the shoals of empiricist and linguistic critiques, which have argued that traditional theories of substance involve metaphysical posits that can't be observed, that are unnecessary to understanding reality, and that in fundamental ways are meaningless.

Political uneasiness.

Many recent thinkers have rejected the notion of essences as artificial, confining, and even oppressive. Existentialists are famous for the slogan 'Existence precedes essence'. By this they mean that we are whatever we choose to be and that neither God nor nature nor society determines what we are. Feminist philosophers have adroitly shown how various conceptions purporting to define what it essentially means to be a woman have been used to keep women in a limited and subordinate position, excluding them from all sorts of things (such as voting, higher education, and owning property) supposedly not proper for them. Some thinkers have gone so far as to suggest that all determinations of the human essence are to be rejected on these grounds.

A contextual approach.

What is considered accidental and essential can also be thought of as context dependent. The colour of a metal may be accidental when the metal is an internal part of an automobile engine but essential in a sculpture. In technical terms, we can say that the metal's colour is accidental *qua* engine parts and essential *qua* sculpture. One can qualify the use of accident and essence in instances such as these and sidestep broader, metaphysical issues about whether the distinction is a fundamental one or merely a useful device. Linda Alcoff proposes a notion of 'positionality' along just these lines.

Madonna is an apposite example of the debate over the essence/accident distinction, since many of her admirers claim she is the paradigm of the post-modern person for whom there is no unchanging essence at all but merely a sequence of accidents. If Madonna's seemingly limitless ability to transform herself is taken seriously, then, *pace* Aristotle and Descartes, Madonna suggests that there is no such thing as essence at all. Philosophers may not use Madonna as their exemplar, but be warned that some will still make a claim that is the same in essence, if not in accident.

See also

4.1 A priori / A posteriori
4.10 Necessary/Contingent
4.11 Necessary/Sufficient
4.13 Realist/Non-realist
5.3 Empiricist critique of metaphysics
5.4 Feminist critique

Reading

*Aristotle, *Metaphysics*, bks 7, 8
*René Descartes, *Meditations on First Philosophy* (1641)
Saul Kripke, 'Identity and Necessity', in *Identity and Individuation*, ed. Milton K. Munitz (1971)

4.9 Knowledge by acquaintance/description

Francophones have a philosophical advantage over Anglophones in that they already have embedded in their language a distinction we have to make explicitly. In English we know (1) people, (2) facts, and (3) how to do things. Translate 'know' into French, however, and you can't use the same word for all three. To talk about knowing people and places, you use *connaitre*, and to talk about knowing facts, *savoir*. (*Savoir* is also used for knowing how to do something – *savoir-faire*.) Have you ever noticed that one can know *how* to do something (like play the cello) but not be able to put that knowledge into words? It is an ancient distinction, one to which Aristotle, for instance, was very much alive. In English, to talk about *savoir* we need to use the phrase 'propositional knowledge', which is knowledge *that* something is the case. So there are at least three kinds of knowing:

Knowing that: knowing facts, propositions, theories (*savoir*)
Knowing as familiarity: knowing a place, a person, a pet (*connaitre*)
Knowing how: knowing how to do something, how to perform a certain act properly or well (*savoir-faire*)

Let's put aside *savoir-faire* for the moment, since the real interest in Anglophone philosophy has been a distinction that has its roots in the contrast between *connaitre* and *savoir* (though none of what follows should be taken as a description of the actual meaning of these words in French).

Russell's approach.

Bertrand Russell made a philosophical distinction between two types of knowledge. The first form of knowledge (more closely related to *connaitre*) is 'knowledge by acquaintance'. This is knowledge we get of things by being directly aware of them – that is, through direct observation rather than the reports of others. The kinds of things of which Russell believes we are directly aware are sense-perceptions (sounds, sights, tastes, smells and feels), memories, introspections, universals (general ideas such as circles, numbers and brotherhood) and possibly our own selves.

Knowledge by acquaintance is, for Russell, the root of all knowledge. It makes possible, however, a second kind of knowledge: 'knowledge by description'. This comes in two forms:

1. *Definite Descriptions* (*the* such and such – e.g. the cat) and
2. *Indefinite Descriptions* (*a* such and such – e.g. a cat)

In each case, 'such and such' will be a word or compound of words standing for things we know by acquaintance.

At this point, we part company from *connaitre*, since, for Russell, to know a person is to have knowledge by description. This is because what we are directly aware of is not a person, but sense perceptions of a body, a voice, and so on. So when I say, 'I know the Queen,' 'Queen', like all proper nouns, is a kind of shorthand for a description that picks out only a single entity and no other: 'the woman with white hair I meet for tea every week'. Note that this description contains only things known by acquaintance.

Put this together and Russell's theory is basically this: we know by acquaintance sense perceptions and universals (white, hair, woman, etc.). From these, we can gain knowledge by description (the woman with white hair I meet for tea every week). When these are definite descriptions rather than indefinite ones, we can replace this description with a proper noun as shorthand (the Queen).

Knowledge as usage.

But is being able to do this – substituting a proper noun for a definite description, and vice versa – knowing? This issue bears on a philosophical problem that gripped Ludwig Wittgenstein, and following him J. L. Austin. Is 'knowing' being in a certain state of mind (perhaps having a direct awareness of sensation, an idea, or a relation of ideas), or is it being able to do certain things (perhaps saying the right words in the right way in the right context)? Wittgenstein's view seems to have changed over the course of his philosophical career but to have settled towards the latter view. Others, like Alvin Plantinga and Rudolf Carnap, resist his conclusion and try to retain a version of the former.

Using this tool.

As with many of the concepts and distinctions in this toolkit, we have a highly specific theory that is subject to the controversies you'd expect. Bertrand Russell's theory of descriptions is far from unproblematic and one could (and some do) spend a lifetime unravelling it. But, on the other hand, there are more general lessons we can take away from this, irrespective of where we stand regarding the ultimate success of Russell's arguments.

Most basically, going back to the starting point of the discussion, unless we can distinguish between knowing *that* (knowing in the sense of being familiar with something) and knowing *how* (knowing how to do something) we're going to end up in a hopeless muddle. Also, there must be something to Russell's distinction between knowledge by acquaintance and description, even if the boundary is drawn incorrectly. Some things we know because we are aware of them and some we know via something we can do – in this case giving some kind of account of them.

Beyond this lies much debate and disagreement. In this sense, the distinction between knowledge by acquaintance and description is more of a start than an end point. You need to know it because to do philosophy without it is to philosophize naively. But once you are aware of it, you can't simply pick it up and use it unproblematically. Like a trench in war, you need it not so much to make progress but to avoid being pushed back and hopelessly defeated.

See also

4.14 Sense/Reference
6.1 Basic beliefs

Reading

*Bertrand Russell, *The Problems of Philosophy* (1912)
Ludwig Wittgenstein, *Philosophical Investigations* (1953)
J. L. Austin, *How to Do Things with Words* (1962)

4.10 Necessary/Contingent

Some philosophical distinctions have a whiff of the esoteric about them, but others are closer to common sense. The distinction between the necessary and the contingent falls into the latter category. In essence, it is the distinction between those things that must be the way they are and those that could have been otherwise. But what sorts of things? It doesn't take philosophers long to start making distinctions, so let's consider an important one here.

Events and claims.

Normally, in discussions of necessity and contingency philosophers distinguish between two types of necessary and contingent things.

Claims that are always true, in all cases, no matter what, are *necessary claims*. It is simply not possible for claims that are necessarily true to be false – and for those that are necessarily false to be true. Contingent statements, by contrast, are claims that happen to be true (or false) but could be false (or true).

Necessary states of affairs are events or states of being that simply couldn't be otherwise. If an event happens necessarily, it is impossible for it not to happen. If, on the other hand, an event is contingent, it is possible that it might either occur or not occur.

As an example of a necessary truth, consider any mathematical truth, say, $2 \times 2 = 4$. This is traditionally seen as a necessary truth, since, given the meaning of '2', '4', '=' and '×', it must always be true that $2 \times 2 = 4$. It could not be otherwise. (Of course, it is true that we could have used the symbols of '2', '4', '=' and '×' to stand for other things, but the necessity we ascribe in this case is not that those particular symbols stand for what they do, but that, given the meanings they have, $2 \times 2 = 4$ is necessarily true.)

If, however, you consider a historical truth like 'George W. Bush is the president of the US from 2001 to 2004,' it seems perfectly reasonable to say that this statement is not necessarily true and that there's nothing necessary about the state of affairs it describes. Had a few things gone differently in Florida before, during and after the US presidential election of 2000, it would have been Al Gore who entered the White House as president, and it would just be plain old Governor Bush. Because there is no necessity about it, the fact that 'George W. Bush is the president of the US from 2001 to 2004' is a contingent truth.

Determinism, Spinoza and necessity.

Conceptually, the distinction is therefore a clear one. As you can imagine, however, things become more controversial once you try to decide what actually is necessary and what actually is contingent. For example, if you are a strict determinist, then you believe that everything that happens is the inevitable consequence of what has gone before. There is no room for luck or free will. From this point of view, nothing is contingent, and all events are necessary. 'George W. Bush is the president of the US from 2001 to 2004' would be a necessary truth, since as a determinist would see it this fact could not be otherwise. Though it looked to us as though the election could have gone either way, in a deterministic universe the result was inevitable. The seventeenth-century philosopher Spinoza is famous for holding that *everything* happens necessarily, and hence all thoroughly true claims are necessary truths. Eighteenth-century philosopher Immanuel Kant tried to get around the problem by holding that from one point of view (that of human experience) everything that happens in the course of the world we inhabit occurs necessarily; while from another point of view (that of a metaphysical world beyond our experience) human actions are sometimes free and contingent. Other philosophers, sometimes called 'compatibilists', have held that properly understood human actions can be legitimately described as both necessary and free.

Quine and contingency.

At the other extreme, if you buy into W. V. O. Quine's semantic holism (see 4.3), then everything becomes contingent. It is always the case that what we judge now to be true we might later judge to be false. Mathematical truths such as $2 \times 2 = 4$ appear to be necessarily true, but we can't rule out the possibility that facts will emerge about the meanings of the terms involved that will lead us to revise our judgement.

So, although it is easy enough to define the difference between the necessary and contingent, it is much harder determining precisely which truth-claims belong under which category.

Example: the existence of God.

The distinction crops up in many branches of philosophy, including arguments concerning the existence of God. Consider God as a hypothesis. If she exists, would she be a necessary or contingent being? God could surely not be a contingent being: it can't be that God exists but might not have. If God exists, God must be a necessary being, and the claim that 'God exists' is a necessary truth. One way of conceiving God this way is to say that it is part of the concept of 'God' that God necessarily exists. What some philosophers have tried to argue is that this means God must in fact exist, since a non-existent God would be a contradiction in terms: a necessary being who doesn't in fact exist. Saying that God does not exist would be as self-contradictory as saying that a triangle does not have three sides. This argument can be found in the work of rationalist philosophers like Descartes and Spinoza. It has its principal roots, however, in the *Proslogion* of St Anselm of Canterbury. Even some modern-day philosophers like Alvin Plantinga adhere to versions of it. A related theological issue is whether or not it was necessary that God created the world.

Problem: the future and the excluded middle.

In section 9 of his text *Interpretation* Aristotle points out something interesting with regard to our talk about the future. Consider the statement 'A sea battle will take place tomorrow' (uttered by someone the night before the Battle of Salamis in 480 BCE). Most of us would say that the statement was on that evening either true or false. But here's the rub: if that statement was either true or false before the battle occurred, then it seems that the future was (and is!) already necessary and determined. This seems an intolerable conclusion for many to draw. One way to preserve the contingency of the future, of course, is to hold that our claims about the future are neither true nor false until the events they predict actually occur, but such an option seems to many equally intolerable. It seems not only practically impossible (we couldn't say that it is true that someone will keep a promise or be there at an appointment); it also seems to violate one of the fundamental principles of rationality – the law of excluded middle – which holds that a statement must be either true or false, but not some third alternative (see 3.3).

You can see that even though things looked pretty simple at the outset, there's a lot going on with these concepts. Although the distinction between the necessary and the contingent has its roots in common sense, you can be sure that in the hands of philosophers it becomes something much more extraordinary.

See also

4.1 A priori / A posteriori
4.4 Categorical/Modal
4.3 Analytic/Synthetic
4.11 Necessary/Sufficient

Reading

Aristotle, *Interpretation* 9
Alvin Plantinga, *The Nature of Necessity* (1974)
Saul Kripke, *Naming and Necessity* (1980)

4.11 Necessary/Sufficient

What does it mean to be a person? When do I have knowledge, rather than mere opinion or belief? These are two major questions in philosophy. Answers to them often set out what the necessary and sufficient conditions for being a person or having knowledge are. Sufficient conditions are what is *enough* for something to be the case. Necessary conditions are what is *required* for something to be the case.

We can see the differences and relations between them by considering a few everyday examples.

Being a UK citizen is a necessary condition for becoming the Prime Minister, but it is not sufficient. It is required of the Prime Minister that he or she be a UK citizen, but if this condition is satisfied other conditions still need to be met to hold the office, among which are winning a number of elections.

Investing an enormous sum of money in the country and lacking a criminal record are sufficient conditions for gaining a US green card, but they are not necessary conditions. This is because there are other ways of gaining green cards, such as being the spouse of a US citizen, or having certain skills deemed important by the US government.

One or many, joint or separate.

Conditions may be singular or plural, and some conditions may be both necessary and sufficient. Being composed of H_2O is a necessary *and* sufficient condition for something being water. Something must be H_2O to be water, and if it is nothing but H_2O that is sufficient to make it water – no other conditions apply. But to be ice, a substance must both be H_2O *and* at less than 0 °C in normal atmospheric conditions, or the equivalent. These two conditions – of atomic structure and temperature – form the *set* of necessary and sufficient conditions for something to be ice.

Application in definition.

Specifying sets of necessary and sufficient conditions is a common philosophical method of defining a concept. For instance, it has been suggested that the necessary and sufficient conditions for 'knowing that X' are that (1) one believes that X, (2) one is justified in one's belief, and (3) X is true. To have knowledge you need all three components. Hence each condition *separately* is a *necessary* condition, though *together* they form the *sufficient* conditions for knowledge. This set of three, then, comprises both the necessary and sufficient conditions for 'knowing that' something is the case.

In personal identity, there are several competing accounts of the set of necessary and sufficient conditions for a person at one time to be the same person at another. Some claim that a form of psychological continuity is necessary and sufficient. On this view, just as long as enough memory, beliefs and character continue to exist, so a person continues to exist. Others argue that this is necessary, but not sufficient, since one also needs to be physically continuous: unless one's body (or at least one's brain) continues to exist, no amount of psychological continuity is enough for one to survive. The set of necessary and sufficient conditions for personal identity includes, therefore, both physical and psychological continuity. Yet others claim physical continuity alone is necessary and sufficient.

But there are some philosophers who would reject the whole model of necessary and sufficient conditions, at least for some areas of enquiry. Wittgenstein thought it would be nonsense to seek necessary and sufficient conditions for something to be, for example, a game. Many things are games and what they have in common cannot be specified by a set of conditions but is rather a kind of 'family resemblance'. The rules that govern the correct application of the use of any word, including concepts like 'knowledge' or 'person', cannot be forced into the straightjacket of necessary and sufficient conditions. Instead, we have to rely on judgement and the observation of how words are used to determine whether someone has genuine knowledge or is the same person over time.

See also

1.10 Definitions
3.9 Criteria

Reading

Ludwig Wittgenstein, *Philosophical Investigations* (1953)
*Patrick J. Hurley, *A Concise Introduction to Logic*, 7th edn (2000)
*Theodore Schick, Jr, and Lewis Vaughn, *How to Think about Weird Things: Critical Thinking for a New Age*, 3rd edn (2002)

4.12 Objective/Subjective

Examinations may be the bane of a student's life, but most people accept them because they offer the chance of an objective assessment of one's work, whereas one's view of one's own work may be subjective and distorted.

We make distinctions like this all the time. We talk about a news report being objective or, if the viewpoint of the reporter is too prominent, too subjective. We talk about taste being subjective, but measurements of pollutants in the atmosphere objective. But do we have a clear understanding of what the objective/subjective distinction really is?

When a judgement or point of view is rooted entirely in one individual's particular perspective on the world, we often call that judgement 'subjective'. In doing so we signal that we suspect that the judgement is partial, probably doesn't take account of all the facts, or fails to rise above the personal viewpoint. When, however, a judgement takes into account all the relevant data, disregards personal prejudice, and finds agreement with other competent and informed people, we say a judgement is objective. By this we signal that the judgement is impartial, well grounded in facts, and rises above the personal.

The subjective is thus what pertains to the (individual) subject, consciousness or mind, while the objective is what stands outside or independently of the (individual) subject.

A tool.

When thinking about issues related to subjectivity and objectivity, consider this model, where S stands for a subject, O for an object, and the arrow the relationship between them.

1. $S_1 \leftrightarrow O_1$
2. $S_2 \leftrightarrow O_1$
3. $S_1 \leftrightarrow O_2$
4. $S_2 \leftrightarrow O_2$

Consider whether all subjects are the same. Suppose S_1 is different in some important way from S_2. Some thinkers, for example, believe that the human male S is different from the human female S, that the human S is different from that of other animals and God, and that each individual S is different from other individuals. Some maintain that no S is identical with itself over time (see Hume). Others hold that language and its ever-changing meanings leave the S indeterminate (see Lacan). If any of these possibilities is true, does it make sense to say that the relations between the relevant Ss and Os (or even the Os themselves) are the same? That is, can judgements of truth, or goodness or beauty ever be the same for different subjects like S_1 and S_2? Is what philosophers call 'intersubjectivity' or 'common or shared subjectivity' possible?

Even if the subjects are the same and intersubjectivity exists, what about the objects? Compare 1 and 3 (or 2 and 4). Different subjects of the type S_1 (or S_2) are likely in life to encounter different environments and circumstances (O_1 and O_2). Indeed, no two people's experiences of the world are identical. This being so, can we expect any given Ss to come to shared judgements? Aren't various subjects really addressing different objects? Is it really meaningful to say we operate in a shared world?

Objectivity and ethics.

The distinction is important in many areas of philosophy. Take ethics. When I say 'Fraud is wrong', can that ever be more than my own subjective judgement? Ultimately, aren't all such moral judgements expressions of how an act seems to me? Others may agree, but this gives us only *agreement among a group of subjective judgements.* Similar doubts arise in aesthetic judgements: how can a judgement like 'Picasso's painting *Guernica* is a great work of art' be anything other than merely subjective?

Some philosophers maintain that what is objective is nothing other than what is common to or has been acknowledged through the agreement of a community of subjects. Others maintain that what is objective is what stands against or independently of subjects, both individual and communal.

Knowledge, perspectivism and the hermeneutical circle.

Not only value judgements have difficulties getting beyond the subjective. Consider knowledge itself. How can objective knowledge be possible? We may be able to rise above our individual viewpoints, but we are still locked within a specifically human viewpoint – and one that is rooted in a particular historical and social milieu. The condition we seem to face of only being able to interpret new things on the basis of pre-existing values and beliefs is called 'the hermeneutical circle'. Is it possible to transcend this condition to get a truly impartial viewpoint?

Thomas Nagel has written on this issue in a book with a title that captures the essence of the problem: *The View from Nowhere.* If subjectivity is the view from somewhere in particular, objectivity must be a kind of view from nowhere. But does it even make sense to talk about a view from nowhere? Surely any 'possible take' on truth has to come from some perspective or another? This is the thought that lies behind what has come to be known as the 'perspectivism' of Friedrich Nietzsche – the idea that all knowledge is always from a particular perspective and that thus there is no objectivity.

Nagel responds to the challenge differently. He invites us to see subjectivity and objectivity not as flip sides of the one coin but as two extremes on a spectrum. At one end we have pure subjectivity: the point of view that is rooted entirely in the individual nature of the subject. At the other, we have a perhaps unobtainable objectivity: where knowledge is freed from all taint of particular perspective. But in between we can occupy positions that are more or less subjective and objective. The less our knowledge depends upon the particular features of our own existence, the more objective it becomes. It may never become fully objective, but that may not matter. If we are not convinced that objectivity is all or nothing, we can see the value in gaining a more objective view, even if we can't leave subjectivity behind altogether.

Nagel's treatment of the objective/subjective divide is an example of how philosophers have moved beyond seeing it as a simplistic dichotomy, where subjectivity is bad and objectivity good, albeit hard if not impossible to attain. The debate is more sophisticated now, but its basic terms of reference are still the same.

See also

Reading

*Thomas Nagel, *The View from Nowhere* (1986)
Crispin Wright, *Truth and Objectivity* (1992)
P. K. Moser, *Philosophy after Objectivity* (1993)

4.13 Realist/Non-realist

> In 1628, William Harvey invented the circulation of the blood.

Many schoolchildren at some point or other make a mistake like this one. As we cram their heads full of information about who discovered this or invented that, all breakthroughs get muddled up together and discoveries and inventions get confused.

But our confused schoolchildren have stumbled across a deeper philosophical problem. When we look at the wide arena of human knowledge, from science to politics, ethics and aesthetics, how much is discovered and how much invented? Is ethics the attempt to find out what good is, just as Harvey discovered what the heart did? Or is it the attempt to construct a moral system, like Stephenson designing and constructing the first steam train?

Varieties of realism.

A philosophical realist is someone who believes the pursuit of knowledge is essentially about discovery. More specifically, it is about believing that there are facts about the external world that are the case whether we discover them or not. This broad realist attitude manifests itself across the whole range of philosophical topics. *Ontological realism* is the view that physical objects exist independently of our own minds. *Epistemological realism* is the view that things are true or false independently of whether we know or believe them to be true. *Moral realism* is the view that acts are morally right or wrong, whether we judge them to be right or wrong or not. *Aesthetic realism* holds beauty to be a real property of works of art, there to be discovered by the discerning viewer. *Metaphysical realism* is the view that what is real exists just as it is independently of the subjects that experience it

Realism is often described as the 'common sense' position, but in this instance common sense may be more diverse. Certainly, common sense would agree that physical objects exist whether we perceive them or not, but common sense may not be realist when it comes to art and morals, for example. With art, it is probable that more people agree that beauty is in the eye of the beholder than believe beauty is an actual property of artworks themselves.

Varieties of non-realism.

There are many ways of being a non-realist, which is to say there are many positive things one could believe that are compatible with the denial that the truth or falsehood of statements involves their representing or mirroring an independent reality (epistemological realism), or in holding that what is real is independent of its relation to those subjects who experience it (metaphysical realism).

In ontology, the main non-realist position is idealism – the view that objects are of their essence non-material and would not exist if there were no mind or spirit. In epistemology, one could be a relativist, arguing that what is true and what is false always depend upon one's historical, social or individual perspective. In ethics one could be a subjectivist, and argue that judgements of right or wrong are no more than expressions of subjective approval or disapproval. In aesthetics, one could argue that judgements of beauty in works of art are no more than expressions of personal taste. In all of these areas of philosophy, there are many other ways of being non-realist too.

À la carte.

It should not be thought that one has to choose between being an out-and-out realist or non-realist. One's position can vary according to the question being discussed. Many people, for instance, are realists about the external world but are non-realists when it comes to ethics and aesthetics. Immanuel Kant went so far as to describe his thought as both 'empirical realism' and a 'transcendental idealism'. Other philosophical movements try to run a course between the Scylla of realism and Charybdis of anti-realism by formulating an alternative way of looking at these issues. Phenomenology is one such example. The distinction between realism and non-realism is a deep one, but one need not make a once-only fundamental choice between the two to determine how one approaches all of philosophy.

See also

4.8 Essence/accident
4.12 Objective/Subjective
6.7 Scepticism

Reading

Hilary Putnam and James Conant, *Realism with a Human Face* (1992)
Nelson Goodman, *Ways of Worldmaking* (1978)
Roy Bhaskar, *A Realist Theory of Science* (1978)

4.14 Sense/Reference

Modern philosophy of language, it is widely agreed, began with Gottlob Frege (1848–1925). Frege bequeathed to philosophy a distinction between 'sense' and 'reference', and one hundred years later, it is still used, discussed and debated.

The basics of the distinction can be made clear enough using an example of Frege's. Consider the two nouns 'the morning star' and 'the evening star'.

As it happens, the morning star and the evening star are the same celestial body (the planet Venus). In this case we have two nouns with two different senses but the same reference. They have the same reference because they refer to the same object. But they have different senses because what one understands by each one is not the same: by 'morning star' we may understand a reflective body that appears at a particular point in the sky in the morning, and by 'evening star' one that appears at a particular point in the sky in the evening. We may not even know they refer to the same object.

Frege extends this account to apply, not only to nouns but also to whole sentences. He argues that declarative sentences (ones that state that such and such is the case) should be regarded as nouns, and so have a sense and reference just as nouns do.

Not so easy.

So far, so good, but the reader should be warned that virtually none of this unpacks in the way one might expect. First, one might be tempted to think that the sense is somehow subjective, especially since Frege says that the thought expressed in a sentence is its sense, not its reference. So sense is somehow equated with thought, which may seem to be subjective. But Frege does not think thoughts, in this sense, are subjective at all. Indeed, it is the thought that one often wishes to communicate in language and that Frege thinks can be communicated in language. But language is not subjective. So thoughts and sense are most definitely not subjective.

The most baffling part of Frege's theory, however, is what he understands the reference of sentences to be. The notion of reference seems pretty straightforward in the case of nouns: the morning star is *that*, you might say, pointing to the star. But what about the reference of a sentence like 'Jimmy Jones makes the thinnest pizzas in Charlottesville'? You can't just point at the reference of that.

Frege says that the reference of such a statement is the set of circumstances that make it true. Frege terms this its *truth value*. But there are only two truth values: true and false. So – and here's the surprising upshot – sentences have only two references: the True and the False. The reference of all true sentences is the True and the reference of all false sentences the False.

In some ways the sense and reference distinction might appear to be a useful tool to help distinguish two features of words and sentences. But viewed in the context of Frege's wider philosophy, it is actually part of some pretty weird metaphysics. As is often the case, therefore, use this tool carefully, because if you try to make too much of it you may find yourself committed to a very specific conception of truth with which you may not want to burdened.

See also

3.17 Masked man fallacy
4.9 Knowledge by acquaintance/description

Reading

Gottlob Frege, 'On Sense and Reference', in *Translations from the Philosophical Writings of Gottlob Frege*, ed. P. Geach and M. Black (1952)
Michael Dummett, *Frege: Philosophy of Language* (1981)
Hans Sluga, *Sense and Reference in Frege's Philosophy* (1993)

4.15 Syntax/Semantics

Language dominated philosophy during the twentieth century. Questions about truth, knowledge, ethics, mind and virtually everything else were all approached via the philosophy of language. If you wanted to understand what consciousness was, for example, you needed to understand what the word 'consciousness' means. And to do that, you had to understand what it is for any word to mean something.

'The linguistic turn' as this emphasis on language was called, is now viewed somewhat ambivalently. Many now judge that language was given too central a role in philosophy and that it was at least as much an obstacle to progress as an aid. Whatever judgement we make about the linguistic turn, it has left an inheritance to contemporary philosophy that cannot simply be sloughed off.

One key part of this inheritance is the distinction between syntax and semantics. Consider natural language first, comparing these two sentences:

The yellow hatred kicked the malicious algorithm.
My dog sick old to sleep needs to be put.

In both cases something is wrong. But what is wrong in each sentence is very different. The first sentence is grammatically a perfectly well-formed English sentence. But what does it mean? Arguably, it means nothing. Algorithms cannot be malicious and they can't be kicked by hatred, which itself cannot be yellow. The second sentence, on the other hand, is grammatically ill-formed, but we can see what it probably means: My sick old dog needs to be put to sleep.

The rules of language being broken in each sentence are thus very different. Whereas the first sentence fails to communicate meaning (the grammar is flawless, but the meaning absent), the second is badly formed (the meaning can be discerned, but the construction is awry).

To put labels to these differences, we can say that the *syntax* of 'The yellow hatred kicked the malicious algorithm' is correct, but the *semantics* is missing or confused: the problem is *semantic*. Likewise, the *syntax* of 'My dog sick old to sleep needs to be put' is wrong, but the *semantics* can be discerned: here the problem is *syntactic*.

In short, syntax pertains to the rules that govern the correct arrangement of words and sentences in language, while semantics pertains to meaning.

Sometimes philosophers refer to the syntactic and semantic dimensions of language as its *formal* and *material* dimensions, respectively. That's why logicians often talk about 'formal' logic. They're not concerned with tuxedos and evening gowns!

Uses in logic.

For the purposes of logic (as opposed to, say, poetry or rhetoric), syntax is about the formal construction of language, whereas semantics concerns not simply meaning but truth and falsehood. The non-natural, symbolic languages frequently used in logic enlist the same distinction. Indeed, pure logic is entirely concerned with syntax: it is the study of which constructions in logic are valid and which are not. In a sense, there is no semantics in pure logic. Although one can say, for example, A v B means 'A or B', the phrase 'A v B' alone is purely syntactic, as it does not mean anything particular about the world. To say 'A v B' is an acceptable construction in logic is rather like saying 'article + adjective + noun + non-transitive verb' is an acceptable construction in English. Both are concerned purely with right and wrong construction, not with meaning (truth or falsehood).

Importance in artificial intelligence.

The distinction between syntax and semantics is particularly important in debates around artificial intelligence. One can get computers to process sentences according to syntactical rules in ways that appear to be meaningful. But what enables a language user to have a semantics is the subject of some debate, and many, such as John Searle, have argued that digital computers only have syntax, not semantics. A computer therefore, unlike a human, cannot discern that 'The yellow hatred kicked the malicious algorithm' and 'The big ugly thug kicked the terrified stranger' are sentences of a very different kind. The heart of his position can be found in Searle's 'Chinese room' experiment (see 2.6).

See also

1.4 Validity and soundness
2.6 Intuition pumps
2.9 Thought experiments
4.7 Entailment/Implication

Reading

*John Searle, *Minds, Brains, and Science* (1984)
Rudolf Carnap, *Introduction to Semantics* (1942)
Richard Larson and Gabriel Segal, *Knowledge of Meaning* (1995)

4.16 Thick/Thin concepts

Although many of the concepts and distinctions in this book were first formulated many years ago, philosophers are still generating new and useful tools. In philosophy one often has the experience of reading a distinction being made for the first time and wondering how on Earth we got on for so long without it.

One such recent contribution is Bernard Williams's distinction between thick and thin ethical concepts. Thin ethical concepts are ones such as 'good', 'bad, 'right' and 'wrong'. Such terms are very general and leave it open as to what precisely constitutes them. In this respect they stand almost as placeholders for a specific theory to flesh out later.

For example, if I say 'one should maximize the good', I really haven't said what you should do. That depends on what the good is. If the good is human happiness, then I must maximize human happiness. But if the good is a life free of sin, I will probably be required to behave in ways rather different from those that maximize happiness – in this life, anyway.

Thin concepts thus allow for wide variations in how they are understood. Thick concepts, on the other hand, carry with them a more substantive (but not necessarily complete) meaning.

We may disagree about when 'gratitude', for example, is ethically required, but we all understand that gratitude is the appropriate recognition of a good deed towards oneself, family or group and that gratitude is a morally virtuous emotion. This is what makes it a thick ethical concept.

Another example of a thick ethical concept would be 'deceit'. Deceit is a morally bad form of deception. Although we may disagree as to whether a particular act should be classified as deceit or, say, a white lie, the term 'deceit' itself carries with it both a clear enough idea of what it is and whether it is morally good or bad.

Use in moral theory.

The distinction is extremely useful in discussions about moral theory. Some debates require thin concepts, some thick ones, and it is useful to be able to distinguish the two and identify which is appropriate. For instance, meta-ethics is the study of the general nature of ethics and ethical claims. An example of a meta-ethical question might be 'Is ethics about objective features of the real world?' To answer this question we need to consider whether statements like 'killing is wrong' describe facts about the world or something else, such as our feelings about the world. In such discussions, thin ethical concepts are all that are required, since we are not arguing about whether this or that moral judgement are correct but about the nature of moral judgements themselves.

When, however, we are discussing substantive issues in ethics, thicker concepts are required. For instance, if I want to argue that assisted suicide is ethically unjustifiable on the grounds that the taking of a human life is always wrong, I need to be able to say why it is wrong and what specifically I mean by wrong. To do this I need a substantive account of ethical concepts such as 'wrong' and 'murder'. General conceptions of what ethics is and the use of mere placeholders won't do.

An advantage of the terms 'thick' and 'thin' over other distinctions (such as meta-ethics versus normative or substantive ethics) is that they don't presume a sharp distinction. Thick and thin are not flip sides of one coin but opposite ends of a continuum, between which terms can be thicker or thinner. That means that this tool captures both a difference between two end points of the spectrum while allowing for the shades of grey in between.

See also

3.11 False dichotomy

Reading

*Bernard Williams, *Ethics and the Limits of Philosophy* (1985)
Clifford Geertz, 'Thick Description: Toward an Interpretive Theory of
    Culture', in idem, *The Interpretation of Cultures: Selected Essays* (1973)
Michael Walzer, *Thick and Thin: The Moral Argument at Home and Abroad*
    (1994)

4.17 Types and tokens

If you found out I had the same car as you, I don't suppose you would care
much about it. But if you found out I had the same fiancée as you, you
might not be so sanguine.

What this example shows is that to talk of the 'same' X is *ambiguous*. In
the example of the car, what's the same is the model. The two cars are
constructed in the same way, look the same and function similarly. When
they roll off the production line, they are (or should be) qualitatively almost
identical. That is to say, almost any quality that the one car has, the other
should have too. If one has a 12-valve engine, then so must the other. If it
does not, then it just is not the same car.

The case of the fiancée is a little different. To say that we have the same
fiancée is not to say there are two fiancées who have virtually the same qualities; it is to say that there is one fiancée whom we inadvertently share. In this
case, my fiancée and yours are not just qualitatively similar, they are quanti-
tatively (or numerically) identical. They are quite literally the same person.

The most common way of distinguishing between these two senses of
sameness is in terms of what philosophers often call 'types' and 'tokens'.
Types are abstract forms of which individual objects are particular tokens.
So, for example, the type 'billiard ball' does not refer to any particular object, but an abstract notion of what a billiard ball is. All particular billiard
balls are tokens of this type.

Origins.

The distinction has its formal origins in considerations of language. Any
particular word is a single type and any particular appearance of it, in speech
or writing, a token. Hence when Hamlet murmured, 'words, words, words',
he was uttering three tokens of the single type 'word'.

Plato clearly had something of this in mind in his theory of forms (*eidē*). There is a good deal of disagreement about just what this theory entails, but its central motivating idea is simple enough. If we ask, for example, 'What is a triangle?' it is not enough to point to any particular triangle and expect that to suffice as an answer. A right-angled triangle is certainly a triangle, but there are many other triangles of differing size and with different internal angles. But what makes all these different things triangles?

Plato's solution was to say that each of the 'many' different things of the sensible world 'participate' in a 'one' or a 'form' (*eidos*) that makes it what *sort* or *kind* of thing it is. There are many different triangles but only one form of the triangle. This form contains the essence of 'triangleness' and particular triangles are what they are because they somehow partake in the form of the triangle. So although there are an infinite number of actual or potential triangles, there is only one form of the triangle, and it is understanding what this form is that enables us to recognize particular triangles.

Plato sometimes seemed to suggest that he believed these forms were a kind of non-physical entity that exist in some other, transcendent world. But put into type/token terms such metaphysical extravagance seems unnecessary. All the particular triangles are tokens of the one type 'triangle'. This 'type' need not be some weird, non-physical entity; it is merely the abstract concept under which particular geometric shapes can be categorized. Of course, this still leaves questions, in particular about the status of abstract concepts. But the type/token distinction has the merit of not in itself implying anything metaphysical, mysterious or supernatural.

Identity.

The type/token distinction is also important with regard to identity. Two things that are the same in every respect, but which are not, in fact, one object, are said to be *type-identical*. Each type-identical object or person is said to be a token of that single type. When we have two terms – for example, my fiancée and your fiancée – but only one referent, we say the two terms refer to one single thing that is *token-identical*.

The distinction may seem obvious, but it is crucial. Take, for example, the claim that mental states are brain states. This could mean one of two things. It could mean mental states are a type of which brain states are particular tokens. On this view, it is possible that there could be other tokens of mental states, such as machine states, or vegetable states. A stronger claim is that brain states and mental states are token-identical. Like our fiancées, there is not one type and several different tokens of her walking around. Rather, the token is the type – there are no mental states other than brain states.

See also

3.16 Leibniz's law of identity
3.17 Masked man fallacy

Reading

Charles Sanders Peirce, 'On the Algebra of Logic', in *Collected Works of Charles Sanders Peirce*, ed. C. Hartshorne and P. Weiss (1931–5)
D. Armstrong, *A Materialist Theory of the Mind* (1968)

chapter 5

Tools for Radical Critique

5.1 Class critique

One of the most important tools developed by critics of a social-political turn has been that of what we'd like to call the 'class critique'. By this we mean criticizing philosophical concepts and theories on the basis of the ways in which they serve or subvert class hierarchy or class struggle.

Although there were certainly earlier precedents, the classic formulation of this critical tool is to be found in the work of German philosophers Karl Marx and Friedrich Engels. Most philosophers before Marx and Engels held that philosophy and other elements of human culture develop through the free action of the mind, independently of the economic order in which they were produced. Marx and Engels challenged this idea, contending instead that the mode of production (e.g. feudalism or capitalism) characteristic of a social order acts as a kind of 'substructure' that grounds and determines the attributes of the cultural 'superstructure' built upon it. For Marx and Engels it is not the dynamics of ideas that determine society; it is the dynamics of the economic base that determine our ideas. This is what is meant by saying Marx stood Hegel on his head.

You might say that for Marx and Engels the economic substructure functions almost like the Freudian unconscious, determining the contents of our conscious minds without our even realizing it. Later class critics like Antonio Gramsci (1891–1937) rejected the classical Marxian thesis that this determination is one directional, maintaining that the culture can affect the economic substructure too.

In either case, how might one use such a tool in philosophical thinking?

Politics and religion.

For example, you might argue (as many Marxist critics have) that the Reformation was not fundamentally a religious innovation but a change in thinking demanded by the newly burgeoning capitalist institutions of Europe. Because capitalism needed to break the communal, local ties characteristic of feudalism, it developed new religious superstructures that emphasized individual conscience over corporate, feudal church authority. Indeed, Marx himself is famous for arguing that essentially religion is a tool used by the ruling class to mollify those it exploits, and by the exploited class to dull the pain of the wounding it receives at the hands of its rulers. Religion is, says Marx, nothing more than the 'opiate of the masses'.

Similarly, Marx argued that the masses of people in purportedly democratic capitalist societies have been duped into various forms of 'false consciousness', such as the belief that liberal political rights – such as free speech and free assembly – were developed for them and are currently enjoyed by them. In reality, says Marx, such rights were developed for the ruling class, are effectively enjoyed only by that class, and in practice are truly only protected for that class or its interests. The US Civil War, which Marx covered as a journalist, was, therefore, not fought to end slavery but to clear the way for capitalist intervention in the American South. Similarly we might argue that US racial segregation ended not because of the political savvy and clever arguments of Martin Luther King and others but because it served the interests of capitalism to end it. The Gulf War, similarly, was fought not to protect the rights of small nations like Kuwait but to protect European and US access to Middle East oil.

To use this tool, then, when scrutinizing a philosophical concept or theory, ask yourself the following questions:

1. In what way does this concept or theory help the ruling economic class maintain its position? How does it serve their economic interests?
2. In what way does this concept or theory help manipulate or attenuate the suffering of the exploited class?
3. How is this term used in practice, not just theoretically?

If you discover that the concept or theory does seem to serve the interests of the ruling classes against the exploited classes, that doesn't in itself show that the concept or theory is wrong. But at the very least it should make you question whether it is based on the power and interest of the ruling classes rather than on sound reasoning.

See also

2.3 Dialectic

Reading

Karl Marx, *Theses on Feuerbach* (1845)
*Karl Marx and Friedrich Engels, *Manifesto of the Communist Party* (1848)
Antonio Gramsci, *Our Marx* (1919–20)

5.2 Deconstruction and the critique of presence

Nearly all conceptions of truth in the history of philosophy have centred on the knower in some sense being *present* to the object of knowledge. Against this tradition, Jacques Derrida (1930–), leader of the *deconstructionist* movement (a movement often collected with others under the vague rubric of *post-modernism*) regards the privileging of presence to be one of the most profound shortcomings of Western philosophy. For Derrida, what's *not* present is more important in our intellectual life. Moreover, he says, pure presence of the sort normally imagined in philosophy is never even achieved.

Derrida took his inspiration from phenomenologist Martin Heidegger's (1889–1976) call in *Being and Time* (1927) for a *Destruktion* of the Western metaphysical tradition. For Heidegger, the difficulty we have endured over more than two thousand years of philosophical thought has been our repeated covering up of being (*Sein*) by 'placing' – putting entities or particular beings in our thinking instead of being. In other words, rather than understand being as it actually is (the being of all particular beings), we have erroneously conceived of being as if it were just another thing. The Heideggerian task, therefore, is to strip away the distorting accretions of our traditions and return our thinking to that largely forgotten, primordial grasp of being itself – a sort of grasp that was more commonly achieved among pre-Socratic thinkers. (See 5.6.)

For Derrida, the problem is slightly different. For Derrida our mistake has been to think about truth and being on the model of 'presence'. On this model, what we take to be true must be based somehow upon that which is or can be immediately, fully and transparently present to us – for example, a direct observation, sensation or impression (empiricism), a clear and distinct idea (Descartes), an intelligible form, an essence (Plato, Aristotle, Aquinas), or the human voice or God.

But, Derrida maintains (using insights he has gleaned from Hegel, Nietzsche, Husserl and Heidegger) that closer scrutiny will show that nothing is or can be immediately present to us in the way demanded by past theorists. Although he aspired to a comprehension of the whole, Hegel recognized that assertions call forth a 'negative moment' – asserting X is simultaneously to assert that it is not non-X. In Edmund Husserl's terminology, meaning appears only against a 'horizon' or world (or set of other meanings) that differs from it.

Philosophies that claim a basis in the presence of the true and the real, therefore, are misleading (even Heidegger's attempt to regain a return to an authentic and resolute comprehension of being). In making this point, Derrida famously criticized past philosophy for privileging speaking over writing, for holding that the spoken voice places us in the direct presence of the other and the meaning of his or her words. For Derrida, speaking can make meaning no more present than writing. The condition that meaning must endure in its failure to achieve pure presence, shorn of absence, Derrida calls *différance*.

Wider import.

Derrida is also concerned about the social, political and ethical implications of ways of thinking purportedly based upon claims to presence. As Derrida renders it, claims to have grasped and privileged presence depend upon an exclusion of difference, impurity, absence and non-being. This exclusionary moment, for Derridians, quickly translates into acts of political and social exclusion. Discursive practice entails certain forms of conduct and political practice. Hence political forms that claim to be founded on, for example, natural law, transcendent rights, the will of God, the will of the people, the demands of history, or the dictates of reason, inevitably exclude, oppress and tyrannize.

Although literary critics allied with deconstruction, such as Paul De Man, have used deconstruction primarily as a technique in literary criticism, the work of Derrida and Derridian deconstructionists has a broader scope. It aims to guide us towards ways of thinking and acting that acknowledge *différance* and eschew basing themselves on claims to pure, clear, univocal, universal, ahistorical, immediate presence.

Using the tool.

In order to engage deconstructive criticism, ask these questions:

1. Does the theory or practice with which I'm concerned base itself on some claim to presence?
2. Is there a way to deconstruct this theory, on its own terms, by showing that the presence it claims does not and cannot be achieved?

If you can find positive answers to these questions, then you will have formulated a powerful critique.

See also

2.3 Dialectic
5.6 Heideggerian critique of metaphysics

Reading

Jacques Derrida, *Writing and Difference* (1967)
Christopher Norris, *Derrida* (1988)
*Peggy Kamuf, ed., *A Derrida Reader: Between the Blinds* (1991, 1998)

5.3 Empiricist critique of metaphysics

People say all kinds of things: some strange, and others ordinary. Consider the following selection.

1. My cat is on the mat.
2. The atmosphere of Jupiter contains ammonia.
3. There is a magnetic field around this object.
4. Unicorns characteristically have a single horn growing from their foreheads.
5. The entire universe, including all memories and all evidence of an apparent past, appeared out of nothing just one second ago.
6. A noumenon is a thing of which it is in principle impossible for humans to have experience.
7. There is one God, and He is a trinity.
8. The forms (*eidē*) described by Plato exist.
9. It is possible that what you experience as blue I experience as red and vice versa, even though the physical structures of our eyes, nerves and brains are in relevant ways the same.

What philosophers have noticed about these and other sorts of statements is that some make claims about the world of human experience, and others do not. Their thinking about the philosophical implications of this distinction has led to the refinement of one of the most powerful critical tools ever developed – the empiricist critique.

The term 'empiricism' derives from the Greek word *empeiria*, meaning 'experience', and the core of the empiricist critique is that philosophical claims departing from the realm of human experience are unacceptable. In general, this critique takes two forms: (1) a critique of meaning and intelligibility, and (2) a critique of truth.

Critique of meaning and intelligibility.

One strategy empiricists have developed has been first to argue that statements are only *meaningful* if they are about or somehow based on human experience, and then, second, to go on to scrutinize various theories, terms and claims to see if they are, on this account, meaningful. If it is not about what humans can experience, it is meaningless.

Claims like 1 above are certainly about matters of experience – through the senses of vision and touch I can experience my cat curled up on the mat by the door. Claims like 2 may not have been connected to actual human experience before the advent of telescopes, space travel and modern chemistry. But statement 2 was never *in principle* beyond human experience; it was only beyond the experience of a specific historical moment. Statement 3 talks about something we don't itself experience but whose presence or absence is rigorously connected to the behaviour of iron filings and various instruments – in other words, things we can experience.

Claims like 5 and 6 are a different matter: they relate in no way to experience and are therefore meaningless, according to some empiricists. Influential philosophers have also argued persuasively that statements like 7–9 have little or no connection to experience either. Much of this hinges on the question of what precisely experience is. Do or can humans have 'experience' of an infinite, eternal and transcendent being as some describe God?

Critique of truth.

You might argue, and some have, that *all* of the above statements 1–9 are meaningful. The problem isn't really one of *meaning* but rather of *testing*. It seems impossible for humans ever to produce a test or a reliable *decision procedure* for working out whether statements like 5–9 are true or false. This has led some to advance the principle that if a philosophical claim can't be disciplined by experience or used to deduce claims that can be disciplined by experience, it is not worth anything.

Perhaps accepting or rejecting such claims is a matter of faith, and that may be so, but can such leaps of faith be philosophically responsible? Without the disciplining of our beliefs through procedures that test them against shared experience, isn't it the case that all beliefs are acceptable? Without the discipline and guidance of experience, anything goes.

These lines of argument have been devastating to a great deal of metaphysics (and even some of ethics and aesthetics), so much so that many philosophers today regard most metaphysics as nonsense. Empiricism has often, though not exclusively, been associated with materialism and political as well as philosophical attacks on old orders such as Platonism, Aristotelianism and religion.

See also

3.14 Hume's Fork
3.29 Testability
6.3 Mystical experience and revelation

Reading

Paul K. Moser, *Knowledge and Evidence* (1989)
Harold Morick, ed., *Challenges to Empiricism* (1980)
David Hume, *A Treatise of Human Nature* (1739–40)

5.4 Feminist critique

Among the most important features of human life are gender and sexuality. Strangely enough, however, it has been only recently that philosophers have begun to assess one another's theories by using gender and sexuality as categories of analysis. But how can you use sex and gender as philosophical tools? Consider the following examples.

Many philosophical theories of ethics describe the passions as unruly, dangerous and amoral forces that must be dominated, subdued, ordered or mastered by reason. Now it is one thing to criticize such theories as being empirically baseless, full of incoherence and inconsistency, but it is quite another to show how such theories reflect conceptions of male and female held by the cultures in which they originated. It is still another to show how they have been used by dominating males to keep females in subordinate positions. Can it be an accident that in, say, Plato's time when men dominated and controlled women, philosophical theories associated reason with men, passions with women, and maintained that a proper moral life entails the dominance of the passions by reason? The pattern of male dominance repeats itself throughout Western social history, and so does the pattern of ethical theories demeaning the passions and valorizing reason. Might the Western philosophical tradition's conception of rationality function as an instrument of social control?

Wide-ranging implications.

And so perhaps it goes with other dimensions of philosophical theory. Might it be that various conceptions of justice bear a masculinist bias? Yes, says Carol Gilligan. Perhaps the binary quality of so many philosophical categories (good/evil, true/false, being/non-being, sense/non-sense) is itself masculine? Yes, says Hélène Cixous. Might our adoration of autonomy and independence reflect something of the males who articulated these concepts? Yes, argues Nancy Chodorow. Might our gender relations somehow be caught up with the dynamics of capitalist exploitation and alienation? Dead on, say Margaret Benston and Heidi Hartmann. Could we even say that our conception of God and being functions in a narrow, masculine and oppressive way? Absolutely, says Mary Daly. What about various conceptions used in determining truth, knowledge and science? Surely, they are free from the taint of gender or sex? Wrong, say Ruth Hubbard and Loraine Code. In short, virtually any field of human thinking may be subjected to feminist critique.

Using the tool.

In using this tool ask yourself the following questions:

1. Does the concept or theory I'm considering in any way reflect the conceptions of male and female, masculine and feminine held by those who developed or embraced it?
2. Might there be some way, even contrary to the intent of its authors, that this concept or theory functions to subordinate women or privilege men?

As with the class critique (see 5.1) it does not necessarily follow from the fact that a concept or theory favours men over women that it is false. However, it should make us suspicious if it does, since we would not expect objective reason to be biased in this way. Some would go further and argue that equality is more important than truth and that if a theory or concept privileges men it should be rejected. Full stop.

See also

5.1 Class critique
5.5 Foucaultian critique of power
5.7 Lacanian critique

Reading

*Miranda Fricker and Jennifer Hornsby, eds, *The Cambridge Companion to Feminism in Philosophy* (2000)
*Rosemarie Putnam Tong, *Feminist Thought: A More Comprehensive Introduction*, 2nd edn (1998)
Simone de Beauvoir, *The Second Sex* (1949)

5.5 Foucaultian critique of power

Do you use language, or does language use you? If you are at all suspicious that language itself might be in the driver's seat, you may be sympathetic to an enormously influential form of criticism that developed over the past 30 years on the basis of the work of French philosopher and historian of ideas, Michel Foucault.

Archaeological method.

In texts like *Madness and Civilization* (1961), *The Birth of the Clinic* (1963), *The Order of Things* (1966), and *The Archaeology of Knowledge* (1969), Foucault undertook to show how our words and concepts have fitted into historical layers of thinking and acting (sometimes called 'discursive formations') that in many ways order our lives and thinking. This view has challenged those who believe that it is the other way around – that it is we who consciously order and control those structures. In short, Foucaultian theory diminishes the importance (perhaps even the very existence) of the individual, human agent and self.

Foucault's view has also been controversial in its claim that it is through these multifarious discursive formations that power is exercised. Hence through the concept of 'madness', seventeenth and eighteenth-century social formations laying claim to 'rationality' excluded those who didn't fit into them. In the nineteenth century the concept of 'madness' was also deployed against those who did not adhere to norms of bourgeois morality, such as the promiscuous.

How might other concepts and institutions of practice – such as family, woman, chastity, school, beauty, virtue, truth – serve as instruments of social order and control? Whom do they oppress or exclude or diminish in power?

Genealogical method.

In *Discipline and Punish* (1975) Foucault tried to show how the concepts clustering around criminality and the techniques of managing those called 'criminal' have changed over time. In tracing out the history of a concept, its changes, and the purposes behind them, Foucault develops what Friedrich Nietzsche called a 'genealogical' method – a method Nietzsche used to explore the concepts and practices of Christian morality. The method, however, is not simply historical. It is also subversive, for it aims to uncover the trivial, petty, arbitrary, and sometimes nasty, purposes and effects of what it investigates. While, for example, many have seen the changes in the criminal justice system as efforts to become more humane, Foucault argues that the changes have, rather, been organized around developing new, more effective techniques of social control. (He later undertook a genealogy of concepts and practices of sexuality.)

If we were to examine throughout history the motives, purposes and struggles that determined the origin and development of apparently innocent concepts, institutions and practices, would we find repellent devices for control, manipulation and oppression?

Microphysics of power.

Unlike other forms of social critique, however (such as Marxism and psychoanalysis), Foucault maintains that there is no comprehensive system of social order (like capitalism). Rather, Foucault argues that there are many different power systems interweaving and operating simultaneously. Hence he himself eschews developing a single complete system of social and conceptual dynamics, instead calling his project a 'microphysics of power'.

Among the most famous objects of Foucault's scrutiny was philosopher Jeremy Bentham's plan for a model prison called a 'panopticon'. (One has actually been built and put into use in Cuba.) The prison has no cells with bars. Instead it is constructed so that prisoners come to believe they are always under the surveillance of the guards – and so, they come to discipline themselves.

Foucault challenges us to ask in what ways we live in panopticons of our own making. How do credit cards, government and company records, computers, security cameras and managerial techniques place us under constant surveillance (including self-surveillance) or the fear of constant surveillance? And how does this affect how we think, act and feel?

Normalization.

Another powerful tool of Foucaultian critique is the analysis of normalization. Foucault argues that in various ways orders of power seek to diminish the range of human possibility by privileging certain beliefs and practices as 'normal'. Hence sexual practices, family structures, religions, ways of speaking and acting that differ from the 'normal' are called 'deviant' and through various oppressive techniques are quashed, reducing individuals to the 'docile bodies' needed to serve rising industrial society.

Foucault, then, offers us a number of powerful additions to our toolkit. When assessing a theory, idea or practice, Foucault enjoins us to ask ourselves what power games might be lurking there – for power is subtle. He also cautions us not to rely on any single system of critique – for power faces us in many different guises, using many different techniques.

See also

5.1 Class critique
5.4 Feminist critique
5.8 Nietzschean critique of Christian-Platonic culture

Reading

Michel Foucault, 'What Is an Author?' *Bulletin de la societé française de philosophie* 63 (1969)

Michel Foucault, *History of Sexuality* (1976, 1984), vols 1–3
Paul Rabinow, ed., *The Essential Works of Michel Foucault* (2000)

5.6 Heideggerian critique of metaphysics

According to Martin Heidegger the course of Western philosophical history
has been characterized by a series of mistakes, and those mistakes he calls
'metaphysics'. In Heidegger's view metaphysics began when Plato addressed
being as an object of conceptual knowledge and made the error of thinking
about being *per se* as if it were like an individual being or entity. Whether it
has been Plato and Aristotle's theories of forms, ancient and modern theories of substance, or the various conceptions of matter that have punctuated
Western philosophical history, we have time and time again repeated this
mistake or 'errancy'. Most recently we've been subject to an especially per-
nicious form of it. Heidegger calls the current form of errancy *das Gestell*,
from the German verb *stellen* (to put or to place). We have come wrongly to
think that it is we humans who put or fix or control the meaning and uses of
things. More destructively, through the various technologies that have pervaded our ways of thinking and acting, we have come to think of the world
as transparent, under our control, and as little more than a pile of raw material for us to appropriate, consume, build things from, and burn as fuel for
our machines.

Forgetfulness of being.

Our condition, however, is not simply one of error. Before Plato we had a
clearer (though never an utterly transparent) grasp of being, so our current
state is really a complex kind of forgetting. The very activities of 'everyday'
living distract us from it. And just as we may never really notice a hammer
and our immersion in a world of human instruments until it breaks, our
distracting immersion in the world we construct for ourselves remains invisible to us until somehow it breaks down. But our incapacity is not complete.
We retain through it all – buried beneath centuries of misleading metaphysics and the hiddenness intrinsic to being – a 'primordial' understanding of
it. Heideggerian critique, therefore, has two objectives:

1.   To show us that our metaphysical traditions have been erroneous and
     forgetful.
2.   To help us retrieve, recover and remember being itself.

Not a thing but no-thing.

Being itself, as Heidegger reveals it, is not an entity or a thing. You might say, in a rather poetic way (and Heidegger does), that it is 'nothing' – or no-thing. (In fact, Heidegger suggests that poetic language may be the best way to express our grasp of being.) Because it is a no-thing, humans – at least those immersed in metaphysics – misconstrue the 'event' of being and try noisily to cover it up conceptually, by placing their own inventions in its place. Generally they do this by trying to grasp something that is purportedly and entirely *present*. Or, seeing the impossibility of this sort of foundationalist gesture, they despair and become nihilists, denying all meaning and being.

For Heidegger being is the place, the clearing, the lighting, the 'there' (*da*) in which entities or particular beings appear or disclose themselves. (Hence in his early work Heidegger calls the being humans endure 'there-being' or *Dasein*.) Heidegger maintains that being is essentially temporal. In fact, *Dasein* is temporality (*Zeitlichkeit*) itself.

Using the tool.

Heidegger is not easy and applying his thought as a tool is therefore difficult. But one can begin to do so by asking some of the questions Heidegger raises about philosophical theories:

1. Does this theory express or depend upon a metaphysic that mistakes for for being a particular kind of being?
2. How does this theory contribute to our continued forgetfulness of be-ing?
3. How does our primordial grasp of being still express itself in this theory despite its errancy?
4. Does this theory try to avoid or cover being by placing some purported grasp of some presence in place of being?
5. Is this theory somehow an expression of nihilism caused by the despair of metaphysics?

See also

4.8 Essence/Accident
5.2 Deconstruction and the critique of presence

Reading

Martin Heidegger, *Being and Time* (1927)
Joseph P. Fell, *Heidegger and Sartre: An Essay on Being and Place* (1979)
Rüdiger Safranski, *Martin Heidegger: Between Good and Evil* (1998)

5.7 Lacanian critique

To what extent does our language determine who we are and how we relate and fail to relate to one another? For French philosopher Jacques Lacan (1901–81) the answer is that it does so to a profound extent. Lacan developed and modified the theories of Sigmund Freud (1856–1939) in the light of cutting-edge developments in logic, mathematics, physics and the structural linguistics of the Swiss thinker Ferdinand de Saussure (1857–1913) in order to produce a new form of language-oriented psychoanalysis. His theories have proven influential in philosophy and are useful in reflecting upon philosophical topics.

For Lacan, in contrast to thinkers like Descartes, the subject is neither fixed nor transparent. Subjects cannot communicate with one another (or even themselves) directly but only through the *signifiers* called 'words' in language. As Philip Hill puts it, this is a bit like the way it is in legal negotiations. Clients (subjects) don't communicate directly with one another but only through the lawyers (signifiers) who represent them. Famously, therefore, Lacan said, 'The signifier represents the subject for another signifier.'

Things, however, become more complicated for the following reasons. First, language doesn't represent the subject passively but turns around and structures the subject. In fact, the subject only comes to be with its initiation in language. Second, the meanings of words are neither fixed nor even fully understood by anyone. Third, repression is required for a subject to assimilate the rules or order constituting a language – or what Lacan calls the 'symbolic order'.

The result of all this is that communication is never utterly clear and complete, that selves are both brought together and separated by language, and that the subject is subject to 'demands' that remain unfulfilled and 'desires' that are rooted not in the individual but in the symbolic order of which it is a part. Because the subject must suffer this condition, Lacan symbolized it as an S with a slash running through it from upper right to lower left $\mathcal{S}$. For Lacan, our language itself is our unconscious.

A critical tool.

But how can these ideas serve us as a philosophical tool? There are a number of strategies.

When analysing a philosophical text, Lacan asks us to look beyond the surface meaning of the words in order to assess the psychodynamics submerged in them. Since our desires are structured through the symbolic order of which we're a part, we can interrogate a text to assess what it presents as objects of desire, need and fear. Consider how, for example, Plato seems to desire in his forms something fixed, something beyond the body and the passions associated with it. Think of Nietzsche's longing for the *Übermensch*. Consider Sartre's longing for good faith, for freedom, and, in a way, an absent God; consider how threatening women seem to him.

What are the 'desires' animating and generated by the text? Are the images and doctrines of the text 'symptoms' of submerged psychic 'demands', guilt, shame or dread? Where is the secret, quasi-sexual pleasure Lacan calls *jouissance* hiding in this text? What here is the repressed 'real' – that is, what is it this text would like to say but finds it impossible to say?

Indeed since language and the symbolic order require repression, Lacanian critique offers us a way to discover just how the oppressive dynamics of our society work. Lacan's identification of various features of the symbolic order as 'phallic' has offered feminist philosophers a point of leverage to destabilize masculinist institutions and practices. For example, Luce Irigaray (1930–) in *Speculum of the Other Woman* (1974) and *This Sex which Is Not One* (1977) has suggested that female *jouissance* includes forms of pleasure that are disruptive to masculinist ways of engaging the world. Because female *jouissance* cannot by definition be accommodated into the orderly, rule-governed ways of thinking, acting and feeling characteristic of the symbolic order, we can expect women's ways of living to offer us models of liberation. Female *jouissance* points to polyclimactic poetics rather than the single climax around which works of art modelled on male *jouissance* (orgasm) are centred. Women's practices of sharing, consultation and non-hierarchical organization present insights into potentially more liberated forms of social and political life. Contemporary philosopher Slavoj Žižek (1949–) has picked up and modified the Lacanian approach to genealogy of culture.

See also

5.4 Feminist critique
4.12 Objective/Subjective
5.2 Deconstruction and the critique of presence

Readings

Jacques Lacan, *Écrits: A Selection* (1977)
Slavoj Žižek, *Looking Awry: An Introduction to Jacques Lacan Through Popular Culture* (1992)
Elizabeth Grosz, *Jacques Lacan: A Feminist Introduction* (1990)

5.8 Nietzschean critique of Christian-Platonic culture

What do many punk rockers, Platonists and Christians have in common? According to a perspective developed by Nietzsche, what they have in common is that they are nihilists (from the Latin *nihil*, 'nothing') – and nihilism is the natural result of the twisted dynamics of our Christian-Platonic culture. How is this the case?

For Nietzsche, we suffer under the burden of three philosophical demands, rooted deeply by Christian-Platonic philosophy in the way we think, feel and act.

Through claims to *transcendence* the Christian-Platonic tradition renders the value of this world derivative, as finding its source in a superior transcendent world – heaven, God, the forms, the ideal communist utopia.

Through the *ressentiment* that pervades it, this tradition demands that the weak be made equal to the strong, and it tears down the strong to achieve this under the guise of doctrines like democracy, socialism or egalitarianism.

In its *will to truth* the tradition propagates a desire and a longing for absolute, fixed, universal, literal, non-temporal, singular, unequivocal, complete, consistent and incorrigible truth.

What's so bad about heaven, equality and truth? Well, the problem is that they are inhuman and unhealthy. They weaken us and undermine the forces that bring real power, joy, creativity and vitality to our existence.

According to Nietzsche, believing in a never-present superior realm – that our world or society is somehow lacking because it doesn't measure up to an 'ideal' world or society – inevitably leads us to devalue our world and the human condition. Demanding that the strong be brought down destroys those free, individual, creative spirits who sustain, invigorate and lead culture. The impossibility of achieving a universal, objective, single truth for all humankind ultimately wears us out and leads us to reject truth and value of *any* kind – even of a more human, provisional and partial kind. In short, Christian-Platonic culture leads us to self-hating, life-thwarting, world-consuming nihilism. For the nihilist, not only is God dead, but everything else might as well be dead too.

The cure.

Fortunately, for Nietzsche there is a cure – if only we can muster the tremendous strength necessary to adopt it. We must 'overcome' Christian-Platonic culture. There are three ways of doing this.

The first is *amor fati*: We must reject appeals to transcendence and embrace this world itself, the body, nature, warts and all, including lusts, competition, pride, and the fact that we will suffer and die. We must love our fate and reject transcendent 'God'.

Second, we must *be or follow the strong*: We must break away from hating the special, the different and the culturally powerful and encourage those who have the creative, individual vitality of cultural leaders. Life should be art and we its artists – or at least the lovers of artists. Blessed are the strong.

Third, we should embrace *perspectivism*. We must forget truth and acknowledge truths – many different perspectives, inconsistency, a literary engagement with the world. We must reject 'God' or absolute truth and morality.

Using the tool.

The tools of Nietzschean philosophy cannot be picked up by just anyone. If you disagree with Nietzsche's basic diagnosis of where we have gone wrong, you will find his tools blunt. But if you buy into the Nietzschean critique, ask yourself to what extent a given philosophy is Christian-Platonic. To what extent does it depend upon a view of truth as singular, objective and universal? To what extent does it deny any meaning and value that can't be rooted in something divine, ideal or transcendent? To what extent does it tear down the special and strong in the name of virtue, morality, equality and (false) love?

See also

5.1 Class critique
5.5 Foucaultian critique of power

Reading

*Friedrich Nietzsche, *Toward the Genealogy of Morals: A Polemic* (1887)
*Friedrich Nietzsche, *The Will to Power: An Attempted Transvaluation of All Values* (1901, 1904, 1906)

5.9 Pragmatist critique

On what basis should we accept or reject certain beliefs? Perhaps the most common answer one might receive to this question would be 'On the basis of whether the belief is true or not, of course.' But how are we best to unpack the meaning of 'true' here? Traditionally, many people have answered that true claims somehow express or mirror the nature of reality, and reality is what it is independent of whatever we think or say about it. The job of philosophy and science, from this point of view, is somehow to produce theories that picture or capture or reflect or represent that independent reality.

Pragmatists, however, think that there's something wrong with this way of conceiving truth, philosophy and science. According to the pragmatists, closer scrutiny will convince you that little sense can be made of what it means to 'mirror' or 'represent' or 'grasp' an independent reality. Moreover, in reflecting back on the history of philosophy, one can see that this sort of *representationalist* position produces more problems than it is worth.

A better option, say the pragmatists, is to think of true claims as those that we agree are more effective in helping us get along in the world; and we should give up entirely worrying about whether or not they represent an independent reality. Accordingly, the theories of natural science are true not because they express the nature of independent reality but because they enable us to manipulate objects in experiments and technologies in ways we approve. Moral theories are 'right' when they enable us to get along with one another and to act as we wish to. Aesthetic ideas need be thought of as nothing more than agreements about what we ought to think of as beautiful (or, anyway, as artwork) and how we ought to arrange, feel and think about the sensible dimensions of our environments. In short, what we ought to adopt as true is what we agree solves problems for us and helps us get along better in the world.

We no longer need to concern ourselves with how things look to God, or from some imaginary and unobtainable, ideal point of view. We no longer need to worry about what lies beyond or below our experience and our engagements with the world. A lot of problems, say the pragmatists, can simply be left behind in this way.

Metaphysics and religion.

Among those features of our intellectual life many pragmatists think we can do better without must be counted metaphysics and much, perhaps all, of dogmatic religion. Many ordinary religious practices and beliefs find support among pragmatists as useful devices for bringing meaning and community to people's lives. On the other hand, many also see religious doctrine as bringing violence, division and intolerance. Whether or not God is a trinity, whether or not the consecrated communion host holds the true presence, whether or not substantial forms exist, whether or not the One descends into three hypostases are questions whose answers serve no purpose and which have proven either useless or downright harmful.

Using the tool.

In assessing a philosophical theory through pragmatist terms of criticism, then, ask yourself the following questions:

1.   Considering all its implications and the practices actually associate with it, does adherence to this theory make our lives better?'
2.   Is anything about this theory useless or, worse, an obstacle to living in a better way?

Changing our thinking along these lines may at first seem strange. But, says Richard Rorty (1931–), just as many Protestants have found religion perfectly acceptable and even superior having abandoned the doctrine of the real presence, so will we find philosophy and life generally acceptable and even superior when we abandon metaphysics and thinking about truth as representation. Or perhaps, on the other hand, we will find ourselves inclined to a position like that articulated by Catholic author Flannery O'Connor who exclaimed when told by a friend that the Eucharist is a beautiful symbol even if it doesn't include the real presence of God: 'Well, if it is just a symbol, then to hell with it!'

See also

5.2 Deconstruction and the critique of presence
5.3 Empiricist critique of metaphysics
5.5 Foucaultian critique of power

Reading

Charles Sanders Peirce, *Pragmatism and Pragmaticism* (1934)
William James, *Pragmatism and the Meaning of Truth* (1907)
*Richard Rorty, *Philosophy and the Mirror of Nature* (1979)

5.10 Sartrean critique of 'bad faith'

Have you ever held something valuable – say a vase, a rare artefact, an infant – in your hands and found yourself, for no apparent reason, terrified that you would drop it? Have you ever stood on a high balcony or on the edge of a towering cliff and found yourself afraid you would fall off or somehow go over the rail? Have you ever found yourself in the midst of a quiet and solemn ceremony and afraid you might shout out some horrible expletive? If you have, you're not alone. French existentialist philosopher Jean-Paul Sartre (1905–80) sees something more than a psychological phenomenon in these common experiences. For him they point to something exceedingly profound about human existence: our absolute freedom.

For Sartre, what's terrifying about holding an infant or standing on a cliff is not simply that some external force or an accident might surprise us and *force* us to do something awful. More deeply, we are anxious because there is nothing stopping us from freely dropping the child or freely hurling ourselves to our deaths. The only thing that can stop us in such situations (indeed, in any situation) from engaging in the most horrendous acts is ourselves – our own absolutely unconstrained *choice* not to do so.

The thing is, being absolutely free is terrifying to people, and in the face of it we often feel emotions like *anxiety* (or what the existentialists call *Angst*), nausea and dread. Because freedom can be anxiety-ridden, people flee from it and attempt to hide from their own freedom, maintaining that they are *not* really free. When people do this, when they try to deny their own freedom, Sartre describes them as acting in *bad faith* (*mauvaise foi*). Bad faith, accordingly, characterizes many philosophical positions.

Examples.

Those Marxists, for example, who argue that human behaviour at any given time is determined fundamentally by the imperatives of history and the economics of any situation, deny that history and the economy develop solely through acts of human freedom. Marxian economic determinism, then, is a philosophy of bad faith. (Keep in mind, however, that Sartre thought Marxism could be reconciled with his philosophy of freedom, and he spent a great deal of effort explaining how – see his *Critique of Dialectical Reason*, 1960).

Naturalism is also, typically, for Sartreans an example of bad faith. Many philosophers, such as Baron d'Holbach (1723–89), have maintained that human beings are continuous with the natural world. Since events in the natural world are determined according to causal laws, and since, these philosophers argue, human actions are just natural events, human actions are necessitated through causal chains, and we are therefore not free. For Sartre, however, human consciousness (what, following Hegel, he calls the *pour-soi*) is discontinuous with the natural world (what he calls *en-soi*). Consciousness *negates* and distinguishes itself from natural objects and processes. And pretending otherwise is bad faith.

Using the tool.

Bad faith is, according to Sartre, never complete. In some fashion, people always know that they're free, and signs of this all-but-ignored self-awareness pop up from time to time. To use this critical tool, then, when scrutinizing a philosophical position, ask yourself the following questions:

1. How, if at all, does this philosophical theory express a denial or endorsement of absolute human freedom?
2. If it denies freedom, how, despite its denial, does the theory – perhaps implicitly and against its explicit intent – nevertheless affirm human freedom?

There is one important caveat to bear in mind, however. The force of the critique is lost if, as a matter of fact, human beings are not free in the way Sartre suggests. This tool, therefore, is premised on the assumption of absolute human freedom. It is not enough to complain that someone is denying their freedom – you also need to be prepared to show them that they have a freedom to deny.

See also

5.1 Class critique
5.6 Heideggerian critique of metaphysics
5.5 Foucaultian critique of power

Reading

Jean-Paul Sartre, *Being and Nothingness* (1943), pt 1, ch 2
Joseph S. Catalano, *A Commentary on Jean-Paul Sartre's Being and Nothingness* (1974, 1980)
Thomas R. Flynn, *Sartre and Marxist Existentialism* (1984)

chapter 6
Tools at the Limit

6.1 Basic beliefs

The project of philosophy is often described in terms of an architectural analogy. The edifice of our knowledge is like a building, and if we are to be safe in that building we have to be sure that our foundations are secure and not built on sand.

This 'foundationalist' approach to philosophy requires that some beliefs act as such foundations. But what sort of basic beliefs could possibly do this? What ought we to select as the bedrock assumptions upon which the edifice(s) of our remaining beliefs is (are) to be built?

Variations on a theme.

The idea of a basic belief has appeared in various incarnations. Ancient Stoics like Cleanthes and Chrysippus claimed that our thought and experience includes 'cataleptic impressions', whose veracity is self-evident. Later, René Descartes resurrected this gesture in his doctrine of certain and indubitable 'clear and distinct ideas'. A. J. Ayer talked about *basic statements*. He defined them as statements the truth values of which determine that of at least one further statement, but no other statements determine the truth value of them. In other words, a basic statement is one that can be invoked to show the truth or falsity of another statement, but no statement is or can be invoked to show its own truth or falsity.

For Ayer, basic statements are typically observation statements. I observe that pure water is a clear, easy-flowing liquid, and this observation can be used in arguments to show the truth or falsity of other statements. For instance, if someone drowned in a thick, opaque, muddy substance, our basic statement can be invoked to show that the person did not drown in pure water.

More recently, Alvin Plantinga has defined 'properly basic belief's as beliefs that are not believed on the basis of other beliefs, but do themselves form the basis of other beliefs. A belief is properly basic when (1) it is basic and (2) I am justified in believing it.

Hence, following Plantinga, if I believe in fairies just because I decide I'm going to, and use that as a basis for other beliefs, my belief is not properly basic, for though it is not based on other beliefs I am not justified in any way in believing it.

Can God be basic?

There is clearly more than a passing resemblance between Plantinga's properly basic beliefs and Ayer's basic statements in terms of how these beliefs function as foundations for knowledge. But the two philosophers differ considerably in what they consider to be properly basic. For Plantinga, properly basic beliefs include more than just observation statements and self-evident logical truths. Perhaps most pointedly, Plantinga maintains that belief in the Abrahamic God is properly basic. It is not that one can't be wrong to believe God exists, but that for some people the existence of God is as evident as the belief that other people have minds, or that we see things, or that there is an independent world. In each case it is possible that one is wrong. Infallibility, for Plantinga, is not a feature of properly basic beliefs.

Plantinga's argument exploits a common limitation in philosophy. David Hume argued that we have no deductive, rational grounds for believing in cause and effect; nor do we, strictly speaking, ever observe causation at work. Nevertheless, we are compelled to believe and act as if causation were real. Belief in causation is thus properly basic: it is not based on any other belief but is itself the basis of other beliefs, and people would accept that we are justified in believing in it. Plantinga aims to show that belief in God is, for many people, just the same. Atheists who argue that there are no grounds for belief in God can be asked why they believe in causation, since there are no demonstrative grounds to believe in that either. The atheist may respond that, on that logic, why isn't belief in fairies properly basic? Moreover, there's wide variation in belief in God, unlike belief in external objects, so in what sense can theological beliefs be basic? And so the debate will go on.

Anti-foundationalist philosophers like the pragmatist Richard Rorty, the post-structuralist Michel Foucault, and the literary theorist Jacques Derrida argue that there are no such things as basic beliefs or statements. But any *foundationalist* approach to philosophy requires something that functions like basic statements or properly basic beliefs. If you wish to pursue a foundationalist course, the difficulty is deciding what is a legitimate basic belief, given that, by definition, they are not grounded in any other beliefs.

See also

1.9 Axioms
5.2 Deconstruction and the critique of presence
4.13 Realist/Non-realist
5.6 Heideggerian critique of metaphysics
6.6 Self-evident truths

Reading

Bertrand Russell, *An Inquiry into Meaning and Truth* (1940)
*James F. Sennett, ed., *The Analytic Theist: An Alvin Plantinga Reader* (1998)
Julia Annas, 'Stoic Epistemology', in *Epistemology: Companions to Ancient Thought 1*, ed. Stephen Everson (2001)

6.2 Gödel and incompleteness

The physicist Alan Sokal once said in an interview, 'Someone, I can't remember who it was, said that he had a rule of thumb which was that whenever anyone on the humanities or social sciences cites Heisenberg's uncertainty principle, that the person should be assumed guilty until proven innocent. I think that's quite fair.'

There is a tendency in philosophical writing, particularly by non-professionals and undergraduates, to pick up one of the great theories of science and draw specious philosophical conclusions from it. When professors and tutors read words like 'I will use Einstein's theory of relativity to show that . . .' their hearts sink.

The problem is that the big theories are usually much more complicated than they seem, and it is only when one takes the time to learn about them in detail that one can understand them well enough to draw any accurate conclusions. Sokal was personally vexed by the tendency people have to draw philosophical conclusions from quantum theory, which is particularly rash given that even professional physicists find quantum theory baffling.

Precisely what?

Philosopher of mathematics Kurt Gödel's (1906–78) incompleteness theorem suffers from a similar fate. The reality is that, unless you've studied mathematics at a very high level, you probably don't understand what Gödel's theorem means, let alone what its implications are for other areas of philosophy. For a start, there are actually two theorems, the second of which is a corollary of the first. According to Simon Singh in *Fermat's Last Theorem* (1997), a mathematically accurate statement of the first theorem is 'To every w-consistent recursive class k of formulae there correspond recursive classsigns r such that neither v Gen r nor neg(v Gen r) belongs to Flg(k) (where v is the free variable of r).'

A more comprehensible, but already somewhat simplified, version of this is that in any formal, consistent logical system capable of describing arithmetic there is at least one sentence that can neither be proved nor disproved within the system.

Why is this so stunning? The explanation of this is partly historical. At the turn of the last century Gottlob Frege and Bertrand Russell had both produced work of the highest calibre and reputation as part of a project of showing that every mathematical truth was provable in precisely the way Gödel showed it to be impossible. Hence Gödel's theorem provided a devastating and fatal blow to the Russellian project of subsuming mathematics within logic.

General application.

More generally, the lesson of Gödel is often taken to be that you just can't prove everything. That's fine as far as it goes. But Gödel's theory doesn't tell you what you can't prove, except for the specific areas of mathematics to which the theorem applies. Even the claim that every consistent theory must contain at least one statement that is not provable within that theory goes beyond the strict confines of Gödel's theorem, which only applies to the formalization of arithmetic. It is tempting to draw all sorts of implications from Gödel's theorem to philosophy in general, but often rash and difficult to do so.

So the general philosopher would be wise not to read too much into Gödel's theorem, but simply to take it as a cautionary tale against the grander ambitions of philosophy.

See also

1.6 Consistency
4.7 Entailment/Implication

Reading

Kurt Gödel, 'On Formally Undecidable Propositions of *Principia Mathematica* and Related Systems', *Monatshefte für Mathematik und Physik* 38 (1931)
Bertrand Russell and Alfred North Whitehead, *Principia Mathematica* (1910–13)
Michael Dummett, 'The Philosophical Significance of Gödel's Theorem', in idem, *Truth and Other Enigmas* (1978)

6.3 Mystical experience and revelation

Philosophy has had at best an ambiguous relationship to the mystical. There have been many thinkers generally known as philosophers whose life and work has been centrally informed by mystical experience – thinkers like the medieval Meister Eckhardt (1260–1327), Hildegard of Bingen (1098–1178), and Julian of Norwich (1342–1416). Even certain elements of some of the most prominent canonical philosophers may be described as mystical. A famous section of Plato's *Symposium* called 'The Ladder of Loves' (210e–211a) has inspired many as a description of mystical revelation – not to mention the way he describes the very uppermost activity of the soul in his famous 'Divided Line' in the *Republic* (532d–534a). Along these same lines Neoplatonic philosophers like Plotinus (*c.*205–70), Proclus (410–85), and the Christian Saint Augustine (354–430) all appeal to mystical-like experiences in their philosophical work. Certain dimensions of the work of Martin Heidegger – such as the '*Augenblick*' and 'Call of Conscience' as they appear in *Being and Time* (1927) – have been thought of as somehow mystical. According to Wittgenstein the sort of 'showing' he talks about in his *Tractatus Logico-Philosophicus* (1921) reveals the mystical (*das Mystische*; 6.44, 6.45, 6.522). And many philosophers have talked about 'intuition' and 'intellection' – but how are these different from mystical experience and revelation? (See, e.g., Spinoza's *scientia intuitiva*; *Ethics*, pt 2, pr. 40. sch. 2.)

Hostility to mysticism.

But, in general, philosophy has not been warm to mysticism, and there are good reasons for this. Broadly, we might say, philosophers reject mystical experience because it doesn't seem well suited to underwrite explanation or knowledge. In particular, it is accused of being unintelligible, unreliable and inconsistent.

It is *unintelligible* because, by definition, mystical experience is to some extent not fully understood, even by those who claim to have had it. Mystical experience is typically described in vague terms as being beyond the grasp of sensation, public observation, intellect and reason. It is also frequently held to be *ineffable* or beyond language. But how can something ineffable, private and suprarational count as a good explanation? How can it serve any explanation at all?

Mystical experience is *unreliable* because it is almost always private, personal and impossible for others to test or scrutinize. Individual personal experience has proven time and again an unreliable basis for knowledge. One of the most important dimensions of establishing knowledge about matters of fact has been corroboration through testing and subjecting knowledge claims to the scrutiny of others. Mystical experience seems impossible to correct or check in this way, but without this sort of disciplining literally anything goes.

It is *inconsistent* because theories based upon mystical experience show very little consistency, as the vast variety of religions and spiritual fads demonstrates. The theories of natural and social science show remarkable consistency and uniformity in comparison with those of religion and metaphysics. Few physicists dispute the laws of thermodynamics. Few biologists dispute evolution. Where disputes arise in the sciences there seem to be agreed-upon and effective ways of ending them. The belief systems based upon revelation and mystical experience, by contrast, have been wildly varying and contradictory. Consider, for example, Judaism, Orthodox Christianity, Catholicism, Quakerism, Buddhism, Islam, Zoroastrianism, Hinduisms, Ba'hai, Egyptian religion, Greek Olympian religion, native American religions, and New Age channelling. Moreover, their disputes seem intractable and without well-defined procedures for settling them. Doesn't this show that mystical experience ought not to be relied upon as a guide in the search for knowledge and understanding of the world?

What if?

On the other hand, mystical experience has been around for a long time. Many people have attested to its power. And if William James is right in his *The Vari-*

eties of Religious Experience (1902), there seems to be sufficient uniformity across various instances of mystical experience to suggest that there might be something to it. Perhaps, paraphrasing Shakespeare (*Hamlet*), there's more in Heaven and Earth than ever dreamed about by philosophy. Perhaps not.

See also

3.29 Testability
5.3 Empiricist critique of metaphysics
6.6 Self-evident truths

Reading

Elmer O'Brien, *The Essential Plotinus* (1964)
Augustine, *Confessions*, e.g. bk 7, ch. 16
*Theodore Schick, Jr, and Lewis Vaughn, *How to Think about Weird Things: Critical Thinking for a New Age*, 3rd edn (2002)

6.4 Possibility and impossibility

Should philosophers be constrained by thoughts of what is possible? After all, according to the explorer Fridtjof Nansen (1861–1930), 'The difficult is what takes a little time; the impossible is what takes a little longer.'

Possibility and impossibility are important in philosophy, as we will see shortly. But first it is necessary to distinguish between different *kinds of possibility*. There are several ways of doing this, but what follows captures the main distinctions that are usually made.

Logical impossibility.

Something is logically possible just as long as it does not contain any contradictions – or, more broadly, so long as it doesn't break the laws of logic. For instance, a square circle is logically impossible, because such a concept is a contradiction in terms. But a flying pig is not logically impossible, since there is nothing about the concepts of pigs and flight that makes the idea of a flying pig incoherent. (This explains why you could have a fictional film in which a pig flies but not one in which any of the circles were square.)

Physical impossibility.

When, however, we think about what is impossible, we don't usually think only about what is logically impossible. We have another idea of possibility, which we might call 'physical possibility'. Something is physically possible if it doesn't break any natural laws, whether or not we have the technology or means to bring it about now. Hence travelling to Mars is physically possible, but (according to most physicists) travelling to Mars faster than the speed of light is physically impossible.

Practically impossible.

We could add a third category of 'practically impossible' to describe things which, though physically possible, are beyond our means now and in the foreseeable future. We might include here notions of technologically or financially possible and impossible.

Application.

Having clear distinctions between these different senses of possible and impossible is important because a lot of philosophical arguments work by considering situations that are not real. Arguments about personal identity consider cases such as teletransportation and brain transplantation. Moral arguments sometimes consider scenarios such as being able to destroy the entire world by flipping a switch or saving it by killing one person. H. Paul Grice (1913–88) put forward an argument in the philosophy of language that entertained the possibility that language users would switch their usages of blue and green at an arbitrary future time.

In each case, one can ask whether the scenarios described are possible or not. But one also needs to decide how relevant this possibility or impossibility is. Sometimes it is argued that it doesn't matter whether the scenario is physically possible or not; it just has to be logically possible.

This is because one of the most important uses of philosophical tools is conceptual clarification and exploration, examining the meaning and implications of a position, argument or concept. One can do this, arguably, by reflecting upon how the concepts under scrutiny apply to any logically coherent situation, irrespective of whether it is physically or practically possible or not.

On other occasions, however, one might argue that the contingency of our actual world is vital, and therefore any argument that goes beyond what is possible in this world is irrelevant. For instance, returning to the philosophy of personal identity, it can be argued that we have to start from the fact that we are the kinds of physical beings we are. To argue from what *might* be the case if the universe operated under different natural laws would there-fore be spurious. As human beings, we are constrained by the laws of nature and, so this line of reasoning goes, it is irrelevant to consider how one might use the word 'person' if these laws were different.

All these issues are complex and open-ended. What we need to do is to be clear about what sense of possibility and impossibility we are employing and to be sure of why we think, in any particular argument, the possibility of the situation being considered is relevant or not.

See also

1.11 Certainty and probability
1.12 Tautologies, self-contradictions and the law of non-contradiction
2.9 Thought experiments
4.4 Categorical/Modal
4.10 Necessary/Contingent

Reading

Michael J. Loux, *The Possible and the Actual* (1979)
*Theodore Schick, Jr, and Lewis Vaughn, *How to Think about Weird Things: Critical Thinking for a New Age*, 3rd edn (2002)

6.5 Primitives

Once in Spain and with a poor grasp of the language, I (Julian Baggini) found myself in a restaurant confronted with a choice of desserts, one of which was *helado*. 'What's *helado*?' I asked the waiter. He shrugged his shoul-ders and replied, '*Helado es . . . helado*'.

My *camerero* was premature in deciding he could provide no further de-scription of what an ice cream is. But are there other words the meaning of which just cannot be explained by other words?

Such words can be called 'primitives'. They are primitive in the sense of being prime (or first), not old or undeveloped. They are words that cannot be further analysed or defined in terms of other words. You either grasp what they mean, or you don't.

Example of 'good'.

G. E. Moore's theory of 'good' would be such a primitive concept. Moore believed that 'good' cannot be explained or defined in terms of other properties of the natural world, such as pleasure, pleasantness or beauty. Goodness is a basic moral feature of reality and to attempt to define it in terms of features of the non-moral natural world is to commit what he called 'the naturalistic fallacy'. Good is therefore a primitive concept because it cannot be explained or defined in terms of anything else. Another example Moore gave was 'yellow'. The yellowness of a lemon cannot be defined in terms of anything else, it is a basic feature of our experience.

That is not to say that one can say nothing about what goodness is, or that it cannot be defined at all. We can help someone to understand what goodness is by pointing out examples of it, explaining how it contrasts with badness, and so on. But in all these activities we are not analysing goodness into its more basic constitutive elements. We are simply using other words or examples to help someone perceive or recognize goodness for what it is.

It might seem that primitives are inevitable. After all, if there were no primitive concepts, then any concept could be broken down into other more basic concepts, which could in turn be broken down into others, and so on, *ad infinitum*. At some point, it seems, there have to be some basic terms that admit of no further analysis. Without primitives, conceptual analysis would go on forever, and we would never have an adequate foundation for our language.

Observation statements and ostensive definition.

The empiricist view is that the most basic concepts are not primitives in the sense outlined but what Ayer called 'observation statements'. On this view, at the foundations of language are words like 'cat' or 'blue', where the meaning is determined by observation. So there should be no point at which one just has to shrug one's shoulders and say, 'X means just X.' One has only reached the most fundamental stratum of language when one reaches a concept where, to explain what the term means, one has to point to some observation. (Some philosophers call this 'ostensive definition'.)

Holism.

There are in fact philosophical theories that maintain that there are no primitives. *Semantic holism* is one. On this view, it is not the case that concepts invariably sit on top of other more basic concepts, with primitive concepts providing the foundations for a vertically structured language. Rather, say the holists, words form a mutually supporting system of interrelated meanings where the support structure is more horizontal. Words have their meanings as part of a whole language where no concepts are primitives but where all words both define and are defined by other words in the language. One can only understand words and sentences in this language by being initiated gradually into the language as a whole. This introduces circularity to meaning, for sure, but not necessarily of a vicious kind. Along these lines Wittgenstein famously said, 'To understand a sentence means to understand a language' (*Philosophical Investigations*).

Philosophers are fond of analysis and are suspicious when anyone claims that a concept is primitive. The suspicion is that there is simply an unwillingness or inability to take the analysis further, or that there is a kind of intellectual laziness in accepting a concept as primitive rather than working harder to understand it in other terms. Empiricism and semantic holism offer two ways of working without the idea of primitives. The rule of thumb is to assume that the Spanish-waiter-style shrug is premature, but not to rule out the possibility that there may be some concepts for which this really is the only sensible response.

See also

1.10 Definitions
3.6 Circularity
3.25 Regresses

Reading

*G. E. Moore, *Principia Ethica* (1903)
*A. J. Ayer, *Language, Truth and Logic* (1936)
Ludwig Wittgenstein, *Philosophical Investigations* (1953)

6.6 Self-evident truths

Isaiah Berlin said that philosophers are adults who persist in asking childish questions. There is a great deal of truth in this. But what philosophers also need to know is when it is necessary to stop asking such questions, 'Why?' or 'How do you know?'

It is normally perfectly reasonable to ask how we know something to be true. But some have maintained that this question is inappropriate in some cases since it is a self-evident proposition – that is, we need provide no further evidence or proof for it. If a proposition is a self-evident truth it stands in need of no further justification because it is in some way self-verifying.

Many philosophers have maintained that there are no such things as self-evident truths. Those that other philosophers wish to defend as self-evident may be divided into three categories: (1) the laws of logic, (2) analytic statements, and (3) basic observation statements.

Laws of logic.

Many have considered the laws of logic to be self-evident. For instance, the law of non-contradiction, which states that something cannot both be X and not-X at the same time, is supposed to be one such self-evident truth. If you have to ask why something can't both be entirely black and not-black at the same time, you just haven't understood what it means for something to be entirely black.

Analytic statements.

Analytic statements are also said to be self-evident. 'All bachelors are unmarried men' is an analytic statement, since 'unmarried men' is already contained within the meaning of 'bachelor'. Therefore, to anyone who understands the meanings of the words in the sentence 'All bachelors are unmarried men' the truth of the statement is self-evident.

Observation statements.

A third candidate for self-evident truth has been basic observation statements. These include statements such as 'I am seeing yellow.' Such a statement, it seems, does not require any further justification; it makes little sense to say, 'How do you know you're seeing yellow?' If I were, on the other hand, to say, 'I am seeing a yellow canary', my claim would not be self-evident, since it is possible that what I am actually seeing is a fake canary or a hallucination. So observation statements are only self-evidently true when they confine themselves to the experience itself and do not make claims as to the real existence or otherwise of what is being observed. 'I seem to be seeing a yellow canary' is self-evidently true to the person having the experience; 'I am actually seeing a yellow canary' is not.

Clear, distinct and adequate ideas.

Descartes's most famous sentence is 'I think, therefore I am', from his *Discourse on Method*, pt 4 (1637). In a sense this putatively self-evident truth ('I am') may be thought of as a kind of observation statement – if we include reflection as a kind of observation. One can see this by considering the formulation Descartes gives in his Meditation 2 (from *Meditations on First Philosophy*, 1641) – 'I am; I exist', rather than the famous statement above. The difference between the two is important. Descartes is not deducing his existence from the fact that he thinks. Rather, Descartes maintains that 'I think; I am' is what he calls a 'clear and distinct' idea, an idea that when clearly and distinctly conceived by the mind is immediately seen to be indubitable and true. (Descartes's theory echoes the ancient Stoic doctrine of 'cataleptic impressions'. Spinoza would later call a similar manner of conceiving, 'adequate'.) The 'therefore' in 'I think, therefore I am' is thus redundant.

Philosophers being philosophers, there is not a self-evident truth in existence that someone hasn't claimed isn't self-evident after all. But unless some statements are self-evidently true, wouldn't we be like Isaiah Berlin's children after all, and would there be any end to our persistent asking, 'But how do you know it is true?' Perhaps there isn't.

See also

1.12 Tautologies, self-contradictions and the law of non-contradiction
4.1 A priori / A posteriori
4.3 Analytic/Synthetic
6.1 Basic beliefs
6.3 Mystical experience and revelation
6.5 Primitives
6.7 Scepticism

Reading

S. Everson, ed., *Epistemology: Companions to Ancient Thought 1* (2001)
R. Descartes, *Principles of Philosophy* (1644), pt 1, Principles 7, 10, 45
*B. Spinoza, *Ethics* (1677), pt 2, def. 4

6.7 Scepticism

Philosophy has a constructive and a destructive side. The easiest side to get a basic grip on is the destructive one. There philosophy casts doubt on arguments and beliefs. It takes great skill to do this well, but virtually anyone can sound something like a philosopher just by learning a few key statements such as 'How can you be sure?', 'Not necessarily,' or 'But what if . . .?'

Using these phrases allows one to play the sceptic. Scepticism has been a great spur to philosophical progress and is sometimes used as a tool in its own right. Descartes's famous 'method of doubt' consisted in relentlessly asking sceptical questions about all his beliefs until he identified the one belief that he could not doubt and so could stand as the foundation of all his knowledge: the fact that he existed. In Descartes's hands, scepticism became a means to the end of certainty.

But scepticism can also be relentlessly negative. The problem is (as Descartes demonstrated) you can ask a sceptical question about virtually anything and not get a cast-iron rebuttal. How can you be sure you're not a brain in a vat, wired up to make you think you're living in the real world? Does the fact that we perceive independent, material objects necessarily mean that such objects actually exist? What if we're just dreaming? Can I be sure that what seem to be other people just like me have minds like my own? Might they not be simple automata?

Perhaps there is no decisive answer to any of these sceptical questions. Perhaps there is always room for the sceptic to pop up and raise his or her doubts. If this is so, then maybe the challenge for philosophy is to recognize when it is appropriate to set aside the sceptical doubt and when it has to be taken seriously. Or perhaps, rather than setting sceptical doubt aside, philosophers have to learn somehow to philosophize within the context of doubt. Perhaps philosophers have to learn to live with the permanent possibility that the sceptic is right without either dismissing the sceptic too easily or allowing the sceptical possibility to stand in the way of philosophy's constructive side.

History.

Scepticism has had a long philosophical history. Conventionally, it begins with the figure of Pyrrho of Elis (*c.*365–*c.*273 BCE), though elements of sceptical thinking predate him – for example, in Socrates (469–399 BCE), who was said to have been wisest because he understood that he knew nothing (Plato's *Apology* 21a). In the ancient Hellenistic and Graeco-Roman world, scepticism attacked various schools of philosophical doctrine, especially the Stoics. During the Middle Ages concern with scepticism receded, but one can find interest in sceptical problems orbiting around the issue of whether or how it is possible to know and talk about God. After scepticism proper resurfaced in the Renaissance it became woven into the early modern project of building a new science and concerns about whether it is possible to know the world. Recently philosophers have puzzled over the question of whether scepticism makes any sense at all, and sceptical gestures have pervaded many of the texts collected under the rubric of post-structuralism and deconstruction.

Scepticism is often defined as involving the claim that knowledge is impossible. But there is something problematic about this definition since the nihilistic claim that 'knowledge is impossible' is itself a *knowledge* claim. Perhaps scepticism is, therefore, self-refuting – indeed, the charge of self-refutation is a strong one to advance against a lot of sceptics. But many sceptics are more sophisticated than this.

Positive scepticism.

Indeed, with regard to its sophisticated versions, it is wrong to think of scepticism as nihilistic or as entirely negative. Sceptics have suggested or tried to show that there is a kind of wisdom, or appreciation, or acknowledgement of human finitude and the fragile character of human knowledge that's not itself properly thought of as 'knowledge'. Sceptics have also tried to provide a kind of therapy for various philosophical pathologies that result from misguided philosophical attempts to understand our relationship to the world, ourselves and others exclusively as issues of knowing. In doing so sceptics have tried to lead people to more moderate, tranquil lives and to make possible an appreciation of what it means to be part of the common life in which humans exist.

The problem of the criterion.

Although sceptical thought is extremely varied, nearly all is united in exploring what has come to be known as the problem of the criterion. Skilful use of this problem can serve you well as a philosophical tool. The problem is this: are there any criteria by which we can, without doubt, distinguish knowledge from error? It seems that every candidate for such criteria has withered under the intensity of sceptical scrutiny. One way this problem has been captured has been as a regress: if something is to serve as a standard for knowledge, we must be able to justify its use as a standard. We cannot use the standard itself to justify it, since that would be circular. We therefore need a different, independent standard to justify the first standard. But that second standard will itself require a different, independent standard, and so on, *ad infinitum*.

If reason is presented as the standard, what justifies reason? If perceptual observation is presented as the standard, what justifies perception? For every claim to knowledge, the sceptic asks, 'What is the basis of that claim?'

Too high a standard?

One way philosophers have answered scepticism has been to argue that the sceptic has set standards of knowledge so high that they can never be met. As A. J. Ayer wrote in *The Problem of Knowledge* (1956), 'Not that the sceptic's argument is fallacious; as usual his logic is impeccable. But his victory is empty. He robs us of certainty only by so defining it as to make it certain that it cannot be obtained.'

Ayer's point is that the sceptic only wins if we accept his or her rules. But why should we accept them? Shouldn't we reject the sceptic's standards because they are necessarily unobtainable? It is not just that we could obtain what they demand if we thought harder or were more intelligent. The sceptic demands something unattainable. But perhaps rejecting scepticism on these grounds is just arbitrarily changing the rules to suit us. Isn't there something compelling about scepticism in any case, even if certain formulations of it seem senseless or excessive?

See also

1.11 Certainty and probability
4.6 Defeasible/Indefeasible
6.1 Basic beliefs

Reading

Sextus Empiricus, *Outlines of Pyrrhonism* (*c*. 200 CE)
Stanley Cavell, *The Claim of Reason: Wittgenstein, Skepticism, Morality and Tragedy* (1979)
*Richard H. Popkin, *The History of Scepticism from Erasmus to Spinoza* (1979)

6.8 Underdetermination

Does the sun circle the Earth or the Earth circle the sun? Almost everyone now agrees that the Earth circles the sun. Why? One might suppose because the evidence has shown that this is true and that the geocentric theory is false. According to one influential theory, however, the evidence can show no such thing – at least not to the exclusion of all other competing views.

The theory of the underdetermination of theory by evidence is most closely associated with W. V. O. Quine, who argued that for any hypothesis (such as whether the Earth circles the sun or vice versa) the evidence will always be compatible with more than one explanation. If this is true, then no body of evidence can ever compel us to accept one explanation to the exclusion of all others. We may have reasons to select one of the theories, but those reasons cannot include the fact that only that one is compatible with the evidence.

Quine is not saying that we don't have good reasons to prefer some theories to others. He is simply making the point about the role of *evidence* in explanation. Empiricist philosophy, which holds that knowledge is derived from experience, tends to work on the assumption that the truth is somehow simply generated from the evidence of observation and experience. What Quine does is to show that the relationship between knowledge and evidence is not so straightforward.

On Quine's view, evidence fits into our system of beliefs like a jigsaw puzzle, and although it is natural to suppose that only one piece of the jigsaw will fit in any one place, the truth is that the jigsaw can be put together in any number of different ways – all of which will fit all the pieces.

Examples.

Consider the sun example. It really is possible to maintain, in the light of all the evidence, that the sun circles the Earth. What one has to do is simply to bite a few bullets. So, for instance, if I wanted to maintain the geocentric view, I might dismiss any counter-evidence you bring to me on the grounds that the people conducting the research are servants of Satan, out to propagate the myth of a heliocentric universe. This may strike you as bizarre, but my explanation will fit the evidence. It just won't fit it in a way that you find plausible. This is why conspiracy theorists are so hard to refute. You can always produce evidence that can be spun to fit theories in a variety of ways, and you can always find ways of dismissing counter-evidence while remaining consistent.

The same core point lies at the heart of Quine's ideas about the indeterminacy of translation. Consider an anthropologist observing members of a foreign tribe using the word *gavagai* whenever they see a rabbit. Quine argues that we can never know whether by *gavagai* they mean 'rabbit', 'Look, rabbit!', 'Sacred rabbit!', 'It rabbits there', 'undetached rabbit parts', or even something else. The problem is that the evidence will always be compatible with more than one translation of *gavagai*. No matter how much we observe the tribe members' behaviour and use of words, the possibility will remain open that the translation we favour isn't quite correct – or, perhaps all of them are.

Perhaps the main lesson of the underdetermination thesis is that, just because a theory can fit the evidence doesn't mean it must be right. 'Fit with evidence' cannot be a sufficient criterion for determining the truth of a theory, since two or more incompatible theories can always fit the evidence. We need a subtler understanding of how we use evidence to support or critique our beliefs.

See also

3.1 Alternative explanations
2.1 Abduction
3.29 Testability

Reading

Robert Klee, ed., *Scientific Inquiry: Readings in the Philosophy of Science* (1999)
W. V. O. Quine, *The Web of Belief* (1970)
Pierre M. M. Duhem, *La théorie physique, son object et sa structure* (1906)

Internet Resources for Philosophers

Episteme Links (www.epistemelinks.com). A virtual warehouse of all kinds of stuff related to philosophy.

TPM Online, *The Philosophers' Magazine* (www.philosophers.co.uk). A web version of the magazine edited by Julian Baggini and of which Peter Fosl is a contributing editor. Plus additional interactive philosophy materials.

Peter Suber's Guide to Philosophy (www.earlham.edu/~peters/philinks.htm). A thoughtful compendium of internet philosophy materials.

The Transylvania University Philosophy Program site (www.transy.edu/homepages/philosophy). Peter Fosl's set of resources and materials in philosophy, including his Philosophical Chronology.

The Internet Encyclopedia of Philosophy (*IEP*) (www.utm.edu/research/iep). It's just that.

The Stanford Encyclopedia of Philosophy (http://plato.stanford.edu/contents.html).

X-Refer (www.xrefer.com). A good resource for short articles on philosophers and philosophical concepts.

Maja's World (http://public.srce.hr/~mprofaca/maja01.html). A short but sweet set of links on philosophy.

Erratic Impact (www.erraticimpact.com). A site especially built for research in philosophy. A very powerful resource.

Peter King's Philosophy Around the Web (http://users.ox.ac.uk/~worc0337/phil_index.html). A useful and well-organized collection.

The Window: Philosophy on the Internet (www.trincoll.edu/depts/phil/philo/index.html). Chris Marvin and Frank Sikernitsky at Trinity College have put together a compelling site.

Philosophy in Cyberspace (www-personal.monash.edu.au/~dey/phil). Dey Alexander at Monash University in Australia has a fine set of resources.

Plato and his Dialogues (http://plato-dialogues.org). Bernard Suzanne's interesting site on Plato.

African Philosophy Resources (www.augustana.ab.ca/%7Ejanzb/ afphilpage.htm). Bruce Janz's site on this topic.

Chinese Philosophy (CPP). (http://main.chinesephilosophy.net). An interesting set of links.

The Notebook (www3.baylor.edu/%7EScott_Moore/Continental.html). Resources on continental philosophy from Baylor University.

Index